The Economics of Killing

'We live in a rich world and yet increasingly people are getting caught in the poverty trap and facing real hardship and pain. We know how to solve these problems – by disarmament and demilitarisation, and putting human and financial resources into dealing with the real enemies of humanity: poverty, unemployment, environmental crisis, etc. Vijay Mehta's excellent book sets out the problems and solutions, and challenges us all to create the political will to implement policies which will bring about real change and give hope to humanity.'

Mairead Corrigan Maguire, Nobel Peace Prize Laureate 1976. Founder, Peace People, Belfast, Northern Ireland

'The Charter of the United Nations starts in this way: "We, the Peoples ... have resolved to save the succeeding generations from the scourge of war"... But instead of better sharing and building peace through social justice and economy guided by the "democratic principles" – so well enshrined in the UNESCO's constitution – and by the Universal Declaration of Human Rights, the sinister proverb "if you wish peace prepare war" has been secularly applied by male rulers. And plutocratic (G7, G8) groups have taken over the functions of the United Nations, and have placed the market in the very core of the world governance ... . The result is a profound financial crisis that hides the most urgent planetary challenges as access to food and health of all human beings, the environmental progressive degradation; the lack of horizons of the humanity worldwide.

The net balance is $4 billion per day in military expenditures while 70,000 persons die of hunger ... .

The book ... is extremely timely and provides – what is extremely important and must be underlined – not only excellent diagnosis but also appropriate treatments. And the first is to reduce the power of the military-industrial complex.'

Federico Mayor Zaragoza, Former Director-General UNESCO; President, Foundation Culture of Peace, Madrid

'It is about time someone exposed the nefarious activities of the military-industrial complex that is destroying the foundations of civilized human existence. It has made killing a proifitable industry. This book is a must-read for all peace seekers.'

Arun Gandhi, Grandson of Mahatma Gandhi; President, Gandhi Worldwide Education Institute, Rochester, New York

'Vijay Mehta depicts ways in which the Western powers can restructure their economies away from the reliance on the military-industrial complex towards making the twenty-first century an era of soft power for a more peaceful and sustainable future.'

Deepak Chopra, bestselling author, *Peace is the Way*, California

'[B]rilliantly links the deepening economic crisis facing the West with the dynamics of militarism that is wreaking havoc on the planet, and thus destroying the prospects for a peaceful and just world and hastening the implosion of the United States. Everyone who cares about the future must read this groundbreaking book, and take action before it is too late.'

Richard Falk, United Nations Special Rapporteur on Human Rights for the Palestinian Territories; Professor Emeritus of International Law at Princeton University

'Congratulations to Vijay Mehta on having grappled with this complex and too often sinister issue. The latest technology, with the clinically remote killing process of drones and the like, makes it all the more urgent and compelling. We are all involved. The subsidies by taxpayers to the arms industry are immense. Were that industry exposed to the full rigours of the market economy, it would be in deep trouble. It is a challenge to us all. Vijay Mehta helps us to face up to it.'

Lord Frank Judd, Minister for Overseas Development (1976–77); Minister of State for the Foreign and Commonwealth Office (1977–79); Director of Oxfam (1985–91)

'This important book identifies the real crisis ahead for the world which is not narrowly environmental but the fact that with rising population we will not have enough food or oil or water to survive. That is the real reason that this book, pointing to the waste in military expenditure, offers the real alternative to starvation, which is cooperation to meet our needs.'

Tony Benn, former MP and Cabinet Minister; President, Stop the War Coalition, London

'Vijay Mehta's book is an essential read for young people, North and South, who must demand dramatic change in global resources management and response to the needs for universal human wellbeing. It presents the case for the implementation of new thinking necessary if they and their children are to have opportunities to live full lives. There must be a new realization that North–South human wellbeing and equality of opportunity requires that prosperity be global. The book exposes the reader to the vicious Northern military-industrial complex, and roles of the media and energy sectors, plus the corrupting role of the arms-dealing five permanent members of the UN Security Council in the profits of endless poverty. As power is shifting to the new emerging powers of the South, this book provides thought and hope that the Northern centuries-old model of brutal human exploitation and blatant use of warfare will be uprooted and changed to support socio-economic wellbeing, equal opportunity and sustainable prosperity. Nothing less will suffice.'

Denis Halliday, UN Assistant Secretary-General (1994–98); Former Coordinator of the UN Humanitarian Program in Iraq

'Vijay Mehta lifts the curtain on a truth which many would prefer concealed. If we were to become instruments of peace instead of war and redirect some of the global trillion and a half dollars spent annually on war and weapons to real human needs there would be no need to create Millennium Development Goals. All those supporting humanitarian NGOs should read Mehta's book and act on it.'

Bruce Kent, Vice President, Campaign for Nuclear Disarmament (CND), Movement for the Abolition of War, London

'Vijay Mehta's book shines a timely light on the role that Western governments play in perpetuating conflict around the world. It is particularly welcome in that it does not just identify and detail the problem – it puts forward an alternative, and one which anyone genuinely committed to peace, justice and equality cannot afford to ignore.'

Caroline Lucas, MP and Leader, Green Party, UK

'Measured against their own proclaimed noble ideals, those in power in the imperialist Western states (and most countries elsewhere) betray their ordinary citizens and the overwhelming majority in the rest of the world. A global pact among elites is based on a hegemonic discourse claiming to provide "development". But it is merely the ideological smokescreen for maintaining control over entrenched interests, based on a power of definition selectively used to fuel the further growth of a military-industrial complex. Such continued minority rule puts the future of mankind – if not the planet – at risk. Vijay Mehta's powerful intervention reminds us of the need to mobilise for counter-models. It is a forceful appeal to find adequate forms of multilateral cooperation in search for an alternative future.'

Henning Melber, Executive Director of the Dag Hammarskjöld Foundation, Uppsala, Sweden

'Vijay Mehta's book is thought-provoking at a time of world economic crisis when fresh thoughts and approaches are sorely needed. I hope it will be widely read, especially by those who may, at first, find its substance unpalatable.'

Sir Brian Urquhart, Former UN Under-Secretary-General for Special Political Affairs

'It is high time for a book like this to be written and read. We are beyond traditional international development cooperation. Globalisation and geopolitics have resulted in a complex network of economic, financial, political and military interests of countries and companies. Vijay Mehta's study of the underlying power relations reveals unpalatable truths. It also points in a different direction: policy making based on true values concerning people's development, transparency, equity and human rights.'

Jan Pronk, Former Dutch Minister of Development and Minister of the Environment, The Hague, Netherlands

'This is a book to challenge and test our comfortable assumptions about how the world works, who wields power and what for.'

Dan Smith, Secretary General, International Alert, London

'It should be obvious to every thinking person on the planet that killing people, maiming them, torturing them, dropping bombs on them, blowing up their homes or destroying their livelihoods is not an effective way to make the world a safer or more peaceful place. All war and violence has ever achieved is to fuel more hatred and to sow the seeds of the next conflict. So who benefits from the world's insane, drug-like dependency on weapons and military force as the "solution" to every problem? Vijay Mehta lays out in this book how the world has got into this situation and how we can get ourselves out of it. The real solutions are all there right in front of our noses! The time has come to start implementing them.'

Tim Wallis, Executive Director of Nonviolent Peaceforce Europe, Brussels

'Vijay Mehta clearly describes the connections that link the global machinery of war with global poverty. This book goes to the heart of the global *problematique* and should be read by anyone who cares about building a more decent, equitable and sustainable world order.'

David Krieger, President of Nuclear Age Peace Foundation, California

'Vijay Mehta has thrown down a challenge to the hypocrisy of Western states that preach human rights and development but promote militarism and chaos. As this fascinating book makes clear, we have a choice to make between perpetual crisis, war and poverty on the one hand and the positive alternatives of demilitarisation, disarmament and social investment on the other. Mehta has issued a compelling call to arms against the military-industrial complex that sustains global capitalism. It is up to us to respond.'

John Hilary, Executive Director, War on Want, London

'Vijay Mehta has written a very important book in the face of current global crises and the interrelated socio-political consequences of militarisation. This current paradigm needs to be overturned in favour of a structure of human rights and responsibilities, where justice is dealt with by law and not arms, and where economic resources are channelled into the real needs of our societies.'

Professor Julia Hausermann MBE, Founder and President, Rights and Humanity, UK

'[This book] is a marvellous read, where Vijay has found exactly the right words to describe the present dangerous world situation, the urgency to solve it and above all, offering insights how to solve it. All this with due respect for our beautiful planet and all its inhabitants. Thank you for this, Vijay!'

Marjolijn Snippe, LL.M International Law, World Federalist and advocate of United Nations Parliamentary Assembly (UNPA), Netherlands

'[This book] challenges politicians, corporations and the media who collude with the military-industrial complex for continuing wars and arms expenditure. …Vijay Mehta skilfully illustrates a paradigm shift for reducing military spending and investing the resulting savings in civilian jobs, health care and education. This book is a must-read for anyone keen to understand the issues and seeking peaceful solutions, whether NGOs, GOs or engaged citizens around the globe.'

Dr Norbert Stute (MD), Founder, BetterWorldLinks.org, Germany & UK

'Government aid budgets have been sorely compromised by insane spending on defence. As a result, we in the development camp are striving for ways to increase and improve aid delivery to meet the scale of humanity's problems; half the world's population is battling hunger and disease. My father's book is the best-case scenario – it shows us how we can swap insanity for our shared humanity.'

Renu Mehta, Founder, Fortune Forum charity and MM Aid Model co-architect, London

THE ECONOMICS OF KILLING

How the West Fuels War and Poverty in the Developing World

Vijay Mehta

PlutoPress
www.plutobooks.com

To the heroes of Arab Spring, Occupy Wall Street and anti-corruption campaigners in India and around the globe. Your efforts resonate with millions across the world.

First published 2012 by Pluto Press
345 Archway Road, London N6 5AA

www.plutobooks.com

Distributed in the United States of America exclusively by
Palgrave Macmillan, a division of St. Martin's Press LLC,
175 Fifth Avenue, New York, NY 10010

British Library Cataloguing in Publication Data
A catalogue record for this book is available from the British Library

ISBN   978 0 7453 3225 3   Hardback
ISBN   978 0 7453 3224 6   Paperback

Library of Congress Cataloging in Publication Data applied for

This book is printed on paper suitable for recycling and made from fully managed and sustained forest sources. Logging, pulping and manufacturing processes are expected to conform to the environmental standards of the country of origin.

10   9   8   7   6   5   4   3   2   1

Designed and produced for Pluto Press by Chase Publishing Services Ltd
Typeset from disk by Stanford DTP Services, Northampton, England
Simultaneously printed digitally by CPI Antony Rowe, Chippenham, UK and
Edwards Bros in the United States of America

Contents

Acknowledgements

The book is the product of many years of peace activism and understanding the folly of militarism and chronic wars for profit, resources and domination. It also reveals the fact that military expenditure and the aid agenda are intertwined and unmasking the relationship can radically assist development.

Such a meaningful book could not be written without the assistance of numerous friends and colleagues to whom I'm grateful. Firstly, special thanks to James Brazier for excellent research and bringing the book to shape. Secondly, I am indebted to my excellent editor, Roger van Zwanenberg for direction, guidance and friendly hand for the publication of the book.

Thirdly, many thanks to members of my family, Renu, Sanjay, Ajay and Shanti for comments, suggestions and support. Lastly, thanks to Raceme and Abdul for other additional works for its completion.

The book is a humble attempt to show how the military-industrial model can be replaced by adopting equitable policies for disarmament, demilitarisation and working for sustainable development, thus ending the cycle of violence and poverty.

Vijay Mehta
London, June 2011

Introduction

'Disasters require urgent action to prevent repetition,' said the world's most powerful economist in September 2010, addressing an audience at Princeton University. 'We do not have many convincing models that explain when and why bubbles start...I would add that we also don't know very much about how bubbles stop either.'[1] He urged the listening scholars to redouble their efforts to plug these gaps in their collective knowledge.

The speaker was Ben Bernanke, the chairman of the US Federal Reserve. Two years earlier the US central bank had faced what the chairman called the 'most difficult challenges for economic policymakers since the Great Depression'. Just as the 1990s ended with the bursting of the dot-com bubble, the 1980s with Black Monday's stock-market crash, and the 1970s with an energy crisis, another decade had finished in economic disarray. Major banks were collapsing and entire countries were facing bankruptcy. Economists had yet again failed to predict the crisis, but Bernanke saw no need for what he called 'an overhaul of economics as a discipline'. The standard models were designed for 'non-crisis' periods, he concluded – presumably those brief gaps between the bubbles, the crises, and the slow, painful recoveries.

More interesting was what Bernanke did not mention. He did not describe what linked the financial crisis to the real economy. He did not mention the rapidly changing economies of Asia, or his country's $14 trillion debt, or its persistent trade and fiscal deficits. He did not talk about its vast military expenditure, which imposes a financial burden on the US government that it cannot afford. He did not mention the inconclusive and bloody wars in Iraq and Afghanistan, which had already cost the US at least a trillion dollars.

The purpose of this book is to do what Bernanke did not: to join the dots between the world of finance, which collapsed so spectacularly in 2008; the real economy, where raw materials are fashioned into valuable objects for trading and the underlying motivation of war and militarisation. Once this analysis becomes clear, the astonishing gulf between the wealth and stability of some countries, and the chaos and poverty of many others, is not a natural gulf. The reasons why the vast mineral wealth of the

1

southern hemisphere has not translated into vast *actual* wealth are, in the final analysis, much the same reasons which caused the US economy to go into spasm.

Underlying this state of affairs was an abusive trading relationship maintained through arms sales and repression. Wealthy democracies collude with light-fingered dictators to share the spoils of mineral extraction and cash crops. These kleptocrats grant military access to the West, which turns a blind eye to internal repression. 'These local events don't worry us,' a French ambassador told *Foreign Policy* magazine, when it asked why French soldiers based in Djibouti did nothing as the African country's government crushed pro-democracy protests in 2011.[2]

The abuse is fundamental to the system of trade, but mainstream journalism often misdirects the public along stale and fabricated narratives which blur the issue. Poor countries fail to develop, the story goes, because they pick the wrong leaders. Foreign companies have no choice but to pay bribes, we are told, because otherwise they could not do business, to the detriment of both sides. When it is discovered that the local dictator has stashed billions of dollars in London or Paris or New York, we are to believe that this was mere oversight on the part of Western authorities, who are then lauded for 'freezing' the stolen assets.

This is the 'few bad apples' account of failed development. Were it not for a few bad apples in countries such as Nigeria, Pakistan, Kazakhstan and the Philippines, these countries would today be prosperous, European-style democracies. Proponents of the 'few bad apples' theory shake their heads sadly and say that were it not for the crooks in charge, then free trade, foreign investment, and low taxation would have transformed the Southern Hemisphere decades ago. All along there is a hint of de Toqueville's old aphorism, 'People get the governments they deserve'.

One purpose of this book is to show that the 'few bad apples' theory is a fiction, one promoted by the West to serve its own mercantile interests. Western governments do not wish poor countries to develop into advanced economies, because they believe that were they to do so this would tilt the terms of trade against Euro-American national interests. The most obvious proof of this posture is their attitude to China, a country where industrial development has lifted 600 million people out of absolute poverty within 30 years.

China, it should be pointed out, is highly corrupt. Despite its many 'bad apples' at all levels of government it has nevertheless achieved GDP growth of almost 10 per cent a year, year in, year out, for over 30 years. This proves beyond all doubt that corruption does not necessarily prevent rapid development. The reason for China's success is because its government acts in the interests of China, not of the West. Its bad apples might be corrupt, but they cannot be paid to follow orders from abroad.

This concept of national independence explains why the West vilifies some dictatorships and praises others. Western politicians rarely miss an opportunity to embarrass China's leaders over their poor human-rights record.[3] Yet they hold hands with[4] the unelected leaders of Saudi Arabia, a country that is considered to be more repressive than China. It is extremely difficult to ignore such double-standards, yet somehow the media are fed with reverence for the senior military officers who are among the primary beneficiaries of military-industrial spending.

Across the world, the hirelings of the Western military-industrial complex control nations, working as cogs in a machine that transfers raw materials to the West at the minimum possible expense to the latter. The system's leading brokers are the elected leaders of wealthy democracies, who sign the resource contracts during state visits. Paying off the locals, however, is delegated to the executives of the supposedly private military-industrial companies and their in-country commission agents. To further insulate the governments, Europe operates a chain of offshore havens in which such transactions can be hidden from prying eyes.

China's military-industrial complex exists for the opposite reason. Its primary purpose is not to acquire basic materials from poor countries (although this is an expanding part of its remit), but to steal advanced technologies from rich ones. The Chinese leadership long ago realised that the difference between poor countries and rich ones is actually quite simple: rich countries have the people and equipment needed to produce valuable hi-tech products, what are today known misleadingly as 'dual-use items' (products, software or technology that can be used for both civil and military purposes). *The Economist* once pointed out that a Rolls-Royce aero engine, which tips the scales at six tonnes, is worth its own weight in silver. An average car, by contrast, is worth its own weight in hamburgers.[5] Given that Peru, one of the world's largest silver miners, can produce only about 200 tonnes of silver a year[6] – equivalent to just 33 Rolls-Royce engines – one can understand why countries with a hi-tech manufacturing capability are so much richer than those which produce only commodities. At the end of 2007 Rolls-Royce's order book was worth $90 billion.[7] A result of its success in selling machines that few other companies can manufacture.

China has proven too big to be coerced into adopting 'low road' development. Smaller countries are less fortunate. Enormous state subsidies for military-industrial giants, exempted from fair-trade rules by the World Trade Organization, make it uneconomic for smaller countries to try to 'catch up' as China has done. Local leaders are bought off with bribes and promises of aid. Worst of all, the West arms its despotic local allies with lethal weaponry. It pays for resources with equipment which fuels local arms-races and wars. Conflict destroys a country's ability to organise itself into a Chinese-style 'catching up' mode. Those who remain in the war-zone are starved, stunted, and deprived of education. The educated middle class flees to the West, where it helps to preserve the knowledge-advantage of its host nation. The investment funds needed for building up industry disappear into slush funds in offshore banks, where they collect interest for wealthy Europeans.

The military-industrial complex no longer operates in the interests of nations, if it ever did. It has acquired a deadly momentum of its own. In the twentieth century over 250 wars were fought and 160 million lives were lost. Militarism survived and thrived throughout a century in which communism, socialism and fascism all blossomed, withered and died. The broken, artificial states created by European colonialists in the twentieth century are the war-zones of the twenty-first century. Over two billion people subsist on less than $2 a day. Every 3.6 seconds, a person dies of starvation. Every 30 seconds a child dies of malaria. Every minute a women dies in childbirth.

There is another model of trade, an alternative to the cycle of financial, economic and military disaster that has operated since the beginning of globalisation. By breaking the cycle of arms sales and the co-option of local officials by Western multinationals and by promoting a broader economic ways in countries that for now only produce commodities, it is possible that the world need not be divided into rich and poor zones. It is not necessary for the rich world to fear industrialisation in Africa and the Middle East. History teaches us that the spread of prosperity is not a zero-sum game but one which benefits all humanity. Human security can only be enhanced by adopting a strategy of disarmament and demilitarisation, freeing up resources for constructive economic, political and cultural development.

This groundbreaking book explores the underlying need for disarmament to create a peace dividend for sustainable development, international peace and security which has been recognised in the international legal framework. However, many states have been reluctant to acknowledge its implications, let alone act on it. Governments and parliamentarians can and must adopt policies and take legislative steps to re-fashion the balance of global trade to promote peace, not war.

The book explores the questions: why does the West sell weapons to its enemies? Where did Iraqis learn to make roadside bombs? Why does the West oppose China's hugely successful development model? It illustrates how US attempts to block China's model of development led directly to 2008's financial crisis. It shows how Europe and the US conspire with local dictators to prevent their countries from developing advanced industries, and how this system has incubated a global terrorist threat. Fifty years after President Dwight D. Eisenhower warned of a military industrial complex, and a decade after 9/11, it shows how freedom of speech and national interests are subordinated to the interests of military-industrial elites, creating a global economics of killing. While outlining the crippling human and economic toll of this systemic economic abuse, the book shows how the military-industrial model can be replaced by adopting equitable policies for Disarmament, Demilitarisation and working for sustainable development thus ending the cycle of violence and poverty.

Part I

Military Industrial Complex – Power, Myths, Facts and Figures

1
How the West's Addiction to Arms Sales Caused the 2008 Financial Crisis

In 2008 Western capitalism collapsed.

Beginning with the failure of giant banks such as Lehman Brothers and Bear Stearns, within a year European countries such as Iceland and Greece were teetering on the brink of bankruptcy. Stock markets crashed and gold markets soared as some of the most famous names in global commerce – AIG, Morgan Stanley, RBS (The Royal Bank of Scotland) – contemplated their own oblivion. Across the world, governments responded by spending trillions of dollars to support a financial system that was once synonymous with buccaneering free-market capitalism. To pay for these bailouts, many states decided to slash social expenditure even as the banks immediately resumed the payment of multi-million-dollar bonuses to their staff.

Much was written about the causes of the disaster. Some blamed the greed of individual bankers, whose poor decisions had exposed their institutions to a rash of failed loans, particularly in the US housing market. Some blamed the Western governments, either for failing to regulate the financial system or for imposing too much regulation, depending on the analyst's politics. Some said the investment scene had become too atomised and complex, a result of exotic new securities and derivatives representing diverse risks.

Doubtless these explanations were correct, as far as they went. But all were superficial. None addressed the underlying, structural causes of the economic cataclysm. They did not explain the presence of huge amounts of liquidity in Western capital markets, nor did they account for the astonishingly low interest rates set by the US Federal Reserve. Most importantly, few of the explanations linked what had happened to the financial markets back to the real economy, the place where base materials are cut from the ground, refined and entwined, marketed and sold.

A MYSTERIOUS BOOM

In 2003, a boom began in the United States. Its catalyst was a financial measure that many Americans thought they would never

9

see in their lifetimes. In July that year the head of the US Federal Reserve, Alan Greenspan, slashed the benchmark US interest rate to just 1 per cent. This interest rate controlled the cost of borrowing across the American economy, but it also influenced decisions well beyond the nation's borders. Borrowing money had never been cheaper.

Banks began lending mortgages to people who would never have had access to such large loans in the past, a housing market that came to be known as 'sub-prime'. These mortgages were broken down into new types of security that could be traded among banks, which used complex derivatives to 'hedge' the very obvious risks that sub-prime lending presented. Across the Union, trailers were swapped for condos, beach huts sprang up on the shores of the Great Lakes, existing homeowners withdrew equity from their properties as if they were giant ATMs. The profits of retailers soared as Americans rushed to purchase their goods with what seemed like an unlimited line of cheap credit.

But where was the cheap money coming from?

The benchmark interest rate reflects how easy it is for a government to borrow money. Government bonds are one place that people with surplus cash can park their money to protect it from inflation. Savers tend to purchase government bonds in times of economic uncertainty, for instance during a recession. Bonds are seen as a safe bet – if the government runs out of money, it can simply print more. Capitalist theory dictates that when demand for bonds is strong the government does not need to offer an attractive interest rate (or 'yield') on the debt. This keeps the cost of borrowing low across the economy, which helps to boost investment and propel the country out of recession.

Conversely, during a boom investors prefer the quick gains to be made on the stock market. They tend to ignore stodgy, low-risk government bonds. So, to entice investors to purchase its debt, the government is forced to offer a higher rate of interest. This increases the overall cost of borrowing and cools the booming economy. On paper, the capitalist model should be a perfectly self-correcting, self-regulating system.

That, at least, was the theory.

By 2003 the US Federal Reserve no longer relied on this logic to borrow, if it ever had. This was because Washington had discovered an almost limitless new supply of cheap credit. It was this bottomless well of cheap money that had allowed Greenspan to cut his benchmark rate to record lows, and it was this bottomless well in which the US financial markets would drown in the financial collapse of 2008.

OVERLOAD

For over 25 years the People's Republic of China had been moving away from communism towards an export-led economic model. Following the return of Hong Kong to China in 1997 the Chinese economy began to accumulate reserves of foreign currency at an accelerated rate (see Figure 1.1). Foreign exchange reserves are a marker of a country that sells more to the outside world than it buys from it. As more and more container ships left Shanghai laden with plastic goods and cheap electronics, China rapidly became the world's workshop.

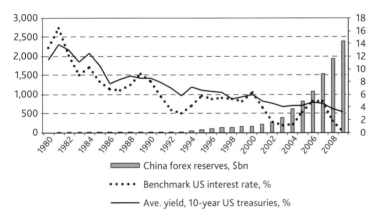

Figure 1.1   Too Much Chinese Money

It was China that was providing the US with its seemingly endless quantities of cheap credit.[1,2,3] By 2009 the gap between US sales to China and what it had bought from China had reached a staggering $227 billion.[4] China used these leftover dollars to buy more US Treasury bonds, ensuring that US interest rates stayed low, and ensuring that American citizens spent more and more on Chinese goods. China and the US were locked in an economic death spiral, hurtling towards the 2008 collapse.

US officials blamed this vicious cycle on China for pegging its currency, the Yuan, to the dollar at a fixed rate. Were the Chinese currency allowed to float freely, they argued, it would appreciate in value, making it more expensive for Americans to buy Chinese goods and thereby correcting the trade gap. There were two major problems with this argument. China's currency was artificially cheap in all its export markets, not just the US – yet it was only China's trade with the US that became so dramatically unbalanced.[5] Secondly, from 2005 onwards China allowed the Yuan to appreciate by more than 20 per cent.[6] The trade imbalance with the US continued to grow unabated. Many economists conceded that monetary reform was a sideshow; something else was going on.[7]

What was it about the structure of US exports that was causing the imbalances? Why did China end up investing so much money in US Treasury bonds? Why did the economic imbalances become so lethal, and why was the situation allowed to culminate so badly?

It is wrong to suggest that China deliberately created a crisis in Western capitalism. In fact, Beijing would have much preferred to invest its surplus dollars in a very different way. When it came to its leftover trillions, China had three choices. It could buy US Treasury bonds. It could purchase US goods and services. Or it could acquire US corporations. Options two and three would have reduced the trans-Pacific imbalances which inflated the various bubbles that burst in 2008. However, there was a problem. The US refused to sell China the goods, services and corporations that it wished to buy, because what China wanted to buy was the US military-industrial complex.

WHY IKE WAS RIGHT

January 2011 saw the 50th anniversary of President Dwight D. Eisenhower's farewell address to his nation. The anniversary reinvigorated discussion of what the former Supreme Allied Commander meant when he warned his countrymen to 'guard against the acquisition of unwarranted influence, whether sought or unsought, by the military-industrial complex. The potential for the disastrous rise of misplaced power exists and will persist.'

Half a century later commentators on both the left and right of the political spectrum have lined up to dismiss and downplay Eisenhower's warning. In the conservative *National Review,* Vincent Cannato claimed that the political Left has been especially eager to appropriate the Republican general's words for political purposes. He concluded that Eisenhower was merely urging fiscal restraint, a warning against wasteful Pentagon spending and procurement policies, rather than pointing towards a construct with autonomous political power.[8]

Some liberal pundits were equally dismissive. David Greenberg argued in *Slate* that Ike's address had been completely misunderstood, calling fulminations against the military-industrial complex lazy, hackneyed, and histrionic. Greenberg condemned what he called the 'mad embrace' of Eisenhower in recent decades by anti-war leftists and so-called realists. While he conceded that the president had worried America could become a garrison state, Greenberg mocked those who saw the military-industrial complex as a conspiratorial, demonic system. Instead, he claimed that Eisenhower's military-industrial complex merely represented an outsize special interest which promoted extravagant military spending.[9]

DEFINING OUR TERMS

Given such scepticism, it is important to define the exact nature of the military-industrial complex. The United States is a useful case-study. Until World War II the US relied almost entirely on an arsenal system. An arsenal was a state-run system of arms factories and warehouses under direct military control. In wartime the government designed and procured munitions and weapons from these arsenals. Once the war ended the arsenals and the military demobilised. Because the US did not have a large standing army, it did not need a standing military-industrial complex.

After World War II, the system changed. The US abolished the old arsenal system and replaced it with a network that fused science, industry and the military. Over three generations thousands of firms, large and small, emerged to equip the military. Other companies were founded to supply these firms, creating a gigantic supply chain that competed domestically but also sought overseas orders. However, the government continued to wield huge power over the complex. In 1993, for instance, industry leaders were called to the Pentagon by Defense Secretary William Perry for dinner – a meeting that came to be known as 'the Last Supper' – to tell their industry to consolidate. In less than a decade, 50 major companies consolidated into six global giants.

The observations in the last two paragraphs are not the words of one of David Greenberg's anti-war leftists or so-called realists. They were made in 2011 by US Deputy Defense Secretary William J. Lynn III on-board the USS *Intrepid* aircraft carrier, now a military museum in New York,[10] to an audience of defence executives. He was quick to assure them that no new 'Last Supper' was on the horizon. If Greenberg and Cannato are correct in their assessment, it seems that someone forget to tell the US government.

The military-industrial complex, or what Lynn called in his speech the 'defence industrial base', produces not only weapons. Increasingly, it also produces 'dual use' items, high-value, hi-tech hardware that commands astronomical prices in overseas markets. Selling these items overseas has become fundamental to the West balancing its trade with developing countries. Were developing countries to decide against buying the output of the West's military-industrial complexes, the balance of world trade would be overturned.

THE CHINA PROBLEM

It is at this point that we begin to understand the events of 2008. US officials are not only convinced of the existence of a US military-industrial complex, but of a Chinese equivalent that must be thwarted in the interests of US national security. For decades China has tried, by fair means and foul, to acquire military-industrial secrets. The examples of this strategy are almost too numerous to mention.

In January 2011, for instance, a US court jailed a 46-year-old man, Zhen Zu Wu, for shipping radar components to the Chinese military.[11] In 2010 Noshir Gowadia, an American engineer, was convicted in a US court of helping China to design a cruise missile based on US designs.[12] He was jailed for 32 years. In 2009 a court in Tennessee sentenced a retired college professor, John Reece Roth, to four years for selling US Air Force drone technology to a Chinese national.[13] In 2008 Gregg William Bergersen, a weapon systems policy analyst with the Defense Security Cooperation Agency, pled guilty to passing information to China about US-Taiwan military cooperation. In 2007 a US court convicted Chi Mak of sending to China details of a quiet energy propulsion project for US warships.[14]

China does not distinguish between military technology and industrial technology. Its strategy exists to acquire both in order to modernise its own military-industrial complex. Those who deny the existence of such complexes need only to read the 2009 Report to Congress of the US China-Economic and Security Review Commission. The report says that Chinese espionage 'is driven by the state-owned research institutes and factories of China's military-industrial complex'.[15]

Dr James Mulvenon, an expert on the Chinese military-industrial complex, argued that profit-driven companies are spun off from Chinese government-controlled defence industrial research institutes and are encouraged to acquire foreign technology in an 'entrepreneurial' fashion.[16] FBI Director Robert Mueller warned that 'China is stealing our secrets in an effort to leap ahead in terms of its military technology, but also [its] economic capability'.[17] Clearly, the US does not see the threat purely in terms of guns and rockets.

THE CAUSES OF A CRISIS

China steals US military-industrial secrets because it cannot purchase them legally. Since the Tiananmen Square massacre of 1989 the US and European Union have enforced an arms embargo against China. At first glance, this embargo does not appear to make much difference to the yawning $227 billion gap between what America sells to China and what it buys from it. After all, even if the US sold as much weaponry to China as it sold to the rest of the world in 2009/10 this would have represented only about one-fifth of the bilateral trade deficit.

However, not only does the US refuse to sell China weapons, it refuses to allow China to invest in US companies which manufacture equipment of a military, strategic or hi-tech nature. It prevents other nations from selling China weapons with US-made components and it is quite possible that, were it allowed to, China would outspend the rest of the world combined on US weapons. Put simply, the US government shuts China out of the part of the US economy most of interest to the Chinese: the military-industrial complex.

The American state has been highly active in blocking Chinese investment in the US. In July 2010, for instance, national-security objections prevented Emcore from selling its fibre-optics business to China's Tangshan Caofeidian Investment Corporation. The companies cited 'regulatory concerns' emanating from Washington for withdrawing their filing with the Committee on Foreign Investment in the United States (CFIUS).[18]

A few months earlier another Chinese entity, Northwest Non Ferrous International Investment, was prevented from taking a controlling interest in a Nevada mining company which had access to tungsten, a metal used heavily by the arms industry.[19] Officials at the Treasury Department, which oversees the CFIUS panel, did not disclose the reason for their concerns beyond the proximity of some of the target company's installations to US military installations.[20]

Telecommunications is another sector that has often been deemed too sensitive to permit Chinese investment. CFIUS has paid particular attentions to the activities of Huawei, a military-backed Chinese telecoms company with expansionist ambitions. Huawei abandoned its attempt to purchase 3Com in 2008 because of US national security concerns. Then, in 2010, a group of Republican lawmakers raised similar concerns of Huawei's plan to supply equipment to Sprint Nextel. Another deal, to buy the server provider 3Leaf, was referred to CFIUS.[21]

The biggest deal to fall victim to such sanctions came in 2005, when the US prevented China from purchasing Unocal, a major oil company. The proposed $18 billion acquisition was described by congressmen as an attempt by the Chinese authorities to 'lock up energy supplies around the world that are largely dedicated for their own use'.[22] Unocal, which possessed substantial interests in Southeast Asia and advanced deep-sea drilling technology, was eventually sold to the US oil major Chevron.

Some deals have slipped through the net. Magnequench, once an Indianapolis-based subsidiary of General Motors, was purchased by a consortium led by Archibald Cox Jr in 1995. Magnequench specialised in the manufacture of rare-earth magnets, a sophisticated component of wind turbines, mobile phones and missile guidance systems.[23] It gradually emerged that Cox was the figurehead for a consortium of Chinese companies led by Zhang Hong, the son-in-law of China's former leader Deng Xiaoping – the man who initiated China's efforts to collect Western military-industrial secrets.[24] Soon the company's new owners began shutting down the company's US sites and shipping production to China.[25] The loss became more significant in 2010, when China imposed restrictions on the exportation of its own rare-earth deposits. 'Pentagon Loses Control of Bombs to China Metal Monopoly' reported Bloomberg.[26]

It is clear that US military and strategic planners are convinced of the existence of a Chinese military-industrial complex. It is also clear that such complexes do not need to be the kind of close-knit conspiracy derided by David Greenberg. It is merely enough to say that the success of the military-industrial complex is of benefit to the people and firms who work within it, a point made by a Canadian intelligence assessment of China's military-industrial complex: 'A variety of actors within the military-industrial complex have strong economic incentives to continue arms sales, and enjoy considerable patronage and protection from domestic and international monitoring.'[27]

Equivalent establishments in the West work in much the same way. Soldiers with business interests, or businessmen with close military ties, are in a powerful position to defend their salaries and the deals that produce them. The US military-industrial complex is diaphanous, comprising pure military technologies, dual-use systems, and industries merely deemed to be 'strategic'. Sketching the outlines of the US complex is made easier by tracking those enterprises that Washington protects from Chinese investment. Military and semi-military manufacturers, oil and hi-tech companies, all clearly fall within the protected sphere. Simply describing the substantial portion of US economic real-estate occupied by these military-industrial enterprises does not, in itself, give life to the autonomous power indicated by Eisenhower's famous warning. But it does illustrate how readily the US government uses its power to protect military-industrial firms, much like the patronage and protection extended by the Chinese government to its own equivalent.

The US has also prevented its allies from selling military technology that includes US components. As a way of circumventing the US embargo, China has tried to purchase weapons from Israel, in the knowledge that many Israeli systems draw heavily on US technology. Israel has become one of the largest suppliers to the Chinese military,[28] a relationship which has strained its ties with Washington. In 2005 the US imposed sanctions on Israel after it sold unmanned drones to China.[29] Five years earlier the US forced Israel to abandon the sale of Phalcon overwatch planes to China, because the Phalcon was based on the US AWACS airborne control plane. China reportedly demanded $2 billion in compensation from the Israelis.[30]

BIGGER THAN THE WORLD?

It is likely that China, were it able, would become by far the biggest market for US arms – at least until it worked out how to make them itself. In January 2010 the US struck an arms export agreement with Taiwan, which China views as a rogue province, worth $6.4 billion – around 4 per cent of the US trade deficit with the People's Republic. Given that Taiwan's annual military budget is only $9.3 billion, compared to the $150 billion that the US believes was China's defence budget in 2009,[31] the US was refusing a market more than 15 times larger than that of Taiwan. The People's Republic could be worth up to $100 billion a year to US arms makers. Between 2004 and 2008, China was the world's largest importer of arms.[32]

A $100 billion reduction in the Sino-American trade deficit prior to the 2008 meltdown would have drained US capital markets of liquidity, causing US interest rates to rise to a more natural level. Pricier loans would have averted the debt-driven bubble. Even the conservative Heritage Foundation has urged the US government to 're-balance' Chinese investment to reduce the 96 per cent that ends up in Treasury bonds.[33]

This $100 billion figure is roughly equivalent to the cost of replacing America's fleet of *Nimitz*-class aircraft carriers with the new *Ford* class.[34] China is currently attempting to construct its own carrier fleet by reverse-engineering an old Soviet ship,[35] but progress seems to be slow. Chinese officials have stated publicly that their inability to buy from the US is the major cause of the trade imbalance. 'The United States bans military items export to China and also subjects military-civilian dual-use items to very rigorous restrictions,' said Chinese Commerce Minister Chen Deming in January 2011, when asked to explain the two countries' huge trade imbalance.[36]

'If there were no such controls, China's imports from the US would rise sharply and the US trade deficit would narrow,' argued Yao Zhizhong, senior researcher on China–US economic and trade relations at the Chinese Academy of Social Sciences.[37] *People's Daily* columnist Li Jia blamed both the US and Europe for restricting hi-tech exports to China.[38] Zhao Zhihao, described in a party mouthpiece as a 'sociology professor', has been even more outspoken. 'China should require the US to cancel or at least temporarily lift its limitations on high-tech exports,' Zhao wrote in the *Global Times*. 'In order to achieve such a goal, powerful media publicity is needed to impose pressure on Americans.' He noted that the US hi-tech embargo covered about 2,500 products, including space-craft components and communication equipment. Zhao concluded that 'the US isn't willing to include its superior products in transactions', which 'naturally leads to an aggravated trade deficit'.[39] The major US exports to China are remarkably low-tech: scrap metal, oilseeds and grains, resins and synthetic rubber feature in the top five.[40]

Xu Chao, a senior official with the State Intellectual Property Office, has added to the Chinese chorus. 'The US has unilaterally blamed China for putting restrictions on the import of US goods, while it restricts the export of high-tech products,' he told a press conference in April 2010.[41] 'It seems contradictory to me.' Although China's imports of hi-tech products have grown rapidly, those hailing from the US declined from 18.3 per cent of imported products in 2001 to just 7.5 per cent by 2009.[42]

Given America's reliance on hi-tech exports, it is not difficult to understand how its attitude to China is damaging its trade balance. Advanced machinery and electronics are critical to the US export basket. According to the US Census Bureau, the major US exports in the first quarter of 2011 were aeroplanes, including engines and parts, electrical machinery, general industrial machines, petroleum preparations (refined from crude oil), generators, scientific instruments, specialised industrial machines, and vehicles.[43] These are exactly the same products that the Chinese are trying to work out how to build for themselves, and which require a high degree of technical specialisation.

Table 1.1   2010 military spending by top five countries (US$bn)

1	USA	700
2	China*	120
3	France	60
4	United Kingdom	60
5	Russia*	59

Source: SIPRI
*estimated

A TROUBLING CONCLUSION

The financial crisis demonstrated that, in its present form, the American economy cannot survive without permitting unfettered sales of arms and dual-use items, even to its enemies. The military-industrial complex is structurally essential to balancing the trade of the world's biggest economy. Even an embargo against just one large customer has a catastrophic effect. By restricting China's purchase of US assets to Treasury bills, in order to prevent the growth of the Chinese military-industrial complex at the expense of its own, the US government presided over a credit-driven disaster that left the country massively in debt, servicing vast interest payments,[44] with unemployment nearing 10 per cent.

Post-crisis, Washington faced two options. It could restructure the US economy away from its dependence on the military-industrial complex. Or it could offer even its most advanced weapons and technologies to China, its biggest strategic rival – a country that is formally committed to recovering control of Taiwan[45] just as the US is formally bound to protect Taiwan[46] and which has a track-record of reverse-engineering foreign technology.

All logic dictated that the US government pursue the first option. Time and again US strategists have warned of what they call China's secret military expansion and the 'misunderstanding and miscalculation' that could arise from it.[47,48,49] In January 2011 the US Secretary of State for Defense, Robert Gates, warned that without a US military presence in Asia China 'might behave more assertively toward its neighbors'. He described questions about China's intentions and its opaque military modernisation programme as a 'source of concern', referring specifically to China's territorial disputes with Japan.[50]

Table 1.2   2004–08 top 19 arms importers

1	China
2	India
3	United Arab Emirates
4	South Korea
5	Greece
6	Israel
7	USA
8	Turkey
9	Egypt
10	Australia
11	Chile
12	Pakistan
13	Algeria
14	Singapore
15	Poland
16	Japan
17	South Africa
18	Venezuela
19	UK

Source: SIPRI

Selling weapons to China would be militarily self-defeating for the US. It would also be unlikely to provide a permanent fix for the trade imbalance. China would begin to reverse-engineer any technology it was able to buy from the US in order to manufacture its own versions, as it has done with Russian equipment.[51] These would be sold on to third-party countries, creating a market for cheaper versions of US weapons. Ultimately, liberalising arms sales to China could exacerbate the trans-Pacific trade imbalance rather than eliminating it.

As stated above, it is impossible to prove the autonomous political power of the military-industrial complex simply by describing those industries that fall within its ambit. To prove Eisenhower's dictum that the complex possesses 'misplaced power', one must prove that it is capable of forcing nations to act against their own interests. If the US is unable to restructure its economy away from its reliance on the military-industrial sector, and is instead forced to hand over America's most deadly technologies to its greatest rivals simply to balance its trade, then the autonomous power of the complex is proven. Those jailed for selling US military secrets to China would be left to reflect on Talleyrand's famous axiom: that 'treason is merely a matter of dates'.

The military-industrial complex does not need to be a monolithic conspiracy in order to wield political power, or to possess a clear goal other than its own survival, or for its effects to be catastrophic. The complex is parasitic on the productive economy not only of the US but of other countries where such defence matrices thrive. It is this cancerous quality, in which the complex spreads under its own critical mass, purely for the sake of its own perpetuation and enlargement, which makes the military-industrial structure a dead weight around the necks of productive and progressive economic forces. It is not China that presents the greatest threat to the US. A much bigger risk to American peace and prosperity is presented by a failure to restructure the US economy and to reduce massively the economic weight of the military-industrial complex.

Table 1.3 Most expensive weapons programmes

	Description	US$bn
F-35	US jet	323
F-22	US jet	77
Eurofighter	EU jet	60
Virginia-class submarine	US submarine	54
B-2 Spirit	US stealth bomber	44
C-17 Globemaster	US transport plane	44
AEGIS System	US anti-missile	43
Trident and proposed 'Son of Trident'	UK nuclear programme	40
J-20	Chinese jet	(est.) 30
V-22 Osprey	US VTOL plane	27

Source: Various

2
What is the Military-Industrial Complex?

In 1921, 30 years before Eisenhower gave his speech, Vladimir Illych Lenin, the leader of Soviet Russia, unveiled his New Economic Policy, the *Novaya Ekonomicheskaya Politika*. The policy laid out a blueprint for a dialled-back form of communism. Instead of the government running every aspect of commerce, the state would instead relinquish control of all but the 'commanding heights' of the economy.[1] These heights were defined as major industries such as energy, steel, banking and heavy manufacturing, as these were viewed as the sectors that controlled the rest of the economy. They were to be organised by the Soviet government's Council of Labour and Defence.

Ninety years on, Lenin might have been surprised to note the similarities between his model and the economy that now exists in the US. The 2008 financial crisis demonstrated that American financial institutions, far from being bastions of capitalism, enjoyed an implicit government guarantee that saw them bailed out to the tune of hundreds of billions of dollars. It became a truism to say that while the banks' profits were privatised, their risks were socialised. Nor was the nationalisation of these risks a left-wing endeavour. The rescue was ordered by the Republican administration of President George W. Bush.

Heavy industry, another of Lenin's 'commanding heights', could also count on taxpayer support. In 2008 US car manufacturers received a $25 billion credit line from the Bush administration to develop cleaner cars, at a cost of $7.5 billion to taxpayers.[2] Under President Barack Obama the government provided a further $60 billion, thus becoming the majority shareholder in General Motors.[3] These sums do not include the government's 'cash for clunkers' scheme, which bribed US consumers to purchase new cars at a cost to the taxpayer of several billion more dollars.[4]

Yet even these 'commanding heights' pale in comparison to the help afforded by the US government to its major weapons manufacturers. The extent of government intervention in this sector begs the question: is the US really a capitalist society? Or has the military-industrial establishment which mushroomed during the long decades of Cold War transformed the US into something more like a Leninist command economy?

THE EVIDENCE

In almost any other environment, the announcement of cuts and efficiency savings worth $178 billion would be a transformative event. This sum is larger, for instance, than the entire economy of Nigeria.[5] It is the amount by which, in 2010, Japan and ten other Asian nations thought necessary to upgrade the infrastructure of Southeast Asia.[6] The total is equivalent to the entire annual exports of India.[7] It is the size of the US e-commerce market.[8]

It is this total, $178 billion, which in January 2011, with little fanfare, the US Secretary of State for Defense Robert Gates announced would be trimmed from the US defence budget over the course of five years. Seventy eight billion would come off the top number and a further $100 billion in cost savings would be redistributed throughout the military. A quarter of the cuts were sourced from the cancellation of a type of amphibious tank that General Dynamics was to construct for the US Marine Corps, at a cost of $14.4 billion.[9] Gates also placed a vertical-take-off-and-landing version of the F-35 Joint Strike Fighter on probation, and he cancelled a surface-to-air missile desired by the army.

Despite being condemned by some elements on the political right as 'weakening America', these cuts were in fact an illusion, a trick of accountancy. What they really represented, reported the *Christian Science Monitor,* 'is the projected savings that would be gained over the next five years by not growing the existing budget'.[10] The newspaper went on to point out that in 2012, the Department of Defense's budget for the fiscal year would be $553 billion – *excluding* around $150 billion for military operations in Iraq and Afghanistan. Although a little less than the Department requested, the budget will nonetheless have grown by 3 per cent on year.

This astonishing sum exceeds the combined military expenditure of the rest of the world. It should be remembered that, although its economy is very large and it provides defence for some of its allies, the US represents only 4 per cent of the world's population. Its 300 million citizens face no conventional military threats to justify such a vast military outlay. The US shares its borders with only two other countries, Canada and Mexico, both of whom are friendly democracies.

Table 2.1   2008 Military spending by region (US$bn)

1	North America	564
2	Europe	320
3	Asia	189
4	Middle East	76
5	Central & S. America	39
6	Africa*	20
7	Oceania	17

Source: SIPRI *incomplete data

HOW TO EXPLAIN?

A pair of vast oceans divides America from the majority of the world's war-zones, most of which are to be found on the African and Eurasian landmasses. In the twenty-first century the Western hemisphere is a peaceful place, at least in relation to the rest of the world. Of the 35 sovereign states in the Americas, only one, Cuba, can properly be called a dictatorship, and it has posed little obvious threat to its giant neighbour since the missile crisis of 1960s. In the southern part of the Western hemisphere, the increasingly prosperous, powerful and peaceable nation of Brazil is setting the standard for its neighbours.

Although it is a trading nation, the US would not be economically crippled by a trade embargo given its vast levels of internal production. Its one Achilles' heel is energy: although the US is the world's third largest producer of crude oil, in 2009 it imported about half its petroleum needs (oil and refined products). Of these imports, roughly 50 per cent came from Western hemisphere countries such as Canada and Venezuela, 22 per cent from Africa, and 17 per cent from the Persian Gulf.[11] We shall assess the role of these imports in US defence spending later.

Militarists have some legitimate responses to these facts. Aside from the crippling cost of overseas operations, the biggest item on the US defence budget is manpower. It is true to say that the US must inevitably pay its servicemen more in salaries and benefits – more than, for instance, the Chinese People's Liberation Army pays its 2.3 million members.[12] The dollar cost is not, perhaps, an accurate representation of the manpower available. The same could be said of its purchasing power for military hardware: America's reliance on US manufacturers makes its military hardware much more expensive than weapons sourced from Russia or China.

Another militarist response is to say that the US is geographically remote from the areas of the world it needs to influence, and that it must therefore spend more to overcome a 'tyranny of distance'. This argument is more tenuous. It presupposes that the US 'needs to influence' unstable areas which in many cases have been destabilised by US intervention or by a political system underwritten by US military power and arms sales. This is particularly true in the Middle East. To quote the Cato Institute, a pro-business American think-tank: 'Our global military activism drags us into others' conflicts, provokes animosity and encourages weapons proliferation. We can save great sums and improve national security by narrowing our goals and adopting a defence budget worthy of its name.'[13]

WHERE DOES THE MONEY GO?

It is worth conducting a brief audit of what, exactly, the US government is paying for with its half-trillion-dollar defence outlay. The military budget represents about 4 per cent of the $14 trillion US economy, even before one considers the contributions to GDP of the various arms manufacturers, their suppliers and contractors, and the dual-use technologies that are supported by defence expenditure. Nor does it include the additional $150 billion set aside for overseas operations.

Conducting such an audit is very difficult. On 21 December 2010 the US Government Accountability Office, which is charged with auditing US government expenditure on behalf of congress, said that it would be unable to do so. It cited 'serious financial management problems at the Department of Defense (DOD) that made its financial statements unauditable'[14] by way of explanation for this failure.

It is not just the military's records that are a problem. Another difficulty is that large sections of military spending are hived off in the budgets of other departments. Military pensions, for instance, fall under the Treasury Department's budget, a system described by the Defense Business Board in 2010 as 'unsustainable' and 'in dire need of repair'. The board estimated that Treasury payments into the military retirement system would grow from $47.7 billion in 2010 to $59.3 billion by 2020[15] – equivalent to an additional 10 per cent of the defence budget.

Nor are nuclear warheads costed into the official defence budget. As of January 2009 there were 2,700 operational warheads in the US nuclear arsenal, with another 2,500 in reserve. According to

Numbers
of personnel

SIPRI, an agreed reduction in the total stockpile was 'occurring more slowly and at this stage is largely on paper', because it consisted of transferring ownership of the warheads from the US Department of Defense to the Department of Energy.[16]

This bureaucratic sleight-of-hand casts doubt over whether the new START treaty with Russia, signed into law by President Barack Obama on 3 February 2011, would genuinely succeed in its goal of reducing the stockpile to 1,550 warheads.[17] Moreover, that treaty came at a cost. Defence commentator Fred Kaplan noted that to persuade hawkish legislators to ratify START, the Obama administration agreed to finance the construction of a new generation of nuclear missiles and submarines.[18]

Despite its various accounting holes, the NNSA (National Nuclear Security Administration) planned to ask for an additional $4.25 billion for its budget between 2011 and 2015. Its current annual budget is approximately $6.4 billion.[19] If one adds such numbers to the defence budget, along with the additional $150 billion for overseas operations, the $53 billion budget afforded to intelligence-gathering,[20] and the various other off-sheet defence expenditures, then the true cost of US government defence spending begins to approach $800 billion, leaving each American household with a bill of $7,000 a year.

THE ECONOMIC EMPIRE

The defence budget is only the tip of the US military-industrial iceberg. The budget supports the economic life of 1.3 million active service personnel and 1.1 million reservists, more than 800,000 civilian defence bureaucrats, and hundreds of thousands of military retirees and veterans wounded in combat. Including their family members, this brings the total number of military-dependent US citizens to over five million.[21]

US military spending is a lifeline for a wide range of other economic interests. Military commissaries provide food to US service personnel and now constitute the seventeenth largest grocery chain in the US.[22] Following the Deep Water Horizon oil rig disaster in the Gulf of Mexico, the Defence Commissary Agency moved to support the livelihoods of fisherman affected by the spillage by buying their produce. In 2009 the US government began legal action against another of these food suppliers, the Public Warehousing Company. It had been supplying food to US troops in Iraq at a cost of more than $30 a day per soldier, for foodstuffs including 'burgers, chicken and crustaceans'. The US Department of Justice accused the company of six counts of fraud.[23]

What, then, of the arms manufacturers? Lockheed Martin is the biggest defence contractor in the US. Based in Bethesda, Maryland, its chairman and chief executive is Robert J. Stevens, a former member of the US Marine Corps. Nearly 80 per cent of Lockheed's revenue comes from the government, which Lockheed furnishes with everything from mail-sorting software to nuclear missiles. The rest of the company's revenue comes from overseas military sales, many financed with US tax dollars, to 40 countries.[24] Lockheed's sales are directly proportional to US military spending.

Who pays the taxes?

To fund the arms manufacturers, the US government must tax productive industries – those that create wealth for themselves rather than draining it from the state. Most revenue is collected from individuals in the form of income tax. In 2009, the Internal Revenue Service collected $1.75 trillion in income tax, as against just $225 billion in corporation tax. Virtually all US income tax is paid by the top 50 per cent of earners.[25] Of these, a great many are physicians. According to *Forbes*, of the 25 best-paid occupations in the US, only two were of a non-medical nature: chief executives and airline pilots.[26] The most profitable *industries* in the US are network equipment, internet services and retailing, pharmaceuticals, and medical equipment, with mining, the manufacture of scientific equipment, and industrial machinery other components of the productive, unsubsidised US economy.[27]

As a 'commanding height' of the US economy backed by the government, the traditional laws of free-market capitalism do not apply to Lockheed, something that Stevens has admitted: 'This is not a business where in the purest economical sense there's a broad market of supply and demand and price and value can be determined in that exchange,' Stevens told the *New York Times* in 2004. 'It's more challenging to define its value.'[28] Stevens' non-market-defined salary was $19.1 million in 2010.[29]

Given such generous compensation, it is clearly in the interests of executives at major arms manufacturers to ensure that the taxpayers' money keeps on flowing. They do this by controlling politicians and officials with access to spending decisions. According to Lockheed Martin, the company has established its own Political Action Committee to divert funds into the election campaigns of tame politicians who 'support national defence, business issues of interest to the corporation, [and] sit on committees with oversight over Lockheed Martin programs.'[30] The company, which has distributed its operation across all 50 US states, also 'supports' the governors' associations of both the Democratic and Republican parties.[31] Put simply, defence companies that rely on tax dollars for their existence use those tax dollars to 'support' officials who will authorise more tax dollars for those companies.

Biological and Chemical

The US stockpile of chemical weapons is spread across eight sites that span North America, each of which are referred to as 'disposal sites'. As of 1996 the Deseret Chemical Depot in Utah held about 44 per cent of the US stockpile of nerve and blister agents. By 2009, the US Army reported that about 60 per cent of the original US chemical weapons stockpile had been destroyed. This left an arsenal of around one million chemical munitions.[32] The US had previously committed itself to eliminating this arsenal by 2004. The US says that it does not stockpile biological weapons but merely conducts research into them.[33]

With 136,000 employees,[34] Lockheed is a tide that lifts all boats – it passes on its government revenues to countless other suppliers and businesses. So do America's other giant military suppliers: Northrop Grumman, McDonnell Douglas (merged with Boeing in 1997), General Electric, General Dynamics, Raytheon and Honeywell. The military-industrial complex is an employer that provides work for millions of Americans at the expense of their fellow taxpayers. It would be less harmful, unfortunately, if the millions whose jobs rely on this corporate welfare operation were paid by the government *not* to work.

Instead, a dangerous idea prevails. This idea is that the US government handing money to US companies is a harmless circulation of wealth around the country. The conservative journal *The National Review* has argued that such defence spending 'boost[s] the economies of local communities and improve[s] thousands of lives'.[35] Lenin would have recognised this argument. It should be said that, in summoning this variant of the broken-window fallacy,[36] the author was referring to lives in the US – the windows are more likely to be broken in the Middle East and Africa.

FOREIGN WELFARE

Corporate welfare for military companies is sometimes routed via third-party countries. The US government provides these countries with grants that they are required to spend on US military equipment. Again, the scale of this expenditure is disguised by government accounting practices: Foreign Military Finance appears in the budget of the US State Department, not the Department of Defense. For 2011 the State Department requested Foreign Military Financing worth $5.5 billion, not including education programmes for foreign military personnel.

Much of this 'assistance' was assigned to countries with their own highly developed military industrial complexes: Israel ($3 billion), Egypt ($1.3 billion), Pakistan ($296 million), and Indonesia ($22 million).[37] In return for their grant the Israelis agreed to purchase 20 Lockheed Martin jets at a cost of $2.7 billion, allowing the US to show a return on the taxpayer's investment.[38] In Egypt the US funds roughly one-third of the national defence budget,[39] a relationship that proved embarrassing to Washington during the demonstrations to overthrow dictator Hosni Mubarak in early 2011.

How can such deals take place in the era of the World Trade Organization (WTO)? State subsidies are precisely the kind of trade-distorting practice that the WTO exists to prevent. But WTO rules offer a crucial exemption relating to the procurement of arms, ammunition or war materials, or to procurement indispensable for national security or for national defence purposes.[40]

Domestically, US arms manufacturers exist in a Leninist economic environment. Externally, little changes. The consequences of this state intervention are alarming, if one accepts market theory. The colossal subsidies that rich nations such as the US provide to their arms manufacturers make it uneconomic for poor countries to manufacture their own defensive systems. While at first this might seem like a victory for disarmament, an analysis of how Western arms makers sell their goods shows otherwise.

It was once thought that for a country to be considered independent, it must have the ability to manufacture its own weapons. This was certainly the mindset around the time of World War II, when adversaries raced to mass-produce more aircraft, tanks and firearms than their enemies. Control of the supply chain was also vital. A 1930s essay by George Orwell suggested that, by this measure, there were only five or six independent countries in the world.

Nothing much has changed in the twenty-first century. Although cheap, low-technology firearms remain a highly effective way to resist military occupation, even against highly advanced nations, few developing countries possess an indigenous manufacturing base. Although some countries such as Pakistan and Ethiopia have learnt to make their own variants of the notorious AK-47 rifle, most states rely on imports from the established arms-manufacturing nations of Europe and North America.

THE EFFECT ON TRADE

US exports, like those of most Western nations, rely heavily on a small number of very big companies. Although small and medium sized enterprises make up 97 per cent of US exporters, they represent less than a third of the total value of US exports, and most sell to only one foreign market (e.g. Canada).[41] A great many US exports are of surprisingly low-value, low-technology items. Surprisingly, quite a few of the 40-foot containers piled onto ships at US ports are filled with scrap paper.[42]

Just 3 per cent of firms produce two-thirds of US exports. Arms manufacturers are a very big deal in this 3 per cent. US overseas arms sales in 2009/10 were $37.8 billion, and will be at least $50 billion a year in the near future, aided by a $60 billion arms deal struck with Saudi Arabia in September 2011[43] as the Obama administration deregulates arms controls in an attempt to sell even more weapons and thereby reduce US indebtedness. As things stand, US weapon exports are equivalent to 30 per cent of the world market.[44]

So it is not difficult to understand why the US Department of Commerce places so much emphasis on defence exports. The Department's Bureau of Industry and Security (BIS) describes its mission as 'to advance US national security, foreign policy, and economic objectives by [...] promoting continued US strategic technology leadership'. Among its duties is 'monitoring the viability of the US defense industrial base'. Again, it is difficult to see how 'defense industrial base' differs from 'military industrial complex'.

The Department's Advocacy Center says that it coordinates US government resources and authority in order to level the playing field on behalf of US companies competing for specific international government projects and procurements. Separately, the Department's

Directorate of Defense Trade Controls 'ensures export compliance in furtherance of US national security and foreign policy objectives'.[45]

Table 2.2   Top ten arms-producing companies (2007)*

1	Boeing	US
2	BAE Systems	UK
3	Lockheed Martin	US
4	Northrop Grumman	US
5	General Dynamics	US
6	Raytheon	US
7	EADS	Europe
8	L-3 Communications	US
9	Finmeccanica	Italy
10	Thales	France

Source: SIPRI *excludes China

Military-industrial exports include not only weapons but 'dual use' items – valuable, hi-tech goods that the US jealously guards. A wide variety of items are defined as dual use, ranging from computers and software to fuel cells, lasers, robotic arms, and optical equipment. The US requires companies to seek dual-use export licenses in situations involving national security, foreign policy, short-supply, nuclear non-proliferation, missile technology, chemical and biological weapons, regional stability, crime control, or terrorist concerns.[46] Its Commerce Control List explains what can and cannot be sold to certain countries. For instance, US companies can sell almost anything to Canada without requiring a license. Exports to China, on the other hand, are hugely restricted.

Looking at the list, a pattern becomes clear. The US is happy to sell technology to countries that already possess it. Poorer countries, even peaceful nations such as Brazil, are frozen out.[47] American firms can sell nuclear equipment to Russia, a long-term strategic rival of the US, but not to Vietnam. 'Regional stability' controls are intended to stop countries acquiring items that are incompatible with US foreign policy objectives or that could alter 'regional stability and military balances'.[48] Countries exempt from these 'RS2' controls include allies such as the UK and Japan, neutral European states such as Sweden and Switzerland, and even former enemies such as Romania and Albania. Non-European developing countries, even reliable US allies such as Colombia, Israel, Egypt, Thailand and South Korea, are frozen out of the 'RS2' products.[49]

Some of these restrictions reflect international treaties, for instance the Nuclear Non-Proliferation Treaty (NPT). However, when the commercial rationale for selling hi-tech equipment becomes too great to ignore, the US unilaterally reneges on such treaty commitments. In 2008 the US government signed a deal with India allowing it to import nuclear equipment from the US, despite India never having signed the NPT. Two years beforehand President George W. Bush had arrived in India with a host of military-industrial companies, including the nuclear specialists Honeywell, to discuss the agreement,[50] despite the region becoming progressively less stable following India and Pakistan's acquisition of nuclear weapons and Pakistan's links to anti-Indian terrorism.

We have already seen how turning down just one large customer – China – can unbalance the US economy to the point of collapse. In most cases, the EU and US are much less scrupulous when pushing high-value military equipment on the governments of poorer countries. Senior officials openly petition to sway the results of defence tenders, illustrating the lack of any clear divide between the state and the supposedly 'private' arms sector. It is worth analysing the various sales pitches used by these taxpayer-funded salesmen.

INDIA AND PAKISTAN: A CASE STUDY OF MILITARY BALANCE

Diplomats promote the theory of a 'military balance' to encourage developing countries to divert tax revenue away from social expenditure and instead to invest in big-ticket weapon systems. One of the biggest contracts on the radar of the global arms trade is India's $10 billion tender to purchase a fleet of 126 fighter jets. This deal attracted feverish attention from the US, Europe and Russia, all of whom sought to capture what would be a massive transfer of wealth from developing India to the advanced economy of the winning bidder.

India's key concern was that its new jets should be superior to the F-16s that Lockheed Martin has supplied to Pakistan since the 1980s, and which it continues to supply.[51] Ostensibly, US arms sales to Pakistan are justified on the grounds that Islamabad is a key US ally against the Taliban, but supersonic jets have not been a major factor in NATO or Pakistani efforts to defeat the Islamist militants. Such weapons are much more relevant to inter-state conflict. Certainly, this is how India, Pakistan's traditional antagonist, views the F-16 shipments.[52]

At this point the so-called 'military balance' enters the equation. A subset of the neo-realist Balance of Power Theory, it centres on the idea that there exists a 'just equilibrium', a situation which provides no incentive for one state to try to impose its will on another through force. Conflicts break out when this equilibrium is disrupted, for instance by one party to a conflict receiving advanced weaponry (such as Lockheed Martin F-16s) from a major power.

Having disturbed the balance of power between India and Pakistan, the US sought to profit from its restoration. President Barack Obama's trip to India in November 2010 was widely reported as a lobbying exercise on behalf of Boeing and Lockheed Martin, which were respectively offering India their F-18 and F-16 jets.[53,54] Obama made mutual security a theme of his speeches: 'In our determination to give our people a future of security and prosperity, the United States and India stand united,' the president told his hosts.[55] Obama was followed to India by hundreds of US business leaders, including those from military corporations such as Boeing, General Electric and Honeywell. After India rejected the US jets in April 2011, the US Ambassador to India Timothy Roemer immediately resigned for what he called 'personal and professional' reasons. The US embassy refused to comment on whether his decision was linked to the failed jet sale.[56] Nevertheless, the US has plenty of other weapons it can sell to India. The fighter contract is only one element of India's military upgrade, which could total $100 billion over the next 10 years.[57]

The motives for bidding for the contract are clear. The deal will extract a vast amount of wealth from India which will support the comfortable lifestyles of Western citizens, either directly through employment (the Stevens example) or indirectly through the tax revenue generated from the winning bidder's profits. Repeat business is likely, as military equipment requires a steady supply of specialised, costly replacement parts.

Winning the bid might also confer a strategic advantage on the supplier nation. The US has used its control of the F-16 supply chain to influence Pakistan's defence policy, refusing to supply spare parts for the jets when the sovereign Pakistani government stepped out of line.[58] More recently, President Barack Obama has warned the Turkish government that its supplies of US weapons and spare parts could be curtailed unless it modifies its policies towards Israel.[59] But this is just a fringe benefit. The main advantage of arms sales is that they financially counterbalance the West's heavy dependence on cheap consumer goods and raw materials from the developing world.

It should be remembered that more people live in poverty in India than do in the whole of sub-Saharan Africa, using an income of less than $1.25 a day as the measure of poverty.[60,61] The fighter deal is worth $22 for each of the 450 million Indians classed as poverty-stricken. The opportunity cost of this outlay is that it could instead be used to make the improvements to communications and infrastructure needed to energise India's impoverished heartlands.

PEACE THROUGH WAR

Alongside the 'military balance', there is another theory propounded by militarists to justify these deals and persuade poor countries to waste their meagre resources. This theory contends that there exists an inverse correlation between arms sales, on the one hand, and deaths in combat, on the other. The theory suggests that the growing lethality and accuracy of national arsenals has reduced the duration and frequency of inter-state conflicts. These effects in turn have supposedly led to a downward trend in annual combat fatalities since the end of World War II.[62]

... and on to Afghanistan

To Pakistan's north-west lies Afghanistan. In 2001 it was invaded and occupied by military forces belonging to the US, Great Britain, and other NATO members, after they had ousted its extremist Taliban government. The occupying powers have made much of the generous amounts of 'aid' they have given to Afghanistan. However, a dossier by Mark Curtis of War on Want provides a rather different picture.

Curtis notes that of the $38.6 billion of aid provided by the US between 2002 and 2009, more than half was actually spent on 'security', training the Afghan police. Much of the rest has in fact been delivered by military personnel as part of the US counterinsurgency strategy. Curtis notes that the US army field manual for Afghanistan refers to this aid as a 'non-lethal weapon' used to buy intelligence information from Afghans. Large sums have been diverted to Western contractors. Curtis quotes the former World Bank director in Kabul, Jean Mazurelle, who said that 'there is real looting going on, mainly by private enterprises'.[63]

Even if one accepts the existence of such a downward trend, there is little reason to attribute it to the efforts of multinational arms dealers. The dilution of national sentiment within trans-national organisations such as the United Nations and European Union are more significant in preventing inter-state aggression, as was the end of the Cold War and the mutual economic interdependence fostered by the World Trade Organization and Bretton Woods institutions.

On the contrary, in the early twenty-first century the growing sophistication of conventional armed forces has driven war underground. The destructive power of modern weapons systems, especially nuclear weapons, has persuaded aggressors to adopt unconventional tactics against their enemies. This has included the sponsorship of insurgent groups who use inexpensive bombs and handguns to destabilise a sitting government, hiding among non-combatants and thereby placing civilians rather than soldiers on the front line. The multi-billion-dollar weapons systems hawked by Western arms manufacturers have proved ineffective against these tactics. Instead, there is an emerging consensus that the only effective weapon against insurgency is sustainable development.

IF YOU CAN'T PERSUADE, STEAL

In November 2010 the US revealed that it had sealed a $60 billion contract to sell hundreds of fighter jets and helicopters to Saudi Arabia.[64] This deal came despite US concerns, voiced in the WikiLeaks data spill, that Saudi Arabia is a major source of funding for al-Qaeda and the Taliban. The leaked reports indicated a rationale for Saudi Arabia's extraordinary outlay on weapons: its concerns over Iran's nuclear weapons programme.[65] Saudi officials have also voiced concerns about terrorism emanating from Yemen.[66]

As with the Indian acquisition, the US equipment sold to the Saudis will not help very much. The threat from Iran is assessed to be a nuclear one, which is of a different order of magnitude to that which can be matched with conventional weapons. At the opposite end of the scale, the supposed Yemeni threat is based on terrorism and asymmetric warfare, tactics which have proved resistant to air power. The diversion of such vast sums into defence contracts may go some way to explaining why, despite Saudi Arabia's oil wealth, the UN ranked the Arab kingdom below countries such as Panama, Libya and Romania in its 2010 Human Development Index.[67]

The US signed arms transfer agreements worth $47.3 billion to Arab states between 2006 and 2009, according to the Congressional

Research Service.[68] In September 2010 a GAO report voiced concerns that while such transactions 'support the U.S. defense industrial base' they were made with an 'absence of documentation' that 'raises concerns that U.S. priorities are not consistently considered before such sales are authorized'.[69] In other words, it appeared that once again the interests of the military-industrial base superseded the national security of the United States.

Table 2.3   2009 Military spending as share of economy (% GDP)

1	Saudi Arabia	11.2
2	Oman	9.7
3	United Arab Emirates	7.3
4	East Timor	6.8
5	Israel	6.3
6	Chad	6.2
7	Jordan	6.1
8	Georgia	5.6
9	Iraq	5.4
10	USA	4.7

Source: SIPRI

The $60 billion contract was equivalent to almost 700 million barrels of crude oil – about two years' worth of US demand from Saudi Arabia's oil fields. Arms deals are one of a limited number of ways that the US economy can pay for this fuel. Without these sales the US would eventually face a balance of payments crisis. Its credit would no longer be accepted; its existing debt would become unmanageable; and it would be unable to honour its Treasury bonds. Such crises struck Argentina in 2001 and Ecuador in 2008. India narrowly avoided such a fate in 1991. This scenario explains the desperation with which US government officials and legislators push arms deals on countries perceived to have surplus cash, like Saudi Arabia.

Corruption plagues the global weapons industry. The typical model runs as follows. An arms manufacturer will hire a local agent in the target country to help win a weapons tender. This individual will normally be a wealthy and well-connected man. The company will hire a risk-mitigation company such as Kroll or Control Risks to make sure the agent has no criminal paper-trail and is reliably discreet. The agent will be formally instructed to desist from bribery and corruption, but he will be offered anywhere up to 20 per cent of the value of the tender if he wins it for his employers.

Such commissions can run into tens of millions of dollars. They provide a huge incentive for illegal collusion between the agent and the adjudicating officials, particularly in countries where officials are poorly paid and where poverty is widespread. Yet so long as the company can display 'due diligence' in hiring the agent, the principle of See No Evil, Hear No Evil prevails. The agents maintain a low-profile and keep their conversations out of the newspapers. They do not need to know anything about the product they are selling; their task is purely to ensure that it is purchased.

The Corner House watchdog notes that half of all corruption complaints reported to the US Commerce Department relate to arms contracts.[70] In July 2010 the US multinational General Electric (GE) admitted that it continued to make use of third-party agents, despite allegations from the US Securities and Exchange Commission that GE agents had bribed officials in Iraq.[71] In January 2010 members of the US Federal Bureau of Investigation arrested 21 arms industry executives at a weapons fare in Las Vegas after FBI agents posing as representatives of the president of Gabon offered a $15 million contract in return for a 20 per cent commission.[72] In India, the career of Prime Minister Rajiv Gandhi was blighted after he was accused of taking bribes from Bofors, a Swedish company which supplied the Indian army with howitzers.

The situation is little different in other parts of the military-industrial trade. One example is the banknote-printing industry. Many countries do not print their own money. Instead, they outsource the paper-making and printing to a handful of secretive European and US companies: Giesecke & Devrient of Germany, De La Rue of Great Britain, Oberthur of France, and Crane, the private family company that makes the paper for the US dollar. In February 2011, following the outbreak of civil war in Libya, the British government intervened to prevent De La Rue from delivering over US$1 billion-worth of Libyan dinars to Colonel Gaddafi.[73] Such control is a useful strategic asset for the supplying nation, allowing its security services to monitor the monetary demand (and therefore economic performance) of other countries.

A newcomer to the industry is the Australian company Securency, which is half-owned by Australia's central bank and which makes currency out of an extruded polymer substrate rather than cotton paper. In 2009 the company was embroiled in an international scandal after *The Age* newspaper reported that Securency's agents had been bribing foreign officials.[74] Subsequent police investigations focused on the agents' activities in Malaysia, Vietnam and Nigeria.

These investigations, it should be noted, were not triggered by the anti-corruption watchdogs themselves but by the newspaper's investigation. Among the agents named by the whistleblower who approached *The Age* was Winnie Mandela, the ex-wife of South Africa's former president Nelson Mandela.[75]

Securency's behaviour prompted the head of Nigeria's central bank, Lamido Sanusi, to demand an explanation from the Australian central bank.[76] However, Nigeria's central bankers have their own explaining to do. Nigeria has its own national printworks, the Nigerian Security Printing and Minting Plc, which possesses what it calls two ultra-modern factory complexes[77] with state of the art printing presses from the Swiss company KBA-Giori. These factories should mean that Nigeria has the capacity to print its currency, the naira, indigenously, without the need for imports.

But when officials are offered ' incentives' to import – incentives of that type that Securency's agents are alleged to have offered in Nigeria[78] – they have no incentive to utilise the local manufacturing base. Indeed, they have an incentive to run it badly. The effect on industrial development is devastating. Consider that thousands of agents are employed worldwide, often working on behalf of multiple foreign industrial concerns, and one begins to see how the West is strangling the industrial development of poor countries at birth.

By being owned by a central bank, Securency had broken one of the cardinal rules of military-industrial trade: to maintain a distance between the 'private' companies of the military-industrial complex and the states that support them. There are no moral shades of grey here. Collusion between the military-industrial complex and poor-country officials is a form of theft. It siphons public funds into the pockets of Western executives and crooked officials. The net effect is that developing governments expend their meagre resources on foreign weapons and other items they do not need, in order to boost the balance sheets of Westerners. The victim-state loses the revenue needed to improve roads, ports and bridges, or to establish an effective system of education, or to provide effective policing, or any of the other public goods needed to promote economic growth. It is the rich stealing from the poor.

There are more subtle forms of bribery. On their visits to poor countries, Western leaders grease the wheels of business deals with pledges of aid. In 2011 Britain's Department of International Development admitted that it was sending direct aid to countries such as Russia, China, Vietnam and Serbia, none of which was viewed as a key priority by relief organisations. The department was also donating foreign aid to India, despite the fact that India has its own foreign-aid budget worth $500m a year[79] as well as nuclear weapons and a space programme. The president of Malawi, Bingu Mutharika, used aid from the EU to buy himself a presidential jet.[80]

CONCLUSION

Countries must pay for what they buy. To do so they must transfer wealth to those countries from which they import. This balancing exercise has led to Western powers placing heavy pressure on developing countries, whether at a military, industrial or political level, to purchase expensive weapons systems that are poorly adapted to their security challenges. If the specious theories of military balance and 'peace through war' fail to convince, then arms manufacturers have proven themselves willing to conspire with corrupt officials to rig tenders and thereby steal wealth from some of the world's poorest people.

So important are big-ticket arms sales to balancing trade that US arms makers exist in a quasi-Leninist economy in which they are underwritten by the taxpayer. Lockheed Martin makes no pretence that it is subjected to the free-market competition encountered by small and medium-sized US businesses. While smaller American companies have to endure capitalism, Lockheed can purchase socialism – it ensures its future by investing in political influence in Washington. Some alleged 'conservatives' justify this socialism along Leninist lines by pointing to the vast numbers of ordinary Americans who owe their livelihood to the Department of Defense's largesse, rather as all Soviet workers were expected to be grateful to the state.

In the export market, this kind of state-socialism fits with the need to balance trade. By extending massive subsidies to military-industrial exporters the US government ensures that they have an unfair competitive advantage against start-ups in poorer countries, and can squash their development at birth. This hampers the ability of poor countries to develop defensive and industrial capabilities internally, allowing the West to enjoy a 'specialism' (or, in fact, a monopoly) in the manufacture of high-value-added armaments and machines.

Low-technology weapons can be an effective means of resisting foreign invasion and occupation – which, after all, is the definition of the word 'defence' – so military-industrial interests play neighbours against each other to ensure continued sales. By selling extremely advanced weapons to the hostile neighbours of a country like India, the US can persuade the Indian government that it needs to invest more in its own military, thus maintaining a notional 'military balance'. Even if the US firm loses that particular bid to a European competitor, it will benefit from similar equations being played out elsewhere – the West can't lose. Bribing warlike countries such as Israel and Pakistan to purchase hi-tech weapons is an effective way of persuading their neighbours to make such purchases.

Through these mechanisms the military-industrial complex has promoted an international cycle of war and poverty. The military-industrial complex forces the US to sell sophisticated weapons, against America's own national interest, to dictatorships such as that of Saudi Arabia, which enforce cultural values that are anathema to those of Americans. At the time of writing, Arab dictatorships were using these weapons to murder peaceful demonstrators demanding greater political freedom in the Middle East.[81] Military-industrial executives share the spoils of corrupt deals with officials in the Third World, as billions languish in poverty. This poverty and corruption promotes a hatred of government that is itself a driver for new conflict, and new arms sales.

3
The Culture of Militarism and Global North's Power of Definition

At the opening of the XLV Super Bowl in Dallas, Texas, the crowd of 106,000 was treated to the sight of decorated soldiers, in full uniform, marching with the Stars and Stripes. Uniformed figures joined in a rendition by *Glee's* Lea Michele of 'America the Beautiful'. The crowd was introduced to Staff Sgt Salvatore Giunta, a recipient of the Medal of Honor for bravery in Afghanistan, to loud cheers. Overhead four US Navy F-18s flew over Cowboys Stadium, although as the roof was closed no one inside saw them. This flyby cost the US taxpayer $450,000.[1]

Such sporting displays are just one of the many ways that Americans signal their reverence for the military. The British journalist Mark Mardell once wrote of his surprise when, sitting on a US domestic flight, the captain of the plane drew attention to a uniformed serviceman on board and asked for him to be honoured, prompting a round of applause.[2] In Tennessee, car-owners purchase number plates with a blue star insignia marking the driver as the relative of someone in military service.[3] Special plates for veterans have been common for years. The Boy Scouts of America, an avowedly patriotic and military-themed organisation, is one of the largest youth movements in the US.

Ritual deference for military service has been found in societies throughout history, from the Greek city state of Sparta, to the Roman Empire, the Aztec nation, the Kingdom of Prussia, the British Empire, the Empire of Japan, and the Soviet Union. Mardell's surprise was strange given that he hailed from a country in which heirs to the hereditary throne enlist in the military as a matter of course and appear in uniform throughout their royal careers. This is a tradition common to many of the world's remaining monarchies, from Norway and Sweden to Thailand and Bhutan. Everywhere, it seems, the personification of the state is closely associated with men and women in uniform. The positive connotations of medals, epaulettes and gold braid continue to outweigh the negative ones.

Explaining why military service is held in such high esteem is not straightforward. The fact that it can be hazardous is not quite explanation enough. Military service is a dangerous job for soldiers in Thailand and Bhutan, but much less so in Norway and Sweden. It is much more dangerous for lower ranks than for senior officers, but officers are afforded no less respect than private soldiers. Even in countries plagued by brutal military dictatorships, popular respect for the military somehow endures despite the disastrous outcomes so often produced by this unquestioned reverence.

A DANGEROUS JOB – FOR SOME

Without question, being a private or non-commissioned officer in the US army is a dangerous job. The wars in Iraq and Afghanistan alone claimed the lives of almost 5,000 US servicemen during the first decade of the twenty-first century. Of those who survived, tens of thousands were repatriated with physical and psychological injuries. US soldiers receive more generous benefits than their counterparts in other countries, but their risks and personal sacrifices are immense, often sustained during conflicts that have little obvious bearing on US security.

The situation of the officer class is somewhat different. In most military structures there is a sharp distinction between the social, educational and financial background of non-commissioned soldiers and those of commissioned officers – those with the rank of lieutenant and above. The risks of military service for these military executives are considerably lower, and the rewards of service vastly higher. The public's failure to understand these distinctions has allowed the officer class to bestow upon itself lavish budgets and privileges, criticism of which is portrayed as 'unpatriotic' or risking the lives of soldiers on the front line.

Officers comprised 17 per cent of the US force deployed to Iraq and Afghanistan, but of the 4,683 Americans killed up to August 2010, they represented only 10 per cent of the casualties, or 471 individuals. On closer inspection this number was smaller still, because it included warrant officers, who are senior non-commissioned officers and specialists below the rank of lieutenant.[4] A study by the University of Pennsylvania found that warrant officers in Iraq had a higher risk of death than any other army rank, at 1.731 (all ranks = 1.00). The risk to officers ranked major or above was 0.46.[5]

The death toll of commissioned US officers serving in Iraq and Afghanistan was similar to that of reporters working in those countries. The Committee to Protect Journalists says that 168 media workers were killed in Iraq between the 2003 invasion and 2010. A further 22 died in Afghanistan. Among those killed included senior journalists from Western news organisations such as Gaby Rado, Terry Lloyd, Rupert Hamer, Michelle Lang, Karen Fischer and Christian Struwe, as well as a great many local reporters.

It can be said without fear of contradiction that journalists receive less popular acclaim than do military officers, in the US or elsewhere. It appears that it is not the dangerous nature of military work itself that earns the armed forces such unquestioned respect. The mortality rates of American fishermen and hauliers are also very high,[6] but politicians rarely single out fishing crews or truck drivers as the embodiment of American bravery and values. The fortitude of ordinary civilians trapped in conflict zones goes entirely ignored.

What other explanations exist for popular deference to the military? It is arguable that US popular culture presents an unduly flattering portrayal of military service. Hollywood sometimes produces movies that celebrate martial values and glorify war. The highest grossing Hollywood movies of recent years were films of the *Lord of the Rings* and *Harry Potter* variety, fantasies which sometimes imparted martial values in an oblique fashion, or presented conflicts in a simplified, good-versus-evil light. Successful films about US military campaigns – *Saving Private Ryan, Apocalypse Now, The Hurt Locker* – contributed to reverence for the military, but they also emphasised the horror and random brutality of war. The most popular film, *Avatar,* actually served as a repudiation of the Iraq War and resource-driven militarism.

More significant is what Hollywood does *not* do. Politicians, reporters, corporate executives and policemen are frequently cast as villains, or in unsympathetic roles. Yet it is extremely rare for American servicemen to be represented as one-dimensional villains or buffoons, even though dramatic representations of soldiers are commonplace. If their actions are villainous, they are usually provided with some context to justify this villainy, at least in part. Hollywood, en masse, mirrors the public's deference for the military, as does the rest of the media.

Even the judiciary is not immune from military exceptionalism. In the US there is a longstanding tradition that civilian courts defer to military authority, as the military's ultimate commander is the president. This deference allowed the president and the military to breach the constitutional rights of 120,000 Japanese-Americans by interning them during World War II.[7] The judicial deference is both legal and personal in nature: during her confirmation hearings, Supreme Court Judge Elena Kagan claimed that she not only respected the US military but 'revered' it.[8] Kagan made this comment after Republican senators accused her of denigrating the US military by restricting its recruitment practices on the campus at Harvard, where she had served as Dean.

If it is dangerous for judges to oppose militarism, then it is disastrous for anyone seeking election. The ritualised 'honouring' of military service has become almost mandatory in US politics. In July 2010 the former Republican vice-presidential nominee, Sarah Palin, joined Glenn Beck, a radical commentator on Fox News network, in a 'Restoring Honor' rally at the Lincoln Memorial in Washington. According to the event's press release: 'This rally will honor the troops, unite the American people under the principles of integrity and truth, and make a pledge to restore honor within ourselves and our country.'[9] Proceeds from the event were donated to veterans' charities.

The most public example of the exaggerated deference for military service, and its political consequences, came during the 2004 US presidential contest, which pitched incumbent US President George W. Bush against his Democratic challenger John Kerry, a senator from Massachusetts. The Democrats had nominated Kerry in large part due to his service in America's futile war in Vietnam 30 years earlier, where he had won two Purple Hearts (awarded to those injured by enemy fire) and a Silver Star for bravery as captain of a Swift boat.

Bush, by contrast, spent the Vietnam War in the safety of the US, where he had enrolled with the Texas Air National Guard. The young Bush enjoyed preferential treatment in obtaining this coveted assignment, which according to the *Washington Post* 'was often associated with efforts to avoid active duty in Vietnam',[10] despite scoring poorly on his pilot aptitude test. Senior Democrats also alleged that Bush had been absent without leave (AWOL) even from this relatively undemanding service.

Rather than presenting a coherent argument against Bush's decisions to invade Afghanistan in 2001 and Iraq in 2003, the Democrats sought to embarrass the president on the basis of his Vietnam record. There was an element of revenge to this. The Republicans had portrayed Bush's predecessor President Bill Clinton, a Democrat, as a 'draft dodger' for accepting a Rhodes scholarship to Oxford University instead of shipping out to fight in Indochina. Kerry's campaign provided a perfect opportunity to make the Republicans pay for this tactic. 'I'm John Kerry, and I'm reporting for duty!' was how the senator announced his decision to run in 2004, saluting his supporters to rapturous applause.

The presidential race quickly degenerated into a debate over Kerry's war record. Bush's chief election adviser Karl Rove understood the danger posed to his candidate by Kerry's status as a war hero. Rove's friend Bob J. Perry, a Texan multi-millionaire, financed the creation and promotion of a political action group called the Swift Boat Veterans for Truth, the sole purpose of which was to muster Vietnam veterans who were willing to denigrate Kerry's war record.[11] This campaign gave rise to the verb to 'swiftboat', as in 'to smear'. Rove's view was that since Kerry had chosen to base his campaign on his war record, he could not object to people questioning that record.[12]

The Swift Boat attacks also targeted Senator Kerry's anti-war activism. Kerry's experiences in Vietnam had persuaded him that the war was a catastrophe. In a 1971 congressional testimony, which he delivered on behalf of other honourably discharged veterans, Kerry said that he had witnessed war crimes committed in Vietnam by US troops. He described stories he had been told by other servicemen in which they had personally raped, cut off ears, cut off heads, taped wires from portable telephones to human genitals and turned up the power, cut off limbs, blown up bodies, randomly shot at civilians, razed villages in fashion reminiscent of Genghis Khan, shot cattle and dogs for fun, poisoned food stocks, and generally ravaged the countryside of South Vietnam.[13]

The Swift Boat Veterans for Truth seized on this testimony. In one TV advert entitled 'Sellout', the veterans said that Kerry's testimony had demoralised troops in the Southeast Asian theatre and 'dishonoured his country and … the people he served with'.[14] The veterans accused Kerry's testimony of endorsing the Vietcong's propaganda and humiliating war veterans. Two years later the veterans group was fined almost $300,000 by the Federal Election Commission for failing to register as a political committee,[15] but by then President Bush was well into his second term. One academic study of the Swift Boat ads found them to have clearly succeeded in weakening Kerry's support.[16]

The 2004 campaign was evidence of the central role that military service, and the concept of military service, plays in US political debate. Destroying the credibility of Kerry's military record became a key priority of his opponents, but this critique could only be delivered by ex-military men who had themselves seen active service. An implicit democratic bar prevents civilian politicians from making the same kind of criticism. Four years later the Obama campaign enlisted General Wesley Clark to downplay the military service of John McCain,[17] Obama's opponent, a former prisoner of war in Vietnam.

Clearly, Bush's political career was threatened by his failure to fight in Vietnam,[18] just as Clinton's was.[19] Kerry, having served in Vietnam, was vulnerable to accusations that he had not fought bravely enough, and was even criticised for campaigning against a conflict universally acknowledged to be a disaster. Pre-empting such attacks has now become a major preoccupation of potential chief executives. During his presidential campaign Barack Obama said that he had considered joining the military after graduating from Harvard University, but was put off because there were no wars going on at the time.[20]

OFFICER'S PERKS

It is clear that, even in the West, civilian control of the military is qualified by uncritical public sympathy for soldiers, sailors and airmen. The origins of this exaggerated sympathy are difficult to define without resorting to an analysis of human psychology, particularly male psychology. What is certain, however, is that in many cases the officer class has used this blanket public sympathy to protect its own privileges, sometimes at the expense of lower ranks. Elected politicians are unable to confront this state of affairs for fear of being portrayed as 'unsupportive' by the generals' allies in the media.

In her excellent book on the military-industrial complex in Pakistan, Ayesha Siddiqa describes some of the perks available to the Pakistani officer class. Many of these, she notes, flow from their privileged access to the vast industrial empire controlled by the military establishment, one of the biggest players in Pakistan's economy. However, there are other perks similar to those enjoyed by officers in the West. This is not surprising: Pakistan inherited its military culture from the British, and its close alliance with the US has transferred other cultural traits.

Siddiqa points out that the Pakistani military-industrial complex originated in part from the age-old British tradition of allocating reclaimed land to loyal military personnel.[21] Urban and rural real estate was provided by the military complex to serving and retired military officials.[22] Real estate transferred to the army included land captured from India in the 1965 war between the countries, a transfer that provided an incentive to the army for further territorial wars.[23] While this arrangement may seem corrupt, similar arrangements still exist in the British armed forces.

Senior officers in Britain receive large residences as a perk of the job. Often these houses have been built especially for officers of a certain rank e.g. a brigadier's house will be larger and more impressive than that of a major. In February 2011 reports indicated that the Ministry of Defence had spent £1.3 million on renting homes for just 30 brigadiers and generals. In one case the taxpayer was paying £6,000 ($9,600) a month to rent a home in London for a general. All of the officers involved earned upwards of £95,000 ($152,000) a year.[24]

Enlisted men also receive subsidised accommodation, but of a very different nature. On returning from Afghanistan in October 2007 the 2nd Battalion of the UK's Mercian Regiment, formerly the Worcestershire and Sherwood Foresters, were billeted in the Cavalry Barracks at Hounslow, West London. Conditions at the base were exposed by a soldier leaking photographs to the *Sun* newspaper.[25] The battalion, which had lost nine men and had 54 injured during their tour of Helmand Province, found walls infested with damp, leaking roofs, rats, two showers between every 15 men, and tiny rooms shared by four men. The base was located directly under the deafening flight path from Heathrow Airport. As one soldier pointed out, the conditions at Hounslow were much worse than would be tolerated in one of Britain's prisons.

British officers are not allowed to keep their grace-and-favour mansions on leaving military service. The British military has replaced the tradition of conferring land upon retiring officers with large lump-sum payments. These payments, which can be worth up to one-and-a-half times the value of final salary,[26] are not well understood by the British public. One report from 2004 suggested that a major (a middle-management rank closer to lieutenant than to general) would leave with a tax-free lump sum of £80,000 ($128,000) in addition to a generous pension[27] and the possibility of a post-military career. Senior ranks are paid even larger sums. The size of these payments is not well-publicised by Britain's Ministry of Defence, presumably because many British taxpayers would be shocked to learn that experienced public servants were being offered such large incentives to stop working.

Even more important are the non-financial perks available to the officer class. Pakistan's military has inherited its educational outlook from the British. Siddiqa notes that in Pakistan, entry to army-run schools is restricted to children of army officers. These elite secondary schools are among the best in Pakistan.[28] By sending their children to these English-medium academies, senior officers are able to secure their children access to Pakistan's best universities and thereafter into elite positions within the state.

Again, a similar situation can be found in Pakistan's former colonial master. British servicemen are offered a Continuity of Education Allowance which subsidises the fees at elite boarding-schools, in theory so that the education of military children is not disrupted when their parents move from base to base. In 2009 this military perk cost British taxpayers £172 million ($275 million).[29] Officially, the subsidy is available to all ranks, both officers and enlisted men. In practice, the vast majority of those who benefit from it are officers.[30]

More than one-third of the school payments are to soldiers of the rank of lieutenant-colonel or above, even though their pay, at £81,000 a year and upwards, already puts them within the top 3 per cent of UK earners. Only 0.1 per cent of privates and less than 10 per cent of non-commissioned officers receive the payments.[31] One obvious reason for this is cost. Although the maximum subsidy is £18,000 a year, parents must stump up at least 10 per cent of the fees themselves.[32] To non-commissioned ranks, this sum is often prohibitive.

Just as in Pakistan, these elite schools control access to British high society. They make up a third of admissions to Oxford and Cambridge universities.[33] It is unusual to become a senior British ambassador, judge, editor, politician or civil servant without a degree from one of these two institutions. It is for this reason that wealthy Britons are prepared to hand over fortunes to 100-or-so elite schools – fees that senior officers claim from the taxpayer. In 2010 just one of these elite schools, Westminster, sent more sixth-formers to Oxford and Cambridge than came from among the 350,000 schoolchildren poor enough to receive free school meals.[34]

BLAMING THE POLITICIANS

It is valuable to understand how senior officers exert pressure on elected politicians to protect these privileges. In Pakistan, the military establishment is so powerful and independent that no politician dares to confront it. British generals, however, are required to be slightly more subtle. Their strategy rests heavily on the dewy-eyed respect which the British public, as elsewhere, affords to servicemen, particularly in a time of war.

The generals' key ally is the *Telegraph*, a broadsheet newspaper with close ties to the military that often acts as the mouthpiece of senior officers. In November 2010 the newspaper reported that an unnamed colonel serving with Britain's elite Special Air Service regiment had quit the army. It was not suggested that this was to enjoy his large lump-sum pay-off. Instead, the *Telegraph* reported his resignation as a protest against proposed cuts to the Continuity of Education Allowance. (Strangely, it also reported the colonel was 'a rather aloof and quiet individual and did not discuss his resignation with anyone'.)[35]

The article proceeded to quote a serving General, again nameless, who blamed threats to the education perk for damaging morale. Damage to morale is hard to measure, but it is not difficult to see how this kind of reporting damages the careers of civilian politicians who control the military budget. The *Telegraph* and other newspapers typically portray equipment shortages as the result of 'government dithering',[36] rather than, say, the result of military funds being spent on school fees rather than body armour. In any clash between politicians and generals, the elected leaders always lose – a direct consequence of the public's ingrained sympathy for soldiers.

Generals sometimes protect their turf by more direct forays into political life. One of the most prominent critics of the British army's alleged equipment shortages in Iraq and Afghanistan was General Sir Richard Dannatt, who until August 2009 was Britain's Chief of General Staff. Described by the *Telegraph* as a 'trenchant critic of the government'[37] General Dannatt frequently used his position to embarrass ministers of the ruling Labour Party over alleged shortfalls of the helicopters needed to transport British soldiers in Afghanistan.[38]

It was only after Dannatt retired in October 2009 that his links with the opposition Conservative Party became clear. He was appointed an adviser to the Conservatives on defence policy and endorsed by the party for membership of the upper house of Parliament, the House of Lords.[39] The shadow foreign secretary, William Hague, was forced to deny accusations that Dannatt was a Conservative stooge.[40] Worse was to come. In parliamentary testimony Sir Sherard Cowper-Coles, the former British ambassador to Afghanistan, said that Dannatt had redeployed battlegroups from Iraq to Afghanistan purely because he feared that, were they not in a warzone, they would be subject to budget cuts. 'It's use them, or lose them', he said.

> In my view, the Army's 'strategy' in Helmand was driven at least as much by the level of resources available to the British Army as by an objective assessment of the needs of a proper counter-insurgency campaign in the province. Time and again, Ministers were pressed to send more troops to Helmand, as they became available from Iraq.[41]

Cowper-Coles continued this devastating testimony by accusing the army of a 'spurious' insistence on rotating brigades through Afghanistan, rather than deploying smaller formations. He said that government ministers were reluctant to question the military advice put to them, for fear of leaks to the press suggesting that they weren't supportive enough of the troops. As a result the Royal Air Force was able to persuade ministers of a needless and expensive deployment of Tornado jets to Afghanistan, even though NATO joint-strategy had made it clear that such jets were not required. Cowper-Coles concluded by saying he thought Dannatt's criticism of ministers regarding equipment shortages was 'unfair', especially regarding the helicopters, because: '27 per cent of the helicopter movements were for moving VIPs around theatre. And most of those VIPs were senior military tourists from London!'

It is worth noting that over the past century more British ministers have died in the line of duty, usually at the hands of the Irish Republican Army, than have British generals. Yet generals are nonetheless esteemed much more highly than politicians. Senior generals ruthlessly exploit this sentimentalism to obstruct attempts to rationalise military expenditure, especially when their own perks are involved. This tendency was much in evidence during debates in the US over funding for the war in Iraq. Democrats who opposed the enormous budgetary appropriations for the conflict were accused of putting the lives of troops at risk.[42]

In an extreme example of military persuasion, in February 2011 *Rolling Stone* magazine reported that a US general had deployed 'psy-ops', or psychological operations, techniques against American senators to persuade them to authorise higher military expenditure. Psy-ops employ advanced forms of propaganda and suggestion to influence the thinking of military targets. The affair only came to light when the leader of the psy-ops team, Lt Colonel Michael Holmes, recounted the episode to journalists from the magazine.[43]

Generals also exploit public sentimentalism to lever themselves into civilian office. Senior service chiefs frequently make the transition into politics. This is especially true of those associated with 'successful' conflicts. Eisenhower, the Supreme Allied Commander in World War II, became president, as did General Charles de Gaulle in France. General Colin Powell was appointed Secretary of State after serving as Chairman of the Joint Chiefs of Staff during the first Gulf War. Wesley Clark ran for the 2004 Democrat presidential nomination after commanding NATO operations in Kosovo. No other profession affords scope for such a direct transition. In many cases ambitious military commanders are only one major war away from high office.

THE POWER OF DEFINITION

The media rarely questions this conveyor belt of khaki-clad politicians. When it comes to warfare, the media debate tends to be confined to a narrow spectrum that sees wars as 'justified' or 'unjustified', 'legal' or illegal', popular or unpopular. Columnists will oppose or support one or other invasion, but without challenging the necessity of war in general or of the many trillions spent each year in prosecuting conflicts and maintaining military hardware and personnel. Instead the debate is closed down into narrow squabbles over weapons of mass destruction, the human-rights record of a regime scheduled for 'change', the legal conditions necessary for invasion, and so on. Practical alternatives to war *qua* war are ignored.

One academic study of the British media's coverage of the Iraq War – the most hotly debated conflict of recent times – found that only 4.4 per cent of newspaper articles about Iraq took the rationale for the war as their main topic, with just 4.7 per cent focusing on domestic protest. Reports of battle/strategy represented 46 per cent of the coverage. The authors noted that these proportions bore a close similarity to studies of US television coverage of the war.[44]

If Great Britain has the world's most rigorously competitive media market, as is often claimed,[45,46,47] it is fair to conclude that the world has reason to worry. Consider, then, the situation in developing countries, which provide the backdrop to most of the world's conflicts. If the media is key to conditioning perceptions of war, then the skewed coverage found in many war-torn countries goes some way to explaining why their citizens accept the unacceptable.

Since their Partition in 1947 the sovereign nations of India and Pakistan have fought three full-scale wars, armed themselves with nuclear weapons, strangled efforts at regional integration across South Asia, impeded each other's trade with the outside world, stirred communal hatreds against Muslim and non-Muslim minorities, supported each other's enemies, bisected and militarised the beautiful province of Kashmir, and mounted a ceaseless campaign of propaganda against one another.

This madness would have been impossible without the collusion of the media. In both countries the press has reflected the elite view that a celebration of nationalism and militarism is a greater priority than preventing countless deaths, both civilian and military. To understand the mentality of the editors, academics, generals and politicians who have united against the masses in promoting hostility towards their largest neighbour, there is one concept that it is vital to understand: 'national consolidation'.

'Today, even as Pakistan engages in whipping up war hysteria, our nation remains steadfastly united and, if anything, the process of national consolidation is becoming stronger,' India's Prime Minister, Manmohan Singh, told an audience of state chief ministers in 2009.[48] The bookish Manmohan, India's first Sikh leader, is far from a typical warmonger. However, in this instance he was playing into a narrative that has kept India and Pakistan at each other's throats since independence.

The principal of national consolidation holds that a country is only 'completed' when its people are united in viewing the nation as a discrete whole, rather than a tapestry of ethnicities or regions. For those who endorse this outlook, the presence of a national enemy is a useful means of consolidating national sentiment and patriotism. India's billion-plus population is made up of many ethnicities, dozens of religious groups, and hundreds of languages. Pakistan faces almost the opposite problem: it is divided into just four provinces, each with distinctive cultures, three of which resent the largest, Punjab, as overly dominant. In both countries the process of 'national consolidation' is therefore incomplete.

The media in both India and Pakistan has been heavily complicit in exaggerating the differences between the neighbours and disguising the countries' many similarities. In 2005 the leader of India's Hindu supremacist Bharatiya Janata Party (BJP), Lal Krishna Advani, visited Pakistan, the land of his birth (Manmohan too was born in what is now Pakistan). Perhaps overcome by his welcome in a country that his party demonises, Advani made some unusually generous remarks about his hosts, including a comment that Pakistan's founder, Mohammad Ali Jinnah, was a secular figure and an 'ambassador of Hindu-Muslim unity'.

The comments provoked a media storm in India. 'In all his decades in public service, did he really have no clue about how India regards its former citizen?' asked one commentator.[49] 'Never mind Jinnah's fondness for drink and food forbidden by Islam,' wrote another. 'Forget too his so-called liberal worldview ... [Jinnah] saw no place for Muslims in Hindu majority India.'[50] Advani, who refused to retract his comments, would later blame the Indian press for the furore and his subsequent resignation as party leader.[51]

Years later, the BJP's political opponents continued to make hay out of Advani's 'softness' towards Pakistan. 'It is the BJP that showed signs of weakness,' Rahul Gandhi of the ruling Congress party said in April 2009. 'It was L.K. Advani who went to Pakistan and spoke in favour of Jinnah. Our prime minster never went to Pakistan.'[52] Any chance of a positive light being shed on Advani's attempted rapprochement between his Hindu hardliners and the Islamic Republic of Pakistan was lost. 'I think we misunderstood [Jinnah] because we needed to create a demon,' said another BJP stalwart expelled for praising Pakistan's founder.[53]

The reporting of violence in Kashmir is especially partisan. When the Indian army shoots Muslims in the disputed province, as it frequently does, Indian newspapers habitually refer to the dead as 'jihadis' even when there is reason to doubt the army's account.[54] For its part, the Pakistani press habitually refers to genuine militants killed in Kashmir as 'martyrs' (شہید). The media in both countries view the aspirations and plight of the Kashmiris themselves as highly secondary to the territorial dispute and military stand-off.

This situation prevails despite the fact that the Indian and Pakistani media are relatively free by global standards, notwithstanding the influence of wealthy proprietors such as the Jain brothers of the Times Group and Mir Shakil ur Rahman of the Jang company. Elsewhere, reporters who challenge the pro-military consensus of a country at war are not merely branded traitors but are subjected to intimidation, violence and murder. The standards of war reporting in India and Pakistan look positively robust when compared to the situation in their southern neighbour, Sri Lanka.

THE TEARDROP OF ASIA

Nowhere has the mantra of 'national consolidation' produced more devastating effects than on the island once known as Ceylon. There, a binary ethno-religious split between the Sinhala-speaking Buddhist majority and the mainly Hindu Tamil minority fell foul of those who believed that for a nation to be a nation it requires national conformity. Following his election as president in 2004 Sri Lanka's president, Mahinda Rajapaksa, launched a war of extermination against the Tamil Tigers (also known at the LTTE), the leading Tamil militant group. His election ended a peaceful four-year period in which the conflict appeared to be destined for a political solution. Thousands of civilians died in the following all-out war.

Journalists who questioned the president's approach soon found themselves in deep trouble. In January 2009 the editor of the *Sunday Leader* newspaper was gunned down by a death squad in Colombo. Two years later the killers remained at large, because, in the words of Rapporteurs Sans Frontieres (RSF), the government 'is doing nothing to solve this murder and in fact is clearly preventing the truth from coming to light.'[55] The government has become an accomplice', the NGO added.

This was not an isolated incident. The state's abuse of journalists has been extensive and President Rajapaksa has refused to heed calls to respect press freedoms.[56] Nor was the government's campaign purely to silence outright criticism of its policies; the repression was also intended to suppress investigation of possible war crimes. In 2006 17 staff of the French aid agency Action Contre La Faim (ACF) were executed in the town of Muttur. All but one of the dead were Tamils, and speculation that the army was behind the killings was heightened by the government's refusal to launch a proper inquiry.[57] In a leaked cable, US Ambassador Patricia Butenis reported that 'responsibility for many alleged crimes rests with the country's senior civilian and military leadership, including President Rajapaksa and his brothers'.[58]

With genuine journalists under siege, and prevented from reaching the battlefront, the Sri Lankan military stepped in to fill the void. The Ministry of Defence launched its own news service to replace impartial reporting with an authorised account of the war's progress and the army's conduct. The ministry ran articles with headlines such as 'Terrorists lose more ground in Jaffna Peninsula'; 'LTTE guns down and hangs fleeing civilians'; and 'Come to security of Safety Zone – Govt. urges all civilians'. The last headline,[59] from

3 February 2009, carried a bitter reminder of why soldiers should not write the news. The army began shelling the 'safety zone' two months later, killing more than a thousand civilians in the process.[60,61]

It would be remiss to go further without stating that the Tamil Tigers had even less respect for press freedoms than the government they were fighting; no independent or critical reporting took place in the Tamil enclaves they controlled. What was shocking was the lack of any attempt by President Rajapaksa to retain the moral high ground. By the time the Tigers were destroyed in 2009, the government's treatment of freedom of expression was barely distinguishable from the terrorists it was fighting.

A COLLECTIVE FAILURE

It is too simple to divide the media into pro- and anti-war camps. For decades the press has found it much safer to be pro-war than anti-war, serving the interests of powerful media barons and political contacts ahead of the interests of the general public. Cartoonish depictions of strutting foreign dictators mysteriously give way to a more 'balanced' commentary in line with government policy (Libya's rehabilitated Colonel Gaddafi). On the other hand, when a friendly dictator falls out of official favour he is quickly portrayed as a Hitler-like figure (again Libya's Colonel Gaddafi, post-rehabilitation, Saddam Hussein, Robert Mugabe). The changes in government posture, and the media posture, are so rapid that they recall George Orwell's Ministry of Truth.

It is not difficult to see how this extreme 'flexilbility' feeds the cycle of international warfare. The media's reverence for the military plays into the hands of those wishing to close down debate over the expense of arms procurement or the privileges available to senior officers. Civilian politicians live in terror of being accused of anti-militarism and must couch all defence-related utterances in circuitous assertions of their patriotism and respect for servicemen. Former generals have a fast track into high office. There, they can represent the interests and views of their former colleagues.

The ultimate victims of this suffocating political atmosphere are the enlisted soldiers trapped on the frontline. They are subject to the whims of senior officers whose lives and privileges differ greatly from their own. Yet ironically it is popular affection for exactly the sacrifices of these soldiers, transferred automatically to higher ranks, that is exploited by the officer class to preserve their privileges and political power.

Although the internet may have placed the traditional media even more in hock to commercial interests than was previously the case, it is the online world that offers the most hope. The WikiLeaks data slippage of 2010 demonstrated how the public could be presented with unmediated access to significant information which bypassed filtration by cosy editorial cliques. The WikiLeaks disclosures so discomfited traditional journalists, noted *Newsweek,* that they were reluctant to defend WikiLeaks founder Julian Assange from threats against his life by US politicians.[62] Such reticence was not the hallmark of a strong, independent press corps.

Ever more, the burden of discovery lies not with reporters but with citizens, who in the internet now have access to a research tool of unprecedented power. It will be up to citizens to evaluate and cross-check sources, to translate documents and to monitor social media in a way that gives them access to an accurate, unmediated version of events that does not rely on a journalist's opaque quid pro quos with proprietors and politicians, officials and insiders. It is this shift in the balance of knowledge that offers the best hope of ending the destructive cycle of militarism and war.

4
Europe and the Remaking of the Middle East

The year 1432 was an important one in the Islamic world. In the early months of that year – 2011 in the Gregorian calendar used by the rest of the world – the Middle East attempted to throw off some of its longest-standing tyrannies. A swift revolution in Tunisia inspired a much longer but eventually successful uprising in Egypt, the most populous Arab state. Protests quickly spread to Bahrain, Yemen, Libya and Oman. Across the region, the twentieth-century political settlement was rapidly crumbling into an uncertain future.

The resignation of Egypt's dictator Hosni Mubarak in February 2011 was swiftly followed by a bizarre visitation. As Egypt struggled without a leader or an accepted constitution, with massive demonstrations continuing to fill Cairo's Tahrir Square, with Iranian warships requesting passage through the Suez Canal and Egyptian refugees streaming over the border from revolutionary Libya, who should arrive but David Cameron, the prime minister of Great Britain, Egypt's former colonial master. Cameron did not come alone. With him were arms dealers from eight military suppliers, including BAE Systems, Qinetiq (pronounced 'kinetic') and Thales[1] (pronounced 'ta-lez').

At the moment of Cameron's arrival the army was easily the most powerful institution in Egypt, underwriting what little government existed at the time. The sudden appearance of a Western leader for talks with the interim rulers legitimised the generals' control at a moment when Egypt stood at the most crucial political crossroads in its modern history. Months later, tens of thousands would gather in Tahrir Square to demand that these generals relinquish power. But this consideration was secondary to Cameron. His goal was to represent Britain's arms manufacturers in the hope of winning sales.

A day later, in Kuwait, Cameron denied that Britain faced a choice between 'its interests and its values' but admitted his country had been guilty of propping up dictators 'in the past'.[2] Under hostile questioning, the prime minister grew agitated. He said that democracies 'like Kuwait' should not have to manufacture their own weapons and that it was 'perfectly right' for British companies like Thales to accompany him on such trips.[3] Cameron's credibility was not helped by the fact that Thales is a French company, and that Kuwait is classed as an 'authoritarian regime' by the Economist Intelligence Unit (EIU).[4] His defence equipment minister Peter Luff was less conflicted in explaining the government's position:

> There will be a very, very, very heavy ministerial commitment to arms sales. There is a sense that in the past we were rather embarrassed about exporting defence products. There is no such embarrassment in this government.[5]

While Cameron was representing the European military-industrial complex in Cairo, in neighbouring Libya jets were dropping bombs on civilian protesters in the capital Tripoli.[6] These Mirage jets were sold to Colonel Muammar Gaddafi's dictatorship in 2006 for around €100 million by the French company Dassault, shortly before Gaddafi visited France that year.[7] France also agreed to refurbish the rest of Libya's air force. As these French-made jets devastated parts of the capital city in 2011, the French oil company Total announced that it was repatriating its workers from Libya. At that point Libya was the world's twelfth largest oil producer, and Libyan oil represented 2.3 per cent of Total's output.[8]

Total's presence in Libya was the result of a production-sharing agreement with Gaddafi's regime. A cable from the US embassy in 2007 noted that Gaddafi's son Saif 'periodically obtains oil lifts' from the Total fields 'which he sells to finance his various activities'. The cable said it was not clear whether Saif's 'lifts' came from the Libyan share of the production or Total's.[9] But it didn't really matter. There was enough oil for both the Gaddafi family and the French to earn billions. The Libyan demonstrators were evidently less happy with the arrangement.

WikiLeaks sheds further light on the role of Western companies in Libya. The US military-industrial complex secured a major foothold: Boeing, Raytheon, ConocoPhillips, Occidental, Caterpillar and Halliburton all tried to enter the Libyan market. They were assisted in this by diplomats, even though those same diplomats recognised Libya as a 'kleptocracy' run for the benefit of the Gaddafi family. The dictator even demanded that the Western oil companies pay compensation, on his behalf, to victims of terrorist attacks ordered by his regime.[10]

The European military-industrial complex does not receive as much scrutiny as the American version, for several reasons. It is smaller, because European governments do not spend as much on defence. With the exception of Great Britain, European countries fight fewer wars than the US. The European complex is more fragmented, because some European governments promote their own state-champions and against other European military-industrial contractors. Even when large pan-European defence conglomerates are formed, national governments tussle for influence over their operations. German Economics Minister Rainer Brüderle has underlined the need for Germany to balance French power within the giant EADS defence company, which makes the Eurofighter and Eurocopter.[11]

The culture of transparency that exists in the US government is actively avoided by European governments, a factor exacerbated by the continent's multiple languages. The result is that middle-ranking European powers such as Britain and France get away with deals that the US would not. American militarists could argue that although the US had sold weapons to Egypt, the Egyptian generals acted responsibly during the overthrow of Hosni Mubarak's government by refusing to fire on unarmed protesters. This is not a defence that France or Great Britain could make in relation to Gaddafi's response to the unrest, which was brutal.

The countries diverged over how to respond to the Libyan crisis. Cameron suggested that Britain could arm the anti-Gaddafi rebels, presumably to get an early foothold of arms supplies to the next Libyan government. He was also in favour of a no-fly zone. France was absolutely against this, with foreign minister Alain Juppe insisting a no-fly zone would need the approval of the UN Security Council – approval he knew would not be forthcoming, because the Chinese and Russian dictatorships on the council would veto any intervention, lest it set a precedent for popular revolts in their own countries. France's real worry, however, was the potential embarrassment of watching American jets shooting down French-made Mirage fighters over Libya, a spectacle that would have a negative effect on future sales.

One reason the military-industrial complex is so profitable is because national leaders undertake sales missions on its behalf. Cameron's opportunism in Egypt was an example of this. So too was Gaddafi's visit to Paris in 2006, when the French authorities allowed the unpredictable dictator to construct a tented compound outside a Parisian hotel. These state-to-state deals are a hallmark of how the military-industrial complex uses its ties to government for profit. Former British leader Tony Blair met Gaddafi in 2007 and with him signed arms deals worth £350 million, including for supplies of anti-tank missiles.[12] Britain also promised to train Gaddafi's soldiers and help with 'defence industrial, technological and equipment matters'.[13]

So great are the 'national interests' involved in balancing trade that elected Western governments become partners in crime to their arms-makers, the oil companies, the miners and plantation-owners. The decision by ministers in Scotland to release Abdelbaset al-Megrahi, the Libyan man convicted of blowing up Pan Am Flight 103 over Scotland in 1988, was allegedly part of a deal to secure access to Libyan oil for British Petroleum (BP). 'The British government and BP wanted al-Megrahi released so that an oil deal being negotiated with Libya could go forward,' said Chuck Schumer, a US senator.[14] While David Cameron conducted his arms tour of the Middle East, Colonel Gaddafi's justice minister, having resigned amid the Libyan uprising, said the dictator personally ordered al-Megrahi to blow up the airliner over Lockerbie, killing 270 people, mostly Americans.[15]

Dictatorships are friends to the military-industrial complex in a way that peaceful democracies are not. Selling arms to dictators is a relatively straightforward process. Despots cling to power by force of arms, so arms are always required. Most dictators are professional military men who are often personally enthusiastic about military expansion and technology. More pragmatically, they rely on the loyalty of the armed forces to keep power, so they must be seen to invest handsomely in military equipment. Finally, given that the West portrays itself as the defender of human rights and democracy, any dictator that is offered arms by a Western power is likely to accept, so as to portray the offer as a Western endorsement of his humanitarian credentials.

It was not only Lockerbie over which the British government showed itself surprisingly eager to forgive the Libyans. Professor David Crane, the Chief Prosecutor in the international probe into war crimes committed in the African state of Sierra Leone, said that Britain and the US placed pressure on him not to indict Gaddafi in relation to the trial. Crane said that, had he refused to comply, those countries would have withdrawn funding for the trial, despite evidence that Gaddafi was instrumental in planning the conflict in Sierra Leone, which claimed 50,000 civilian lives. 'Welcome to the world of oil,' the professor said when asked why the West had protected Gaddafi.[16]

Great Britain has some unique tricks for selling goods to despots. For the past decade Prince Andrew, the second son of Queen Elizabeth II, has served as the UK's Special Representative for Trade. Andrew, a former naval officer who flew helicopters in the Falklands War, works extremely hard in this capacity. In 2010 he undertook 337 overseas trade engagements on behalf of British industry. Of the prince's 22 foreign visits in 2009/10, two-thirds were to countries governed by what the EIU calls 'authoritarian regimes'.[17] Significantly, a high proportion of these regimes were absolute monarchies: Abu Dhabi, Dubai, Oman, Qatar, and Saudi Arabia. In those countries the Special Representative could engage in prince-to-prince discussions that were unavailable to rivals such as France and the US. Such interaction between constitutional and absolute monarchies assists the latter by legitimising monarchical rule and blurring the distinction between the functional legislature of Great Britain and the rubber-stamp parliaments of the Middle East.

Britain's military-industrial complex has exploited this confusion over where Arab royalty ends and Arab government begins. The £43 billion al-Yamama arms deals struck between Saudi Arabia and British Aerospace (BAe) were allegedly the result of £100 million ($160 million) annual payments to Prince Bandar bin Sultan, the son of the Saudi defence minister Prince Sultan.[18] BAe Systems eventually paid $400m in fines after admitting false accounting and misleading statements.[19] However, an investigation by Britain's Serious Fraud Office was shut down by the British government in 2006 on grounds of 'national security'. The then prime minister, Tony Blair, explaining this act of legal sabotage, said that: 'I don't believe the investigation would have led to anywhere except to the complete wreckage of a vital interest to our country.'[20] A US ambassador reported that Prince Andrew denounced the corruption investigation as 'idiocy'.[21]

European states are adept at recovering their payments. The local strongmen who share the spoils of resource-extraction are encouraged to 'invest' their ill-gotten gains in European assets, so they are 'safe' should misfortune strike them in the form of a popular revolt. West London is full of empty multi-million-dollar houses sold as secure assets to dictators and powerbrokers in Britain's former colonies, for instance the King and Queen of Jordan.[22] Egypt's deposed leader Hosni Mubarak owned a mansion in London's Belgravia district.[23] Prince Andrew sold his £15 million house to an offshore company owned by a billionaire from Kazakhstan.[24] The situation in the French capital Paris is little different. Following his rigged election victory in 2010 the president of Gabon, Ali Bongo, celebrated by purchasing a Parisian townhouse for €100 million.[25]

Indeed, the French vie with the British as masters of Africa. Writing in *Foreign Policy* magazine in 2010, Boubacar Boris Diop credited General Charles de Gaulle's advisor Jacques Foccart with establishing France's position after the de-colonisation of Francophone Africa. 'His methods were simple,' Diop noted. 'Install trusted African politicians, some with French nationality, as the heads of these 14 new states and maintain the firm, French grasp on their natural resources.' With almost 60,000 troops on the continent, he added, the French Army could rush to the dictators' aid at a moment's notice 'and had already agreed to do so as part of defence agreements in which certain key clauses were kept secret'.[26] French spies were available to assassinate their opponents.

Unlike the US, Europe has a specialism in the manufacture of luxury goods: bespoke suits and designer dresses, sports cars and limousines, perfumes, even jewel-encrusted mobile phones courtesy of Vertu. The local overseers of European resource extraction are among the leading customers for the ostentatious and expensive wares of Europe's luxury emporiums. Britain's elite private boarding schools welcome the children of foreign powerbrokers, a fact that gives those men even less incentive to finance public education in their homeland.

Foreign Policy reported that Teodorin Obiang, whose father runs Equatorial Guinea, a major oil producer, owns seven Ferraris, five Bentleys, four Rolls-Royces, two Lamborghinis, two Mercedes-Benzes, two Porsches, two Maybachs, and an Aston Martin. In March 2011 it emerged that Obiang Jnr had ordered a yacht costing $380 million from a German company[27] – more than three times the amount that Equatorial Guinea spends on health and education each year. In 2004 a US Senate report found that oil companies paid millions of dollars into bank accounts held by regime officials at Riggs Bank in New York. The oil companies named by the report included Amerada Hess, ChevronTexaco, ExxonMobil, and Marathon.[28] The senators urged them to adhere to the principles of groups such as the Extractive Industries Transparency Initiative (EITI), at the time led by that well-known scourge of dubious deals, Tony Blair.

To avoid such unpleasantness, Europe operates a network of supposedly 'independent' offshore havens through which shadowy deals can be processed. Low taxation is usually cited as the appeal of these places, but their lack of transparency is actually more important. In most cases, these micro-states lack systems for monitoring unusual cash-flows or a media sophisticated enough to investigate them. All major European countries operate their own havens. France uses Monaco, an 'independent' principality on its southern coast, and shares another one, Andorra, with Spain. Belgium and several other countries use Luxembourg. Germany has the princely micro-state of Liechtenstein. Italy has San Marino.

Then there is Great Britain, which requires its own paragraph. The UK operates havens in the Channel Islands, such as Jersey and Guernsey, but also the Isle of Man, which sits in the Irish Sea. All are supposedly 'independent' and therefore beyond the reach of British financial investigators, as is Gibraltar, a British possession on the southern tip of Spain. However, Great Britain also operates protectorates in the Caribbean such as the British Virgin Islands, the Cayman Islands and the Turks and Caicos, all of which are notorious offshore financial havens. Firms in the City of London, when asked to transact deals for shadowy foreign interests, route the funds via these territories.

European governments turn a blind eye to the spending habits of their local partners, at least while those partners are still of use. If they are ousted, however, these same governments then make a great show of 'freezing' the assets of their former placemen. In January 2011 Switzerland 'froze' the bank deposits of Tunisia's ousted leader Zein al-Abidine Ben Ali and his family. The *Financial Times* noted that the Swiss had previously protected the assets of Zaire's Mobutu Sese Seko, Sani Abacha of Nigeria, Ferdinand Marcos of the Philippines, and Haiti's 'Baby Doc' Duvalier.[29] Britain followed suit by announcing that it had 'frozen' the assets of Gaddafi in London, including his son Saif's $16 million house in London's Hampstead.[30] The US is still in possession of $223 million of Cuban assets it froze in 1963.[31] Yet politicians and the press represent these 'freezings' as swift and decisive measures to punish a dictator. It often takes a curiously long time for European countries to repatriate such funds to their country of origin; legal questions, ignored when the money was first 'invested' or laundered, suddenly emerge.[32]

It is a mistake to assume that it is just Britain and France which engage in such activity. Most EU countries are equally guilty, including those Scandinavian countries that promote themselves as bastions of peace and harmony. After the outbreak of civil war in Libya, Sweden 'discovered' €1 billion-worth of assets belonging to Gaddafi.[33] The organisation Swedish Peace notes that Sweden, per head of population, sells more arms than any country in the world.[34] In 2010, Daimler, a German engineering company, agreed to pay the US government $185 million in fines to settle charges that it had bribed its way to contracts in 22 countries. Siemens, another German military-industrial concern, had to pay $1.6 billion.[35]

BY HAPPY COINCIDENCE

A glance at a map shows that the boundaries of European countries are ragged lines that reflect a tortuous history of national formation. They often follow geographical features such as the Pyrenean mountains which divide France from Spain or the Rhine river that demarcates sections of Germany's borders with France and Switzerland. The boundaries of the Middle East and Africa tell a very different story. Ruled onto the map by European bureaucrats, these straight lines were the markers of the colonial domination of subjugated Africans and Arabs.

The reason the bin Saud family rules the country bearing its name is because the Sauds were appointed to do so by the British. After the clan captured Riyadh in 1902 the British Empire entered into increasingly close relations with the bin Sauds. The British engineered the transformation from what the British Library describes as:

> a small sultanate in central Arabia in the early 1900s, to an economically powerful modern state on the eve of the Second World War ... British economic and strategic concerns were involved in the development of the Saudi oil industry and the closely related evolution of Saudi Arabia's northern, eastern, and south-eastern boundaries, as well as the southern Saudi boundary with Britain's Aden colony and protectorate in south Yemen.[36]

This transformation did not merely entail the creation of Saudi Arabia but also its relationship with what were once known as the Trucial States, a string of British protectorates on the Arabian Peninsula coastline. In 1968, when the British cancelled their protectorate status, the Trucial States became the United Arab Emirates. The 'Aden colony' became Yemen, while to the north and west the British handed Jordan and Iraq to the house of Hashem, a rival Arab clan.

The support of these clans proved crucial to Britain and France during World War I, because the Ottoman Empire was allied to Germany and was viewed by Muslims worldwide as their leading representative. In his magisterial account of the creation of the modern Middle East, *A Peace to End All Peace,* David Fromkin describes how Britain and France divided up the captured Ottoman territory between them after the war. Fromkin notes that originally these subdivisions were never envisaged as 'countries' by the European colonial powers – they were intended to be French and British spheres of interest. It was only when the US took a firm stance against imperialism that nationhood was conferred on French possessions such as Lebanon and Syria.

Occasionally, Western politicians admit the West's role in the creation of the today's failed and failing states. 'I don't want to try to insert Britain in some leading role where, as with so many of the world's problems, we are responsible for the issue in the first place,' David Cameron said on a trip to Pakistan, referring to the Kashmir dispute.[37] 'Colonialism wasn't simply the creation of unnatural borders or unfair terms of trade,' President Barack Obama told Ghana's parliament in 2009. 'A colonial map that made little sense bred conflict, and the West has often approached Africa as a patron, rather than a partner.'[38]

The European military-industrial complex evolved to ensure the continued extraction of cheap resources from these former colonies. During the colonial period, this process was simple. Britain, France, and other colonial powers would simply dispatch ships to their colonies to collect resources – cotton, gemstones, tea, coffee, bananas, tobacco. Indigenous workers were paid enough to keep them alive, and powerful local interests were either destroyed by force or paid-off by the imperial administration.

In the post-colonial environment, the situation has changed – slightly. Ships still arrive to transport raw commodities back to Europe for processing. Local interests are still bought off, but it is embarrassing for European governments to be caught making such payments directly. So while ministers and civil servants broker arms-for-resources deals with dictators like Colonel Gaddafi, the slush funds, bag-men and offshore bank accounts are operated by military-industrial companies. Some of these, such as the British firm QinetiQ, were privatised only quite recently.[39] This private status means that when the regime eventually collapses, the Western government is two or three degrees removed from the system which kept their local overseers in power and heavily armed.

In a few cases, former colonial possessions have been strong enough to reject this kind of exploitation. Instead, they developed for themselves the internal processes needed to transform raw materials into valuable goods. India, despite heavy pressure from the West, maintained a policy of import-substitution for over 40 years after independence. By the time it embraced export-led growth in the 1990s, at least some of India's exports were manufactured items, rather than basic natural resources. In most cases, however, the Western powers have cornered the valuable hi-tech 'specialisms' for themselves, ensuring that the economies of their former colonial possessions remain little more than mines, plantations, oil wells and subsistence farms.

India's strength was its size, which allowed it to preserve an internal economy that insulated it against foreign pressures, assisted by a partnership with the Soviet Union. Elsewhere, the former colonial powers were far more adept at keeping the post-colonial countries small and pliable. This is particularly true of French Africa and, until very recently, of the Muslim Middle East. Divide and rule succeeded for almost a century. Oil revenues which could have paid for refineries and research centres were frittered by puppet regimes on European sports cars and mansions. The ordinary inhabitants of these post-colonial extraction zones were left intellectually and physically impoverished.

THE POWDERKEG

It is hard to imagine a more perfect recipe for war than the situation prevalent in the Middle East. There, a lattice of artificial states, almost all of them invented by European colonialists in the twentieth century, is governed by a tiny, unelected, fabulously wealthy elite armed by the West to oversee the exportation of oil. Education, property, material wealth and political power are concentrated in the hands of rulers who in some cases were placed upon their thrones by departing Europeans. Brutal secret police forces suppress even the most basic human rights. Freedom of expression is confined to the interiors of mosques. Many Arab countries rely on labour imported from Asia and kept in conditions of near-slavery.

Within this landscape lies Israel, perhaps the most artificial of the states created by the departing British Empire. In the 1800s a Zionist movement emerged in Europe to seek a national homeland for the Jewish diaspora in what was once the Biblical kingdom of Judea. Zionist groups purchased farmland in Ottoman Palestine, often from absentee Arab landlords, and evicted the Arab tenants to replace them with immigrant Jews.[40] When Palestine passed from Ottoman to British control, the Balfour Declaration of 1917 made the establishment of a Jewish homeland the official policy of the British Empire.[41] The rise of Adolf Hitler in Germany expedited Jewish migration to Palestine and the establishment of the state of Israel.

Immediately after the British withdrew in 1948 the new Jewish state was invaded by Lebanon, Syria, Egypt, Iraq and Jordan, but the well-organised Israelis repelled the Arab forces and expanded their own territory. War and ethnic cleansing by Zionist militias displaced half a million Palestinian Arabs from their homes, many fleeing to the West Bank. Yet the Arab dictatorships soon turned their military humiliation, and the mistreatment of the Palestinians, to their long-term advantage. Arab regimes used Israeli Jews as scapegoats for their own failings. Anti-semitism became as prevalent in the twentieth-century Middle East as it had been in nineteenth-century Europe.

This outlook was much in evidence during the Arab uprisings of early 2011. Yemeni President Ali Abdullah Saleh said the regional unrest was 'plotted by Israel'.[42] Anti-Gaddafi graffiti showed the colonel with an Israeli flag stitched to his shirt,[43] despite Gaddafi once demanding that Israeli Jews be thrown into the sea.[44] In Egypt, Mubarak tried to stifle news of the revolt by describing foreign journalists as Israeli spies, an accusation that led to the sexual assault of a CNN correspondent, who was attacked by a mob yelling 'Jew! Jew!'[45] In Lebanon, on the other hand, Hezbollah claimed that Israel was doing its utmost to *protect* Mubarak's regime.[46]

There were signs, however, that this scapegoating was losing its power. The protesters in North Africa knew that they were not following orders from Tel Aviv or New York. Some Arab commentators began to question whether Israel was, in fact, the root of all their troubles. Abdulateef al-Mulhim, a former commodore in the Saudi navy, wrote that he had 'since childhood, been hearing about an invisible thing called the Israeli conspiracy'. He wrote:

To this day, I see Arabs blaming Israelis for young Arab drug addicts, their poor education, the Iraqi invasion of Kuwait, bad roads, corruption, lack of democracy, unemployment, 9/11, the division of Sudan, the upheaval in Tunisia and the unrest in Egypt. If Israel can do all these things, then the Israelis are either super humans or we simply enjoy blaming others for our failings.[47]

The writer Nick Cohen pointed out that anti-semitism is useful to authoritarian regimes because, unlike standard forms of racism, it is a power fantasy.[48] Anti-semitic conspiracies portray democracy as a sham, engineered from behind the scenes by shadowy Jewish cabals. The only real form of government is therefore despotism, as endured by most Arabs. By reinforcing the power of dictatorships this conspiratorial outlook served the interests of the Western military-industrial complexes. Ironically, it also served the interests of Israel, which enjoyed relatively stable relations with Mubarak's Egypt and Gaddafi's Libya. The myth of Zionist conspiracies could therefore be viewed in itself as a Zionist conspiracy.

THE CHANCE OF UNITY

Now, the picture has fractured. Since the end of the colonial era the strategy of divide-and-rule has served the interests of Europe and the US in the Middle East. There are strong reasons to believe that this system cannot last and that the era of tyrant kings is coming to an end. What replaces it will decide the future of the world's energy supply, the military-industrial complex, and possibly even the fate of Israel. There is a chance that the map of nations drawn up by Europeans could be redrafted by Muslim Arabs.

Any campaign to alter the cartography of the Islamic world, even by peaceful means, is immediately dismissed by Western militarists as 'extremist'. This is an accusation thrown at genuine extremists who seek to bring about a new pan-Islamic Caliphate by violent means, such as al-Qaeda. However, the 'extremist' label is also applied to Islamic groups such as Hizb-ut-Tahrir, which seek a pan-Islamic state via peaceful means. British government documents make reference to 'non-violent Islamist extremism' in reference to such organisations, a description never applied to communist or secessionist movements in the UK.[49]

Most tellingly, Western militarists even described secular pan-Arabists such as Ba'athists and Nasserists (after Gamal Abdel Nasser, the former ruler of Egypt) as 'extremists'.[50,51] When this fact is taken into consideration, it becomes clear that it is not some austere version of Islam that the West finds 'extreme'. On the contrary, the West arms and finances Saudi Arabia, the most oppressive Islamic regime in existence. The 'extremism' of concern to the West is any attempt to forge the Islamic world into a large and powerful political formation, like India, which can exert monopoly control over Middle Eastern oil and independence from Western influence. Pan-Africanism has encountered exactly the same hostility in Western capitals, for the same reasons.

There have been attempts at such a state in the past. For three years, between 1958 and 1961, the United Arab Republic (UAR) was a single nation which united Egypt and Syria. The US embassy in Damascus described the union as 'far from an attractive solution'. It was 'acutely aware of increased pressure an enlarged Arab state would exercise on west-oriented neighbours'. However, so popular was the cause that diplomats urged the US 'to appear relaxed and mildly sympathetic'[52] especially as it came soon after the Suez Crisis in which Egypt had defeated French and British imperialism. Also in 1958, Hashemite Iraq and Jordan united to form the rival Arab Federation, but this lasted only six months before it was overthrown by a military coup in which the prime minister was assassinated, a coup that led in time to the regime of Saddam Hussein in Iraq.

The current national system in North Africa represented the colonial footprint of France (Algeria, Morocco, Tunisia), Italy (Libya) and Egypt (Great Britain). From the sixteenth to the nineteenth centuries North Africa was the Islamic Maghreb (مغربى or 'west'). It was little more than a string of coastal settlements ruled by Islamic noblemen who launched piratical raids against European and American shipping. They enjoyed a trading relationship with the Ottoman Empire, which until World War I was the only non-Christian state to qualify as a Great Power. At one point the Ottoman Empire spanned three continents, but it collapsed following World War I.

Neo-Ottomanism has become a preoccupation of Western strategists, amid signs that Turkey might be rediscovering its Muslim identity after decades of Kemalist secular rule enforced by the powerful Turkish military, the second-largest in NATO, which is closely linked to the US military-industrial complex. Turkey's new 'look east' policy is a result of France and Germany's refusal to countenance Turkish membership of the European Union, despite British and American support for the idea. With only a tiny portion of Turkey lying inside geographical Europe, momentum has built for Istanbul, formerly Constantinople, to resume its leadership of the Muslim world.

Turkey, led by the reform-minded Islamist Recep Tayyip Erdoğan, could become a template for the new polities emerging from the wreckage of Middle Eastern dictatorships. This would be a best-case scenario for the West, but would still cause huge problems. Erdoğan is a critic of Israel, which he has described as the 'main threat to regional peace'.[53] His government has proven willing to use energy supplies as a bargaining chip towards EU membership.[54] Erdoğan is sufficiently independent to sign game-changing energy deals with Russia and offer the hand of friendship to Iran. Multiplied across the Middle East, even the moderate and democratic Turkish model would pose a severe threat to Europe's security environment.

This challenge would become even greater if Turkey led moves towards EU-style regional integration. Such a project, already envisaged by multilaterals such as the Organisation of Islamic Conferences, would marry Turkey's crucial importance as a transhipment route for energy to the countries holding the hydrocarbon deposits. An 'Islamic Union' would be a superpower able to exert great power over Western countries dependent on its energy resources. Europe's policy of divide-and-rule in the Middle East is largely intended to prevent the emergence of such a transnational entity.

The European military-industrial complex exists to extract national resources at preferential rates, and to arm the despotic governments of corrupt, artificial nations against both their neighbours and their own people. History may yet record the Islamic year 1432 as the point when this military-industrial arrangement collapsed. A fundamental alteration in the terms of trade between Europe and its former colonies could now take place, to the benefit of the latter and the detriment of the former. If this proves to be the case, Europe can have little cause for complaint, given its atrocious history of extracting oil and other resources at the expense of dispossessed Arabs and Africans.

Part II

Military Spending and Its Ill Effects

5
Negative Effects of Conflicts on Global and Human Security, Refugees, Forced Migrations and Urbanisation

Urbanisation has become a cornerstone of what is viewed as economic progress. The migration of rural populations to cities is a byword for rapid development in countries ranging from the United States and Australia to Thailand and Nigeria. The centripetal force exerted by cities on village life is usually explained as an economic trend, with impoverished villagers making the decision to journey to the city in search of a wealthier life. This, however, is only half the story. Urbanisation is also the result of conflict and sometimes the cause of it. Increasingly, military-industrial establishments use the widening philosophical gulf between urban and rural dwellers as an excuse to plunder outlying areas.

If all the world's refugees are counted together, their total population as of 2011 is equivalent to that of the Netherlands.[1] Not all refugees are driven from their homes by conflict. Poverty, starvation and internal repression are other motors of displacement. But war remains the major reason for disorderly cross-border migration and internal displacement.

It was once the case that refugees were concentrated in purpose-built camps. These camps became emblematic of the human tragedy of 1980s war-zones such as Afghanistan and Ethiopia. However, since 2007 the majority of refugees have instead merged into urban centres, where they are far less visible to the wider world. This trend is a direct result of the war in Iraq, where Shia death squads have sought revenge for the privileged status that Sunnis enjoyed in Saddam Hussein's Iraq, forcing many Sunnis to take refuge in Damascus, Amman and Beirut.[2]

Iraq's Christian population, once about 1.5 million, is believed to have fallen to around half that total, as the community has come under siege from the Islamic State of Iraq organisation, a Mesopotamian offshoot of al-Qaeda.[3] The majority of these refugees have fled either to the semi-autonomous Kurdistan in the north of

Iraq or to Syria and Lebanon. By its own crude and brutal standards, al-Qaeda has largely succeeded in making Iraq a more Islamic state than it once was.

THE WAR IN PAKISTAN

Less scrutinised than the war in Iraq is the one being played out on the border between Afghanistan and Pakistan, where President Barack Obama has chosen to escalate the conflict he inherited from his predecessor. The consequences for Pakistan in particular are alarming. They illustrate the cyclical nature of violence, as violence and chaos follow displaced populations as they migrate around the region.

At the present time, Obama is playing what has been described by Peter Singer of the Brookings Institution as a game of 'whack-a-mole' with al-Qaeda in the mountains of north-west Pakistan.[4] The game is played as follows. US forces receive intelligence that a leader of the Taliban, or a member of al-Qaeda, is hidden in a particular building. The US military then dispatches a Predator or Reaper drone to the target. The game ends when the drone drops a 500-pound bomb or Hellfire missile on the suspect, performing a summary execution of the suspected militant and any family members or neighbours who might be standing within 20 metres of him.

Unsurprisingly, given the number of innocent women and children who have been killed and injured in these 'precision' strikes,[5] and given the Pakistani army's own offensives in the north-west, tens of thousands of civilians have elected to leave their *watan* (وطن), their homeland, an important concept in South Asian village culture.[6] Many of these Pashtun tribesmen have uprooted themselves to Karachi, a sprawling southern port that is Pakistan's largest city and its economic hub.

Karachi is no stranger to refugees. After India and Pakistan portioned themselves in 1947, the city received more than a million Indian Muslims who preferred to cast their lot with the newly founded Islamic state rather than to risk a loss of status in Hindu-majority India. These émigrés, who included the parents of General Pervez Musharraf, Pakistan's most recent military dictator, established their own political party, the MQM, to protect their interests in Karachi. This protection often descended into violence, with members of the MQM fighting turf wars with parties associated with the indigenous population such as the non-ruling Pakistan People's Party.

Now the MQM has a new enemy. The influx of tribal Pashtuns from the north-west has once again altered Karachi's balance of power and promoted inter-ethnic violence. A wave of tit-for-tat killings has claimed hundreds of lives among both the MQM's supporters and on the Pashtun side.[7] These killings have spread internationally. In September 2010 MQM politician Imran Farooq was stabbed to death outside his home in London, which is also home to MQM leader Altaf Hussain. The MQM has also accused the Pashtun migrants of harbouring members of the Taliban in Karachi.

In January 2011 Karachi's crisis became a national crisis. The MQM walked out of the federal coalition government. One of the reasons it gave for this was to protest at the government's failure to impose security in Karachi.[8] Given that the leader of the opposition was, as WikiLeaks revealed, unacceptable to Pakistan's powerful generals, the collapse of the government set the scene for yet another military coup.[9] Although the MQM soon reversed its decision, the sequence of events illustrated how military action in remote areas transmits unrest into urban centres and national governments.

There are echoes of Karachi's situation in cities throughout the world. In Bogota, Colombia, those displaced by the country's decades of conflict have been the subject of death threats from paramilitary groups.[10] Over 500,000 Chechens have been displaced by war in the Russian Caucasus,[11] but those who have reached Moscow have been treated as potential terrorists subject to arbitrary imprisonment and expulsion.[12] Tamils who fled Sri Lanka's war-zones for the capital Colombo experienced similar treatment.[13] Refugees from Burma's brutal military dictatorship have encountered a sometimes hostile reception in Cox's Bazaar, Bangladesh[14] and Bangkok, Thailand.[15] In the United Kingdom an academic study found that media reports were responsible for encouraging racist attacks against asylum seekers in London.[16]

It is for these reasons that refugees in many urban areas try to disappear, keeping out of sight of the authorities even when they try to help them. 'Invisible' refugees are often unreachable by NGOs, a problem that faces the estimated 40,000–100,000 refugees in the Kenyan capital Nairobi.[17] The legal definition of forced migrants also tends to become blurred in urban areas, as the refugees usually live alongside other immigrants, some of whom may not have been forced, as well as members of the local population.

We have seen how the growth and demographic composition of many cities is driven less by economics than by conflicts in outlying areas. Sadly, feelings of historic injustice tend to endure. Decades from today the urbanised descendants of displaced villagers will still resent the chaotic and violent means by which they became city-dwellers, and this resentment will breed disorder. Such disruption is not factored into the costs of war, but civil unrest in major economic hubs has obvious implications for national prosperity.

Strip-mining the middle class

One particularly disastrous part of the refugee crisis is middle-class emigration. A country's educated population is its greatest asset. These are the people who organise the economy, who provide the bedrock of civil society, who treat the sick, preside over court cases and engineer a country's roads and bridges. Without them, no society can develop beyond a subsistence level.

South Africa's health minister has said that 'if there is a single major threat to our overall health effort, it is the continued outward migration of key health professionals, particularly nurses'. The British Medical Association has likened Europe's poaching of African medical staff to 'rape'.[18] Some reports indicate that there are more Malawian doctors in Birmingham, England, than there are in Malawi.[19] In December 2010, *Mining Weekly* reported that South Africa, a country reliant on the mining industry, had only 500 practising mining engineers, with a similar scarcity of middle managers.[20] The UN estimates that African countries spend an estimated $4 billion annually to plug the skills gap.[21]

The US and Europe, which do their utmost to turn away poor Africans, accept these immigrants with few questions asked. By stripping poorer nations of their educated workforce, they put an end to any chance of those countries becoming their technological rivals. Had the US suffered from a similar brain-drain during its early development, it is unlikely that engineering marvels such as the Hoover Dam, the interstate highway system or New York's skyscrapers would ever have been built.

A GULF IN PHILOSOPHY

Rapid urbanisation brings another threat to peace. Across the globe a political divide has opened between city-dwellers and villagers.[22,23,24] The latter tend to be more traditional, less wealthy, and more mistrustful of state institutions than the inhabitants of urban areas. When Barack Obama referred during his 2008 presidential campaign to his opponents 'clinging to guns and religion' he was referring to small towns in the American Midwest,[25] but he could easily have meant the members of the Taliban who, as president, he has enthusiastically blasted with Predator drones.

Table 5.1   Top ten most peaceful countries (2009)

1	New Zealand
2	Denmark
3	Norway
4	Iceland
5	Austria
6	Sweden
7	Japan
8	Canada
9	Finland
10	Slovenia

Source: SIPRI

In the United Kingdom, rural activists who resisted attempts by the Conservative Party to impose urban candidates on their constituencies were dismissed as members of a 'Turnip Taliban'.[26] In Iran, the protests in the capital Tehran that met President Mahmoud Ahmadinejad's 2009 election victory were not replicated in smaller settlements, where the president's brand of millenarian conservatism remained popular.[27] In Venezuela, Hugo Chavez's radical government relied on the support of the rural poor, whereas the privileged urban elite overwhelmingly favoured the opposition.[28]

This urban-rural split has become a primary catalyst for military coups. Chavez claimed that the United States exhorted the Venezuelan military to overthrow him in the failed coup of 2002, an allegation supported by coup leader Admiral Carlos Molina, who said 'we felt we were acting with US support'.[29] Chavez hailed from the poor rural province of Barinas, whereas the middle-class Molina was born to a rich family, raised in the capital Caracas and represented the interests of Venezuela's wealthiest citizens.

Not all leaders in Chavez's position manage to escape overthrow. Thailand's prime minister, Thaksin Shinawatra, was hugely popular in the country's rural north and north-east.[30] In 2006 he was forced from office by a military junta which shared metropolitan Bangkok's distaste for the prime minister.[31] It should be noted that, as with Chavez, this was not the whole story – Thaksin's business dealings were highly questionable and made him a billionaire while in office – but the contempt with which his rural supporters were held by the military-industrial elite was emblematic of urban elites in many other countries. For years afterwards Bangkok was paralysed by demonstrations staged by pro- and anti-Thaksin groups.

Table 5.2   Top ten least peaceful countries (2009)

1	Iraq
2	Afghanistan
3	Somalia
4	Israel
5	Sudan
6	Congo (Dem. Rep.)
7	Chad
8	Pakistan
9	Russia
10	Zimbabwe

Source: SIPRI

In Pakistan, the military junta led by General Pervez Musharraf launched a minor war against tribal chieftains in the south-western province of Baluchistan. The generals claimed that men like Akbar Khan Bugti, the *nawab* of the Bugti clan, were feudal lords who kept their people in conditions of medieval serfdom. The chieftains countered that Musharraf's government was a Punjabi colonial enterprise bent on stealing the region's natural gas. Both sides were largely correct in their assessment of the situation, but it was the *nawab* who wound up dead in a cave,[32] whereas General Musharraf retired to a comfortable life in the West.[33]

In Honduras, President Manual Zelaya, the son of a rancher, introduced subsidies for small farmers, increased the minimum wage by 80 per cent, opposed privatisation and guaranteed free education for all children.[34] This was a mistake in a country in which a handful of families owns 90 per cent of the wealth and where, according to the BBC, journalists tend to exercise self-censorship to avoid offending the political or economic interests of media owners.[35] On 1 July 2009 Zelaya was seized by the military and forced into exile, in what the Obama administration described as an illegal coup.[36] Washington then threw its support behind Zelaya's right-wing replacement.[37]

It is significant that the military-industrial complex has become so closely associated with metropolitan interests, because most contemporary wars are fought in remote areas. These urban capitalists often portray leaders who enjoy widespread rural support as 'populists' who can legitimately be deposed by military means. By ensuring that rural voices are excluded from government it becomes much easier for military-industrial interests to enact policies without reference to the views of outlying communities, such as land grabs, exploitative resource extraction or colonisation by another ethnic group. This disenfranchisement sews the seeds of civil war.

Nepal provides a sad example of this divide. For most of its history the Himalayan nation was run by and for the Hindu communities clustered around the Kathmandu Valley. Nepal's autocratic monarchy enforced a highly centralised form of control through the 'panchayat' system, which atomised grassroots politics at the village council level and allowed only indirect election to higher assemblies. The Tibeto-Burman Buddhists who populated more remote parts of the country were frozen out of the establishment, as were the ethnically Indian castes who farmed the southern border. It was from these communities that Nepal's Maoist rebels recruited, setting the conditions for a ten-year civil war which claimed more than 10,000 lives.[38]

THE TALIBAN

No group better exemplifies the divide between urban and rural viewpoints than the Taliban. Drawn from the Pashtun tribes which straddle the Pakistan and Afghan borders, these militants advocate the enforcement of customary law and customs that are little unchanged from those practiced by the Prophet Mohammad in the deserts of Arabia. As such, the Taliban have been portrayed in the West as enemies of civilisation and practitioners of a barbarity.

It is not difficult to see why the Taliban have attracted this reputation. On more than one occasion the militants have overseen the stoning to death of women charged with adultery.[39] Their destruction of Afghanistan's giant Bamiyan Buddhas was an act of cultural vandalism inspired by the Koran's prohibition of graven images.[40] Women under the Taliban's control are forced to hide their entire body under a burqa, under threat of disfigurement. The Taliban have staged hundreds of attacks on girls' schools,[41] thereby denying future generations the well-established economic benefits of an educated female population. The Taliban have also sheltered militants associated with some of the world's most deadly terrorists.

It is not easy to see how anyone could view the Taliban's rule as beneficial. However, there is one public service offered by the militants that has earned them the respect of many ordinary

Pashtuns. By establishing Islamic courts, the Taliban bypassed the corrupt and cumbersome legal process found in both Pakistan and Afghanistan. This allowed property disputes and other civil procedures to be concluded much more quickly and cheaply than they would be by the official courts. Petty criminals were also dealt with in a more robust fashion, thereby deterring banditry.

It should be remembered that this kind of customary law was tolerated by the British before their withdrawal from empire in the 1940s. In 2009 the central government of Pakistan legislated to restore these customary laws to their former standing, albeit with a right of appeal to the secular courts.[42] This was an attempt to undermine the Pashtun support for the Taliban, which had co-opted groups committed to the restoration of these laws.[43] The legislation served as a belated acknowledgement that central solutions imposed on remote areas often prove a source of conflict, no matter how well intentioned they might be.

ANTI-REFUGEES: INTERNAL MIGRATION AS A SOURCE OF CONTROL

We have seen how conflict in rural areas is a driver of chaotic urbanisation and inner-city violence, often one imposed by urban elites in the quest for material profit. There is another trend that exactly mirrors this process. Some states have found that the best way to secure control over valuable natural resources in outlying regions is to flood those regions with migrants from urban centres. As the indigenous community is transformed into an impoverished minority, the result is civil unrest, which is then crushed by military power.

In July 2009 the city of Urumqi was torn apart by race riots. Urumqi is the capital of Xinjiang province, the only state in the People's Republic of China with a Muslim majority, at least until very recently. The Muslims, known as Uighurs, speak a Turkic language familiar to inhabitants of the Central Asian 'stans'. Xinjiang, once known as East Turkestan, is home to some of China's most significant hydrocarbon deposits, and these are critical to China's rapid economic expansion.

The province is vital to China not only as a source of energy deposits but also as a transhipment route for oil and gas piped from Central Asia and Russia.[44] The Uighurs, however, have seen very little of the new prosperity. Of the $2 billion tax revenue that Beijing extracted from the province's petrochemical industries in 2005, only $35 million was remitted to Xinjiang's local government to spend on improving the lot of the local population.[45] Rather than using the mineral wealth to benefit the Uighurs, the Chinese authorities have adopted an approach to internal suppression that is draconian even by their standards.

Under the banner of former US president George W. Bush's 'war on terror', the Chinese government has characterised Uighur political groups as 'terrorists' and 'separatists'. The teaching of Islam in the province in tightly controlled, with imams required to attend political education camps.[46] According to Amnesty International, 'the Chinese authorities continue to pursue a language policy that purports to make the school system in the XUAR "bilingual" but which is in fact making Chinese the sole language of instruction.' Furthermore, 'Chinese state has failed to protect Uighurs from employment discrimination which has resulted in extremely high rates of unemployment among Uighurs'.[47]

Sadly the Uighurs, their opinions and culture, are becoming increasingly irrelevant. In 1949 they made up 96 per cent of the province's inhabitants. Today, this proportion has fallen to barely 50 per cent, with at least 40 per cent of the population now composed of Han Chinese immigrants from elsewhere in China.[48] The Beijing government has deliberately incentivised the Han colonisation of Xinjiang to replace the Muslim majority with a Han one, including by relocating to the province Han displaced by the Three Gorges dam in Hubei province.[49]

It was this set of circumstances that ignited the Urumqi riots in 2009. Chinese officials claimed that 197 people died in the violence. China's solution to the civil unrest was a military one; witnesses described military personnel with automatic weapons shooting unarmed civilians.[50] The true character of China's presence in Xinjiang was revealed as a military occupation stripping a non-Chinese people of their mineral wealth, and colonising the region to secure a permanent dominance.

Xinjiang is not the only region that the Chinese are colonising. Tibet has also seen a massive influx of Han Chinese, again part of a government drive to extinguish local cultural difference. This process has been described by Tibetan spiritual leader the Dalai Lama as 'cultural genocide'.[51] As in Xinjiang, the use of the Tibetan language is being deliberately phased out.[52] There are no reliable figures to detail the extent of the Han influx, but Tibet's capital Lhasa is now heavily Han and looks little different to cities in the rest of China.[53]

THE FUTURE

Tensions between the urban metropolis and the rural hinterland have probably yet to reach their peak. In the developing world, urbanisation continues apace, as does the chaotic upheaval of rural populations fleeing from conflict. This process will inevitably place more and more political power in the hands of city-dwellers. The temptation for wealthy urbanites to use social and economic issues to impose military solutions on outlying areas will become a motor for new wars.

There is a risk that much of the world could revert to a period resembling Europe of the Middle Ages, a time when predatory city-states such as Venice and Milan deployed military power at the behest of their own mercantile interests, and against those of rival cities, with no reference to the broader wellbeing. This prospect could even involve the secession of wealthy cities that come to resent the financial burden of developing impoverished rural areas. Such arguments are voiced in the Indian metropolis of Mumbai by nativist parties like Shiv Sena.[54]

There are some reasons to hope that the divergence between urban and rural outlooks can be narrowed. The spread of communications technology has reduced the physical necessity of urbanisation, bringing new opportunities to smaller settlements. Well-managed economic development in rural areas can increase their prosperity and reduce the attractiveness of violence and urban migration. Such advances, however, require governments to take a long-term view – and to resist the quick gains that military-industrial interests foresee in the exploitation of non-urban territories.

6
War and its Ill Effects on Health, Environment and Development

If you are poor, uneducated and living outside an urban area, you are many times more likely to suffer the consequences of war. As the previous chapter described, you will be viewed by the urban military-industrial complex as little more than an outmoded obstacle to economic 'progress'. But worst of all, for people relying on traditional, agrarian forms of life, your environment will be poisoned in the name of this progress. Globalisation has allowed the rich world to export pollution to developing countries at an astonishing rate.

In 2008 Nancy Pelosi, then the Speaker of the US House of Representatives, explained her opposition to drilling for oil in Alaska's Arctic National Wildlife Refuge and off the US coastline. 'I'm trying to save the planet,' she told the Politico website[1] when asked about her opposition to Republican attempts to lift the moratorium on offshore oil and gas exploration. Many US conservationists felt the same way. Despite studies that indicated Alaska could become the eighth largest source of oil in the world,[2] the arctic wilderness remains untouched.

American politicians have been far less brave when it comes to telling their countrymen to decrease their energy consumption. The US consumes about one quarter of the world's oil production. Much of this energy is simply wasted. It is typical for US truck drivers in Colorado to leave their engines running while they eat lunch, to keep the air conditioning on. Many households leave their water boilers on all day, even when no-one's at home, rather than using a timer switch. However, Americans are increasingly intolerant of pollution in their own back-yard. Pelosi's comments tapped into the popularity of the environmental movement, without offering any solution to where the oil would come from instead.

The result of this contradiction has been that rather than sullying their own national parks, Americans have exported pollution overseas. It is now much cheaper for dirty industries such as oil, plastics, and chemical production to operate in far-flung jurisdictions where there is little emphasis on environmental control. Often their neighbours are people with low levels of literacy and formal education, a lack of human capital that leaves them powerless to navigate political and legal systems to protect themselves from environmental damage. In some cases the pollution damages local agriculture to the extent that locals have little option but to work for the polluting industry.

One of the best documented examples of this kind of abusive relationship is in the Niger Delta, where international energy companies have made a fortune extracting and exporting oil. The Delta's oil represents a huge proportion of Nigeria's economy, yielding wealth of $600 billion since the 1960s.[3] Rather than enriching the local population, however, the effects for the people of the Delta have been catastrophic. Frequent oil spills blight their lives and their livelihoods. The majority of the 31 million inhabitants do not have access to clean water or healthcare. According to Amnesty International, which sent a field-research team to the Delta in 2008, 'at night often the only light visible for miles is from flares burning unwanted gas'.[4]

The astonishing and kleptocratic relationship between rich, oil-consuming nations and their local overseers in the Nigerian government has not gone unnoticed among the Delta's inhabitants. A profusion of armed groups has emerged with various goals: some to protest at the exploitation and damage being done to the Delta, others simply to extract a share of the wealth through kidnappings and pipeline-taps.[5] Inevitably, to protect their own ill-gotten wealth, Nigeria's elite has turned to Western arms suppliers for equipment to fight the gangs. Between 2000 and 2005, British arms sales to Nigeria rose tenfold, including armoured vehicles and heavy artillery.[6]

Just as pollution causes conflict, conflicts cause pollution. War has a hugely detrimental impact on infrastructure. Damage to power lines, for instance, increases the use of generators for electricity. Their exhaust fumes vastly increase the output of toxic fumes in settlements. Damage to bridges and roads means that vehicle journeys become much longer, again increasing emissions. Damage to sewerage systems can poison supplies of fresh water and pollute whole neighbourhoods with effluent. The health effects are exacerbated by hospitals having to cope with combat casualties as well as the failing infrastructure.

Then there are the environmental problems associated with the munitions themselves. Rather than becoming 'cleaner' as technology has advanced, in many cases the toxic fallout of modern weaponry is far greater than that of weapons of the past. According to Iraq's Environment Minister Narmin Othman, one of the greatest environmental challenges faced by her war-torn country is the use of depleted uranium rounds used by the US military.[7] Depleted uranium is one of the heaviest materials known to man, 1.7 times the density of lead. This density makes it a highly effective material for making armour-piercing ammunition, as most armour is made of less dense materials. Depleted uranium is now used in a wide range of ordnance, by many countries. It was used extensively by US forces in the Gulf War and the 2003 invasion of Iraq.

Depleted uranium is also highly toxic. The US Department of Defense has long denied its impact on public health, but the scientific evidence has become incontrovertible. A study by the University of Southern Maine, entitled 'Depleted Uranium Induces Neoplastic Transformation in Human Lung Epithelial Cells', found that depleted uranium is a human lung carcinogen. In 2009 an inquest in Great Britain into the death of a soldier from cancer heard evidence from Professor Christopher Busby, who had studied the radiation levels of depleted uranium dust in Iraq. He said it was 'more likely than not' that the soldier's cancer had been caused by exposure to the dust.[8] Since 1993, cases of leukaemia in Iraq's southern port of Basra have quadrupled.[9]

Depleted uranium is just one example of militarised radioactive materials. The construction of nuclear weapons relies on highly enriched uranium or plutonium, which entail the costly and dangerous construction of nuclear reactors. As more and more countries seek nuclear weapons, it becomes increasingly likely that these reactors will be subjected to a successful military or terrorist attack, with severe consequences for anyone living nearby.

More than 20 years after the Chernobyl nuclear disaster in Ukraine, the exclusion zone around the plant remains uninhabitable. The difficulty of storing nuclear waste is yet another magnet for terrorism and potential hazard to health. Again, people living in outlying areas that have been colonised by a wealthier economic group are most at risk. Tibetans have long claimed that the People's Republic of China uses Tibet as a dumping ground for nuclear waste.[10]

Children are disproportionately affected by unexploded conventional ordnance. Their tendency to play and explore makes them the principal victims of the 110 million hidden landmines buried around the world, often in poorly marked minefields. African children have been particularly badly hurt. UNICEF estimates that there are 37 million mines embedded in the soil of at least 19 African states. Those who survive the initial blast are left with crippling disabilities which are all the more debilitating when the only local sources of income are through manual labour.

No less dangerous are delayed explosives dropped from the sky. Cluster bombs and weapons designed to destroy a building or airstrip and then seed it with bomblets that do not explode immediately. They explode when someone disturbs them, for instance people trying to repair the damage caused by the initial blast. Many of these bomblets go undetected for years after being dropped, often until a child spots one of the orbs and tries to pick it up. Laos is still plagued by millions of bomblets dropped by US forces during the Vietnam War 40 years ago. Some 12,000 Laotians have been killed by them in the decades since.[11]

This appalling record has done nothing to deter the US from using these weapons. An investigation by *USA Today* in Iraq found that the Americans had used 10,800 cluster weapons and their British allies almost 2,200 in the conflict, with hundreds of civilian casualties.[12] According to Iraq's Environment Ministry, there are 500,000 unexploded cluster-bomb fragments in that country alone.[13] In 2008 the international Convention on Cluster Munitions was adopted in Dublin, Ireland, but the weapons continue to be used. In 2011 it was revealed that the Libyan army was firing Spanish-made MAT-120 120mm mortar projectiles, each of which carries and distributes 21 submunitions, into civilian areas of the rebel-held city of Misrata.[14]

THE MALNUTRITION-INFECTION COMPLEX

The cumulative impact of environmental poisoning, either through resource extraction or armed conflict (and often a mingling of the two) has a devastating effect on childhood development. One effect in particular goes under-discussed given its vast repercussions for wider society. In war-torn countries, vast numbers of children are affected by growth stunting. This condition is not simply a question of children being shorter than average. In fact, it describes a wide variety of associated disadvantages that combine to destroy the futures of both individuals and nations.

In clinical terms, stunting 'predicts generalized functional impairment on a wide range of biological, behavioural and social dimensions in children and adults from developing countries'.[15] Stunting is a result of a 'malnutrition-infection complex' which, like the military-industrial complex, is an interrelated pattern of harmful effects. A combination of poor diet and illness in young children combines into 'an intense period of growth retardation is generally between 3 and 12 or 18 months ... At the end of this process, marked departure from normality will have often occurred.'[16]

According to the United Nations children's agency UNICEF, around a third of children in the developing world – 195 million individuals – are stunted. In India and other South Asian countries, about half of all children are afflicted, with 61 million in India alone. Stunting is a major cause of death for children under the age of five. One of the reasons it is difficult to deal with is that it is self-perpetuating; stunted mothers tend to have stunted children, especially when the mother is living in unsanitary or deprived conditions.[17]

Both common sense and numerous academic studies have linked stunting to conflict. One study into the link between crop failure, stunting and civil war in Rwanda found that children of both sexes born in the war-zone were more than a standard deviation shorter than the average height for their age. The study noted that height was not the only indicator affected: stunting leads to 'less cognitive achievement and human capital accumulation, lower productivity and wages, and higher mortality'.[18]

Other studies have found that children in the war-torn north of Sri Lanka are smaller than children elsewhere on the island.[19] A useful summary of why stunting is prevalent in war-zones is suggested in a study published by the *Journal of Nutrition*:

Conflict can lead to food insecurity and chronic underproduction; it is also associated with political and economic instability, loss of caregivers, and inadequacy of health environments and services for children. Also, expenditures on the military lower the national investment in health, education, agriculture, and environmental protection.[20]

Famine and war go together. In the modern era, a vast range of NGOs and charities have emerged to monitor food security worldwide and deliver food aid to communities in need. When they are prevented from doing so, it is usually by conflict. In Africa especially, warring parties have often captured relief supplies of food to give to combatants. Women and children go without, and malnutrition and growth-stunting swiftly follow.

This is an appalling outcome for the individuals concerned, but it is also necessary to highlight the wider effect of stunting on development. As mentioned, stunted children tend to find learning difficult. Studies of students in Chile have found that under-nutrition in early infancy was 'strongly and significantly inter-related' to lower brain development and intelligence[21] in later life. Other studies have found that children who suffer malnutrition in early infancy suffer from psychosocial problems in adolescence, such as aggressive behaviour.[22] Given that child soldiers are found in war zones across the developing world, often armed with high-powered rifles, this conclusion is particularly alarming.

The economic impact of growth-stunting is highly damaging. Productivity is based on the ability to learn. If a national population is handicapped by infant malnutrition then it becomes much more difficult to develop a modern economy. Literacy and numeracy are vital to a great many skilled roles across a very wide expanse of the industrial and service economy. Unless a country can develop these two sectors then it will forever rely on the primary sector: agriculture, plantations, mines and oil wells. These unrefined resources will simply be exported to those countries which already possess an educated workforce – the kind of workforce that can make the bombs, mortars and artillery shells to maim and starve native populations into a state of malnourished, stunted helplessness.

THE MILITARY THREAT OF UNDER-DEVELOPMENT

As mentioned, the country that suffers the most from childhood stunting and the associated lack of human development is India. Contributing to this widespread problem is the existence of violent conflicts that rage across the country's hinterland, often unnoticed by the wider world. These conflicts are characterised by the alienation of communities who live in remote areas, pursue traditional forms of economic life, and whose culture and language exists outside the Hindi-speaking mainstream. Their lack of human development makes them outsiders.

India's prime minister, Manmohan Singh, has claimed that the country's most serious internal security threat comes not from Islamic militants sponsored by Pakistan, but from the Maoist revolutionaries known as Naxalites.[23] These guerrillas are highly active in impoverished eastern Indian states such as Orissa and Bihar, and they have proven resistant to military campaigns against them. Naxalites typically recruit from eastern and central India's marginalised tribal communities.

These tribesmen pursue traditional ways of life outside mainstream Indian society and often speak languages not taught within the school system. Their lack of literacy and broader human development has made them frequent victims of land-grabs, and subsidies intended for them are often either not claimed or are siphoned off by corrupt officials. Such hardships make these tribal groups natural enemies of state institutions and an obvious constituency for those who wish to lead an armed revolt.

Military responses to the Naxalite uprising have conspicuously failed. It is unlikely that India's multi-billion-dollar investment in new fighter jets will alter this situation. Indeed, their purchase makes it worse, by diverting resources away from investment in the human development of tribal groups. According to the United Nations' State of the World's Indigenous People's report, since the early 1990s there has been little change in the deep poverty experienced by India's tribes, even though the rest of the population has become wealthier.[24]

'Deprived of formal education and with little access to capital, they fail to find work, either self-employed or within regular jobs, ending up in casual employment or in agriculture.'[25] The report adds that: 'One recurring issue raised by indigenous peoples in United Nations fora has been the use of militarism as a pretext to gain control over natural resources, including land, minerals and oil, without restitution or compensation.' Again, it should be noted that when developing states purchase hugely expensive, foreign-made military systems, this much reduces the available resources for human development, compensation and restitution, thereby increasing the scope for internal conflict.

Africa continues to present the most disheartening example of the connection between militarism, resource-theft and poverty. The World Bank's *2011 World Development Report* was the first edition to make this nexus of effects its central theme. Correctly, it said that breaking this relationship required 'determined national leadership', 'responding at a regional level', and 'renewing cooperative efforts'. It noted that in many countries the violence of war has been replaced by rampant violent crime and political gangsterism, with 'new forms of violence interlinking local political conflicts, organized crime, and internationalized disputes'.

The report noted that West Africa is now seriously affected by drug-related violence, while East Africa is plagued by pirates. Firms in sub-Saharan Africa lose a higher percentage of sales to crime and spend a higher percentage of sales on security than any other region. It pointed out that youth unemployment is consistently cited in citizen perception surveys as a motive for joining both rebel movements and urban gangs. Inequality between richer and poorer households is closely associated with higher risks of violent crime, and corrupt governments fuel grievances. 'Stemming illegal financial flows from the public purse or from natural resource trafficking is important to underpin these initiatives,' it concluded.

This scattering of facts is correct, as far as it goes. Yet the report talked around the problem. Ask any African why lawlessness is so high and he will tell you it is because most African countries are controlled by criminals. Foreign businesses actively seek out and support criminal politicians in Africa, recruiting them to participate in what the report politely calls 'resource trafficking'. As a result, Africa has some of the world's richest politicians and some of its poorest people. These leaders steal their country's national wealth (the report's 'illegal financial flows from the public purse'), and hide it overseas.

Because the money is not invested in competitive industries at home, youth unemployment is inevitably high – a narrow economic base restricts the number of available careers and job openings. These leaders cannot afford ever to lose power, because they would go to jail, so they rig elections and suppress the populace, often aided by foreign military assistance and arms. The West has been known to assassinate African leaders who try to defy the system, for instance the Congo's Patrice Lumumba.[26] The result is that the unemployed either join criminal gangs or resistance movements. Most crucially of all, if the politicians in charge of the police and judiciary are viewed as criminals, then criminality becomes acceptable to many ordinary people who would abide by the law in a well-governed state.

Without explaining this narrative, progress is unlikely. 'Corruption' is a particularly misleading expression. All nations that have progressed rapidly from being poor to being wealthy have experienced extensive corruption, including the US. The difference lies in whether a country's wealth is hoarded in domestic bank accounts, from where it can be invested in national development, or whether it flies out of the country. Africa is an example of the latter trend. A 2008 study at the University of Massachusetts estimated capital flight out of sub-Saharan Africa between 1970 and 2004 at $420 billion or, if the interest was included, at $607 billion.[27] This, it reported, made the impoverished region a net creditor to the rest of the world. The vast interest earnings on this flow make it a highly profitable proposition to Western banks. A 2010 study showed that banks are not merely passive conduits for capital flight from Africa, but that they actively facilitate it.[28]

Their own wealth denuded, poor African countries are left with no option but to borrow from the West, which attaches conditions to the aid that make it even easier for Western corporations to buy the services of greedy officials and ministers. By controlling the narrative, however, the Western media has attributed the problem of 'corruption' exclusively to the Africans involved. The role of US and European multinationals, who pay the bribes, take the resources, arm the dictators, and hide their money, is reduced by the media to that of victims, forever forced by circumstance to grease the palms of crooked Africans.

HUMAN DEVELOPMENT IN AFGHANISTAN

Education in all its various forms, whether formally in school or via other avenues, such as learning through work and information disseminated by the media, is what is meant by human development. In Afghanistan, the US has recognised that resolution to the conflict hinges on this kind of development. Announcing his new strategy for Afghanistan in March 2009, President Barack Obama said the following:

> Our efforts will fail in Afghanistan and Pakistan if we don't invest in their future. That is why my budget includes indispensable investments in our State Department and foreign assistance programs. These investments relieve the burden on our troops. They contribute directly to security. They make the American people safer. And they save us an enormous amount of money in the long run – because it is far cheaper to train a policeman to secure their village or to help a farmer seed a crop, than it is to send our troops to fight tour after tour of duty with no transition to Afghan responsibility.[29]

In October 2010 Mark Silensky, a senior analyst at the US Department of Defense, authored a report entitled *An Irony of War: Human Development as Warfare in Afghanistan.*[30] He contended that only by building a state that was appreciated by the population of Afghanistan could the Taliban insurgency be defeated: 'The Afghan insurgents will be defeated, primarily, by creating a generation of Afghans who see the government as their ally in building an economically promising future.'

Silensky drew a parallel with General John J. Pershing's campaign to end Moro insurgency in the Muslim south of the Philippines, a campaign which Silensky says was won largely as a result of its focus on human development and institution-building. He argues that the British response to the Malayan emergency of the 1950s was again successful due to its emphasis on human development, whereas the French counter-insurgency operations in Algeria and Indo-China failed because they were based on force.

In September 2010 the commander of the international forces in Afghanistan, General David Petraeus, noted that promoting literacy had become a key goal of his operation: 'It's pretty difficult to enforce a law you can't read or to perform maintenance using a technical manual if you can't read it.'[31] Petraeus admitted that he had been sceptical of the literacy campaign for Afghan soldiers and police until he had seen the results.

Sadly, it is less clear that the US has realised the broader need for human development beyond the armed forces. The 'civilian surge' for Afghanistan announced by Obama following his election as US president in November 2008 has brought around 1,100 experts to support Afghanistan's 30-million-strong population as they attempt to rebuild their country after three decades of war. These experts include agronomists advising local farmers on how to improve their crop yields and administrators supporting the work of government departments.

Yet this 'surge' is tiny in comparison to the vast military escalation that Obama ordered in Afghanistan, with 30,000 additional US troops being ordered into the war-zone. An additional $33 billion authorised by congress was allotted to the troop surge in July 2010.[32] Despite Obama's recognition of the crucial role that human development must play if Afghanistan's wars are ever to end, nine years after the US-led invasion the emphasis remains overwhelmingly military.

CHANCES FOR THE FUTURE

In September 2000 the member states of the United Nations agreed to achieve eight Millennium Development Goals (MDGs) within 15 years. Five of these were aimed directly at the issues of pollution, under-nourishment, child health, maternal health and environmental sustainability. Since 2005 the UN has produced annual reports on the progress towards the targets set out by the Goals, with a view to ensuring that the commitments made by the world leaders are met.

More than a decade on, progress towards the MDGs has been sluggish. The most recent report on progress toward the goals said that the world's population of under-nourished people has continued to grow, and that in some areas progress towards hunger reduction has stalled or actually gone backwards. The report said that a quarter of children under the age of five were underweight due to a lack of food, or inadequate water, sanitation and health provision, or because mothers are poorly educated about childcare.[33]

The effects of the 2008 financial crisis, caused by the imbalance between the US and Chinese military-industrial complexes, ensured that poverty rates would be higher in 2015 than would otherwise have been the case. In 2010, 1.4 billion people were living in what the report called 'extreme' poverty, with an income of less than $1.25 a day. The effects on people living in remote areas were particularly marked, it added: 'Children in rural areas are nearly twice as likely to be underweight as those in urban areas.'[34] This urban-rural disparity has increased since 1990.

Nevertheless, the report concluded that apart from in sub-Saharan Africa and Western Asia, the MDG poverty targets would be met by 2015. The vast bulk of progress has been in East Asia, specifically China. In an independent report in 2006, the economist Peter Svedberg noted that China has managed to halve the incidence of child-stunting within five years,[35] a result of rapid gains in economic prosperity.

The only regions in which poverty had increased since 1990 were war-torn West Asia, which includes Iraq, Iran and Afghanistan, and parts of post-Soviet Central Asia. Progress has been made in reducing the number of underweight children in all regions – except again in war-torn West Asia.[36] The report pointed out that 'conflicts are a major threat to human security and to hard-won MDG gains'.[37] It also noted that physical disability, for instance from land-mine blasts, had a devastating effect on human-capital accumulation. Disability 'doubles the probability that a child will never attend school'.[38]

Western countries are hardly breaking the bank to change this situation. In 2009, expenditure on official development aid was $119.6 billion, a 2 per cent fall on the previous year. To put this figure in context, it was $58 billion less than the US is planning to trim from its defence budget (and defence contractors) over the next five years (see Chapter 2). Denmark, Luxembourg, the Netherlands,

Norway and Sweden were the only countries to meet or exceed the agreed international aid contribution of 0.7 per cent of gross national income.

China's extraordinary success in curbing poverty was achieved through rapid industrialisation. It is not at all clear that Western governments wish other poor countries to replicate the Chinese model, however. In 2011 the government of Great Britain announced that it would no longer help to fund the United Nations Industrial Development Organization (UNIDO), which works to enhance the technical and trading competitiveness of poor countries.[39] The UK said this was because UNIDO's goals – economic self-sufficiency for poor countries – were not aligned with UK development objectives. Nor, apparently, were those of UNESCO, the United Nations Educational, Scientific and Cultural Organization, which works to improve literacy, scientific attainment, teacher-training programmes and other attempts to improve the development of human-capital.[40]

A cynical observer might conclude that the West does not relish the prospect of other countries following China's industrialised growth model. This model requires a genuine commitment to public education, technical attainment and a willingness to challenge the West's dominance of high-value production. Instead, the US and Europe seem to prefer sending inadequate quantities of aid to victims of the status quo. Oil and minerals are very cheap when they can be extracted with no concessions to the health and safety of people living near the wells and mines. Sending medicine and food to those affected is cheaper and less politically sensitive than the economic alternatives.

When the trade in raw resources leads to conflict, as it has in the Niger Delta, the West simply arms the affected government against its own people. The intellectual and physical stunting of the affected population by war and pollution makes that population even less likely to achieve China-like levels of human development and economic prosperity. A Chinese proverb states that to give a man a fish feeds him for a day, but teaching him to fish feeds him for a lifetime. Until this philosophy is applied to international aid, then the abusive cycle of militarised resource-extraction will continue to exact a horrendous toll on those countries reduced to a perpetual life of primary-sector pollution and subservience.

Part III

The Folly of Chronic Wars – For Profit, Resources and Domination – More Weapons – More Wars – More Profits

7
Terrorism and Non-State Actors, and How to Make Them Stop

When it comes to funding and arming dictatorships, Europe and America have begun to experience an intractable problem. Although their local overseers are happy to enrich themselves, and to obstruct any kind of development that might threaten the West's monopoly on advanced production, many of their subjects are less content. Arming the regimes has kept a lid on domestic upheaval, to a point. But in some cases, dissatisfaction with tyrannical rule has led to violence not only in those countries but also directed at their Western allies.

DEATH IN LONDON

On 7 July 2005 London endured a morning that the British capital would rather have remembered for different reasons. It should have been a moment for rejoicing. The day before, jet fighters had overflown the city, not for reasons of security but for purposes of celebration. They had streamed red, white and blue smoke over the historic Square Mile to celebrate London's award of the 2012 Olympics, an event made all the sweeter for being snatched from the favourites Paris.

Workers who arrived in their offices early the next morning soon began to wonder why so many of their colleagues were late arriving. Otherwise, it seemed like a typical Thursday. But by around 10am news reports were interrupting coverage of the Olympic victory to report some kind of power blackout on the London Underground. The radio spoke of troops on the ground at Covent Garden. Sirens began to echo across the city. As the true nature of events became clear, that wail would become a cacophony.

Four British Muslims, three of them of South Asian heritage and one a convert, boarded underground trains that morning. They had travelled to the capital from the neglected cities in the north of England in which most British Muslims live. With them they carried backpacks containing bombs. During London's rush hour, when the underground trains were at their most crowded, they had detonated their explosives. One of the bombers, having found the Northern Line shut for maintenance, blew himself up on a bus in Tavistock Square.

Fifty-six people died in the attacks, including the four bombers. About 700 were injured. Such was the scale of the carnage that to store the human remains the authorities commandeered Artillery Gardens, an army cricket pitch in the heart of the city, in which they erected a marquee. Two weeks afterwards the events would claim another victim when the police, panicked into action, gunned down a man on another underground train after mistaking him for a terrorist. He was actually an unarmed electrician from Brazil.

The attacks became known as 7/7. They raised many questions. Britons understood instinctively that their country's foreign policy had somehow inspired the attack but beyond that, agreement ended. Was it Iraq? Afghanistan? Sceptics pointed out that the threat of terrorism predated both those conflicts. Was it Britain's support for Israel? Where had the bombers found their explosives? Who had trained them? The answers to these questions existed, but they differed from the account given by the British authorities.

HOW TO MAKE A BOMB

Learning to make bombs takes time and specialist training. It is not a skill that can be picked up through trial and error, any more than bomb-disposal experts can learn their trade through improvisation. Armies around the world prize their bomb-disposal experts highly. Likewise, terrorist groups protect their master bomb-makers at all costs. Without them, the threat posed by international terrorism would be much reduced.

Ibrahim Hassan al-Asiri is an example of such an expert. Western intelligence agencies say that al-Asiri, a Saudi who works for al-Qaeda in the Arabian Peninsula, designed two bombs hidden in computer printer cartridges that were discovered on US-bound flights in 2010. These devices employed the high explosive PETN. The PETN replaced the carbon-based toner, which had an atomic number close to that of PETN and therefore appeared the same on the airport X-ray scanners. By matching the atomic numbers of the other bomb components to those of the various parts of the printer, the master terrorist bypassed the best technology available to the West.

According to al-Qaeda, the bomb cost $4,200 dollars to manufacture. Al-Asiri had also used PETN to make a suicide bomb which his younger brother hid in his underpants in a failed 2009 attempt to kill Saudi Arabia's security chief. Saudi officials said the bomb used a chemical fuse that could not be picked up by a metal detector.[1] The same type of chemical detonator and explosives were concealed in the underwear of a young Nigerian man who tried to blow himself up on a jetliner in 2009, leading led investigators to conclude that al-Asiri was also behind that operation.[2,3]

A high degree of sophistication is required to build bombs that can bypass airport security. The Saudi interior ministry claims that al-Asiri acquired his skills in Yemen, where he was trained by al-Qaeda operatives in the use of explosives, toxins, and hand-held missiles.[4] Arguably it is these trainers, rather than al-Asiri himself, who pose the real threat. While they operate, al-Qaeda will be able to instruct new generations of bomb makers able to construct sophisticated devices with the potential to bring about mass civilian deaths.

Large bombs are harder to build than small ones. One reason that al-Qaeda was able to destroy Saudi Arabia's Khobar Towers building in 1996, killing 19 Americans and injuring a great many more, was because the CIA underestimated the skill of the terrorists. The *New York Times* reported that CIA security experts believed al-Qaeda was unable to construct a bomb with more than 200 pounds of explosives. The Khobar Towers bomb, built into a truck, was 5,000 pounds.[5] This mistake may have contributed to an erroneous belief among investigators that Iran was behind the attack. However, an investigation by Gareth Porter of Antiwar.com suggested that US officials deliberately misled the public as part of a deal with the Saudi authorities, who were embarrassed by their own links to al-Qaeda.[6]

Contrary to popular opinion, it is not simple to download bomb-making instructions from the internet, particularly for powerful bombs based on sophisticated explosives like PETN. Recognising this difficulty, in 2010 al-Qaeda tried to assist 'lone wolf' terrorists by uploading to the web an English-language guide to bomb-making, but again this concentrated on bombs made from easy-to-obtain household products. Even this document warned readers that making bombs was a 'sensitive task' and that 'your first mistake is your last mistake'. The book was written by students of Midhat Mursi al-Sayid 'Umar, another al-Qaeda bomb expert, who graduated in chemical engineering from Alexandria University in

Egypt and who also fought in Afghanistan.[7] He was killed in a US drone strike in Pakistan in 2008.

Even sophisticated militant groups such as the Irish Republican Army (IRA) lost many bomb makers in the process of constructing explosives. Such losses came despite the IRA operating a specialised training programme to spread bomb-making skills throughout the organisation, which it developed over a period of decades. The IRA also had access to professional-grade electronics and explosives from overseas.[8] To date, al-Qaeda has failed to cultivate a generation of do-it-yourself terrorists. Successful attacks such as the 7/7 bombings require help from experts.[9]

THE MYSTERY OF IRAQ

So building bombs is not straightforward, especially when the bombs are very powerful. Yet this presents a riddle. Within a couple of months of the US invasion of Iraq in 2003, Iraqi insurgents were detonating explosive devices of enormous size. In August 2003, for instance, a car bomb in the Iraqi city of Najaf killed 125 people, including a senior Shia Muslim cleric.[10] Ten days earlier a truck bomb at the UN headquarters in Baghdad had killed 23 people including UN chief Sérgio Vieira de Mello. By 2007 the insurgents were staging synchronised car bombings that were claiming hundreds of lives at a stroke.[11] They were building bombs capable of shredding armoured vehicles,[12] something the IRA never managed in three decades of violent action.

Many of the insurgents were once army officers in the Saddam-era military, who lost their jobs as a result of the invasion. This fact was noted in a 2005 article in the *Financial Times,* which also noted that US commanders ventured several and sometimes contradictory explanations for the huge number of bomb attacks in Iraq.[13] Former Iraqi officers had stashed large quantities of explosives in remote desert hideouts for use in car bombs against the occupying US forces.[14] But conventional military training does not instruct soldiers on how to build car bombs, suicide vests, and explosively formed projectiles.

One explanation was presented by the journalist Barry M. Lando in his book on Iraq, *Web of Deceit.* During his research Lando travelled to Sierra Vista, Arizona, to interview Roque Gonzalez (spelt 'Rocky' in the references), a former warrant officer in the US special forces. Gonzalez told him that Saddam's elite troops had trained in 'unconventional warfare' at the US Army's John F. Kennedy Special

Warfare Center and School at Fort Bragg, North Carolina, during the 1980s. At the time the US was concerned that Iraq might lose its war with Iran. So it authorised the 'unconventional' training to ensure that Iraqi soldiers would be able to fight a guerrilla war if their country was overrun by the Iranian.[15]

What was this 'unconventional warfare'? The *Leader's Handbook to Unconventional Warfare*, published in 2009 by the Fort Bragg school, offers some strong clues. 'Unconventional warfare' is the planned 'development of a resistance movement following an invasion', it says.[16] It trains operatives in how to set up an 'insurgency to coerce, disrupt or overthrow a government or occupying power'.[17] Such insurgencies can employ various tactics, including 'dramatic small-scale attacks, such as bombings and stand-off rocket attacks'.[18] The US army teaches 'the full spectrum of required functions' and has 'provided the trainers and advisers to resistance forces', instructing them in 'guerrilla warfare and underground organizations'.[19] The *Handbook* says that one function of these underground movements is the fabrication of 'special materials' such as 'improvised explosives, weapons, [and] munitions'.[20]

The *Handbook* lists as an example of such US support the case of Nicaragua's Contras, whose operations were being planned and supported by the US at about the same time as the Iraqis were receiving their training at Fort Bragg. The Contras used explosive devices in a way mirrored by the Iraqi insurgents 20 years later. They mined roads to destroy army trucks, with scant regard for civilian casualties.[21] According to the Landmine & Cluster Monitor, the Contras used these explosive devices 'to disrupt economic life and destabilize the government'. These bombs and landmines caused the great majority of civilian casualties during Nicaragua's civil war.[22]

Also in the 1980s, the US armed and trained rebels in Afghanistan to fight the occupying Soviet army. The Soviet invasion of Afghanistan in 1979 had strengthened the military dictatorship of neighbouring Pakistan, presenting it with an external threat to justify its existence.[23] The 'scientific atheism' enforced by the Soviets across Central Asia allowed Pakistan's military to clad itself as the defender of Islam.[24] This made the Pakistani military a perfect vehicle to train the Islamic resistance in Afghanistan, the mujahideen (مجاهدين, literally, 'men of jihad'). The Pakistani military would go on to train a host of other militant groups, especially those targeting India.[25]

Rather than just instructing the Afghans directly, Fort Bragg trained Pakistani officers with bomb-making techniques to transfer to the leaders of the Afghan resistance, including those who would later form the Taliban. One such Pakistani was Colonel Sultan Amir Tarar, known as 'Colonel Imam', a senior officer in Pakistan's Inter Service Intelligence (ISI). He had studied explosives at Fort Bragg in 1974 and became a key figure in 'Operation Cyclone', the name for the US support operation for the Afghan mujahids, recruiting and training key militants such as Jalaluddin Haqqani and future Taliban leader Mullah Omar. Despite being a keen Islamic radical, Colonel Imam was murdered in January 2011 by a faction of the Taliban.[26,27,28]

The Taliban now use Colonel Imam's bomb-making techniques against US soldiers in Afghanistan. Like the Iraqis, the Afghan fighters are adept at improvising roadside bombs and mines. These Improvised Explosive Devices (IEDs) killed 360 US and allied soldiers in 2010.[29] 'The mujahideen used the same kind of IEDs in a different form against the Soviets,' noted US Secretary of State for Defence Robert Gates in November 2009, apparently without irony. It should be remembered that on at least one occasion, Gates received a personal tour of mujahideen training camps from the late 'Colonel Imam'.[30] Gates concluded: 'Let's go back and look at the playbook that they used against the Soviets to see if there's something we can learn.'[31]

One obvious lesson would be, 'don't train terrorists'. US officials have admitted that the man who instructed al-Qaeda chief Osama bin-Laden was an Egyptian, Ali Mohamed, who in 1981 learnt his own skills during four months of training at Fort Bragg, where he too was instructed in 'unconventional warfare'.[32] While at Fort Bragg, Mohamed maintained close links with the Office of Mujihadeen Services in New York, which recruited and raised funds for the Afghan resistance and later formed the basis of al-Qaeda.[33]

The US authorities claimed that his terrorist career was more a result of their own incompetence than any deliberate stratagem. Mohamed, they said, had simply fallen between the cracks of any number of institutions which together constitute America's bloated military-intelligence establishment.[34] After all, he would hardly be the first Fort Bragg graduate to backfire spectacularly. Fort Bragg trained Manuel Noriega, who declared war on the US on behalf of his native Panama in 1989, leading to the US invasion of that country.[35] Fort Bragg trained Los Zetas, a Mexican special forces unit that is now one of Mexico's most deadly drugs cartels.[36]

Given this record, it is highly probable that the devastating campaign of terror waged by the Iraq's insurgents, killing hundreds of thousands of civilians, drew upon skills imparted in North Carolina. The roadside bombs, the textbook insurgency techniques, the sheer swiftness with which Iraqi militants deployed these tactics after the invasion, all point to training in 'unconventional warfare'. Time and again, groups armed and trained by the US army as its proxies have transformed themselves into potent threats to peace.

CONNECTIVITY

The US is not the only country to sponsor terrorism. During the twentieth century the Chinese government backed numerous communist insurgencies in Southeast Asia, including those in the Philippines, Malaya and Burma.[37,38,39] The British state colluded with Protestant paramilitaries to kill members of the IRA in Northern Ireland.[40] Iran does not deny its links with Hezbollah in Lebanon and Hamas in the Palestinian Territories. The Soviet Union and its allies in the communist Warsaw Pact supplied arms to Soviet-backed insurgent groups. According to Human Rights Watch, this support has led to some of these ex-Soviet states continuing to falsify licenses and end-user certificates to supply terrorist organisations with weapons and systems.[41]

Often the most deadly terrorists were those who were first recruited as agents by Western intelligence agencies. 'Colonel Imam' was not the only Pakistani officer to walk a fine line between US operative and Islamic militant, and to die because of it. In April 2010 Khalid Khawaja, another ISI agent, was found dead in a ditch near the town of Mir Ali. He was murdered by an unheard-of group calling themselves the 'Asian Tigers'. Before they killed him they forced Khawaja to admit, on film, to working for the CIA. Once Osama bin-Laden's personal pilot, Khawaja had fought with the mujahideen in Afghanistan. According to one account, he had 'virtually announced' the 9/11 attacks on New York two months before they took place.[42] Khawaja was one of the last people to speak to the *New York Times* journalist Daniel Pearl before Pearl's murder in 2002.

In 2007 Pearl's story was made into a Hollywood movie starring Angelina Jolie, called *A Mighty Heart*. Pearl had travelled to Pakistan to research the background of a British terrorist, Richard Reid, the so-called 'shoe bomber'. In the event, he was murdered by a different British terrorist, a man named Omar Sheikh. Whereas Reid was a petty criminal, Sheikh was highly educated, a graduate of the London School of Economics. Well-placed sources say that he was also an agent of the British secret service MI6.[43] In an extraordinary incident in 2009, Sheikh used a mobile (cell) phone smuggled into his jail cell to ring the president of Pakistan. He pretended to be the Indian foreign minister and threatened all-out war.[44]

The hoax would have been funny had it not come soon after state-backed Pakistani militants had massacred 164 people in Mumbai. The perpetrators of that attack were an outfit called the Army of the Pure (لشکرطیبہ or Lashkar Taiba), one of the many anti-India groups established by Pakistani intelligence using the 'unconventional warfare' techniques it had learned from the Americans. In 1999 Omar Sheikh was sprung from an Indian prison by another of these groups, the Mujahideen Movement (حرکت المجاہدین, Harkat al-Mujahideen), whose origins were also in the Afghan war against the Soviets. The militants achieved this jail break by hijacking Indian Airlines Flight 814 and threatening to kill the passengers. After the prisoners were released the hijackers simply ordered the plane to fly to Afghanistan, where they were met by the Taliban and ISI agents.[45]

Time and again, the terrorists of the twenty-first century can be traced back to the Afghanistan of the 1980s and 90s. For four years, between 2005 and 2009, the most wanted man in Southeast Asia was Noordin M. Top, another master bomb-maker. A Malaysian, he worked for the region's al-Qaeda offshoot, Jemaah Islamiah. Top was responsible for bombs used in a string of devastating attacks on chain hotels and nightclubs catering to foreigners. He learnt his bomb-making skills from Dr Azahari bin Husin, also a Malaysian, a university mathematics lecturer. Azahari gained his explosives expertise in the Taliban-controlled Afghanistan of the 1990s.[46] The militant known as Bangla Bhai, whose group detonated 500 bombs simultaneously across Bangladesh in 2005, trained and fought in Afghanistan.[47] So did the ringleader of the 9/11 attacks, Mohammed Atta.[48]

INTERFERENCE

The pattern of Western interference, much of it incompetent, in the affairs of Afghanistan and other Muslim states is a guide to why the 7/7 attacks on London took place. Since the end of the colonial era, the West had supported some Muslim dictators while training terrorists to fight others, for instance the pro-Soviet Afghan government. Rarely has the West tried to encourage Muslims towards the same freedoms or democracy enjoyed by its own citizens. In the most extreme cases, such as Saudi Arabia, the only place that political discussion can take place is the mosque.

Like the US in Iraq, al-Qaeda seeks 'regime change'. Its goal, first and foremost, is not some globe-spanning Islamic empire but the overthrow of Saudi Arabia's dictatorship, which is armed and funded by the US. There is no disagreement among experts on this point.[49,50,51] Al-Qaeda's secondary goal is to eject pro-Western dictators from other Muslim countries. To do so, the organisation stages attacks not only in those dictatorships but on the countries that support them. The 7/7 attacks on London were explicitly for this reason.

It was no coincidence that some of the bombers were ethnic Pakistanis, or that they had visited Pakistan before the attacks.[52] At the time, Pakistan was run by a dictator bought and paid for by the West. General Pervez Musharraf was a leader who admitted that he spoke English better than he spoke Urdu, his own national language. From 2001–08 the US paid his regime billions of dollars in no-strings military aid, much of which disappeared into the pockets of senior officers, according to the US Government Accountability Office. In return, the general turned his guns on the Taliban. When he was finally ousted in 2008, Musharraf retired to London,[53] where he had once attended war college as a guest of the British military.

Musharraf was just the latest in a long succession of pro-Western Pakistani dictators. Their record of governance is appalling. Pakistan is one of the world's most under-taxed economies, with the government's revenue collection equivalent to only 10 per cent of GDP. The result is that public services are abysmal. One in ten of the world's out-of-school children is Pakistani.[54] However, the military elite does not suffer. It has independent sources of finance, and therefore no stake in improving the situation.

In a video released after 7/7, the bombers and their al-Qaeda backers explained their motives. The film was introduced by Osama bin-Laden's deputy, the Egyptian doctor Ayman al-Zawahiri. He congratulated those Pakistanis prepared to fight against 'humiliation and slavery' and urged others to attack 'the Crusader agent Musharraf' who worked 'in service of America and Britain'. One of the bombers spoke of the 'humiliation and anger' that Muslims feel while living under puppet regimes.

To say that the official British report glossed over this explanation would be an understatement. It gave a reduced and largely irrelevant account of what was on this tape,[55] omitting the reasons given by the bombers for why they had chosen to attack London. The British authorities instead described the attacks as 'Islamist terrorism', which they defined as terrorism with 'a religious justification',[56] as opposed to a political cause.

This was a gross distortion. Islam is a religion. 'Islamism' is and always has been a political doctrine, one invented in the 1940s[57] by a Pakistani theoretician, Abul A'la Mawdudi. Rather than a spiritual movement, Islamism was intended as a 'Third Way' between communism and capitalism, using a literal and highly selective reading of Islamic texts to create a totalitarian economic and socio-political system.[58] Terrorist violence necessarily ignores key elements of the Muslim faith – for instance the bar on killing innocent civilians, particularly Muslim ones. Al-Qaeda has killed far more Muslims in Iraq than members of any other religion.

There was a time when the US was quite happy for 'freedom fighters' to attack not only local regimes but also their puppet-masters. During the 1970s and 80s, the IRA staged attacks inside the disputed province of Northern Ireland but also on the British mainland. They were assisted in this campaign by fund-raising among Irish Americans, permitted by the US government. Senior US politicians such as Senator Edward Kennedy and Congressman Peter T. King were vocal supporters of the IRA, even after the group blew up pubs full of civilians in Guildford and Birmingham and almost killed Margaret Thatcher.[59] In a staggering piece of hypocrisy, King now chairs the US House Homeland Security Committee, from where he condemns Islamist extremism.[60,61]

The IRA emerged because Northern Ireland's Catholic minority was systematically frozen out of institutions by the Protestant majority. Its campaign ended when the British government forced these institutions to accept the Catholics on an equitable basis. Political reform can end terrorism elsewhere. However, for that to happen, the military-industrial trading relationship between the rich and poor worlds must be dismantled.

Where there is no space for open political debate, terrorism is an inevitable consequence. The Euro-American practice of arming and funding dictators who prevent development and oversee the exportation of raw resources has made the West a target of terrorist violence. Al-Qaeda is a manifestation of the anger and humiliation felt by people living under puppet regimes. In the Middle East these feelings of humiliation were further inflamed by the rapid democratisation of Africa, South America and Southeast Asia following the end of the Cold War, leaving Arabs almost the last prisoners of despotism.

The wave of revolution that swept across the Arab world in early 2011 was the best hope in a generation for putting a stop to al-Qaeda's violence. Frustrated politicians who might otherwise have turned to violence suddenly had a chance to test their ideas against the popular will. However, this reform will only take place if the West accepts that it can buy oil not just from tame dictatorships, but also from plural democracies.

8
China's Periphery – The Military-Industrial Mess that Could Destroy a Bright Future

On 17 February 1979 a new war broke out in Asia. As dawn rose over the Mekong River, 21 infantry divisions of China's People's Liberation Army streamed across the length of the southern border into Vietnam.[1] The sheer number of Chinese soldiers – perhaps as many as 250,000 – reflected a belief among generals that the vast population at their disposal was a great military asset. Such was China's confidence that, two days before the invasion, its leader Deng Xiaoping had announced China's intention to conduct a limited attack on Vietnam.[2]

Complex tensions existed within the communist bloc at the time. During Vietnam's war with the United States, Cambodia, China and the Soviet Union (USSR) supported the North Vietnamese forces against the US-backed South Vietnam. After the fall of Saigon in 1975, the geopolitical picture fractured. Vietnam moved firmly into the USSR's orbit, leasing the Cam Ranh Bay harbour to the Soviet navy. US President Richard Nixon visit to China in 1972 marked the start of a long Sino-American rapprochement. China and Vietnam quarrelled over the ownership of islands in the South China Sea. Cambodia began a series of border raids into Vietnam.[3]

In response to these border incursions, in late 1978 Vietnam invaded Cambodia, then known as Kampuchea. Vietnamese forces swiftly captured the capital Phnom Penh and ended the genocidal regime of Pol Pot, the leader of the Khmer Rouge. Pol Pot, a Chinese ally, fled the capital 'dangling from a helicopter' and was forced to hide in the jungle until his death in 1998. China was incensed. It viewed Vietnam as an upstart that had become too cocksure as a result of its victory over the US and its capture of Cambodia, and as part of a Soviet plot to 'encircle' China.[4] China resolved to teach Vietnam a lesson.

At first the Chinese invasion appeared to be going well. The People's Liberation Army quickly captured three provincial capitals, Cao Bang, Lang Son, and Lao Cai.[5] The cost of these gains was immense, however. The Chinese had expected regular Vietnamese army divisions to meet them at the border and engage in a conventional fight. Instead, these divisions remained in a defensive formation around Hanoi, leaving the 150,000-strong Vietnamese border militia to do the fighting. This militia was battle-hardened from fighting the US, adept at guerrilla warfare and equipped with leftover American equipment.[6]

This communist militia retreated into the hilly terrain of the captured settlements, as they had done in the famous defence of Dien Bien Phu 23 years earlier. The militia began to inflict crippling casualties on the Chinese armies. Three weeks after the invasion the Chinese withdrew from Vietnam. Foreign observers estimated that as many as 63,000 Chinese soldiers died in the incursion.[7] A British diplomat who posed this figure to a Chinese general said the commander merely laughed and replied: 'We have a lot of people!'[8]

China claimed that it had achieved its military objectives, but it was very hard to see what these were. Bilateral relations were poisoned for a decade. Overseas the campaign was widely viewed as a disaster and as evidence that China was a 'paper tiger'. The Vietnamese maintained their occupation of Cambodia. Hundreds of thousands of Hoa people – Vietnamese and Cambodians of Chinese descent – were forced to become refugees due to reprisals by the Vietnamese military. Many became 'boat people' living in squalid conditions in neighbouring countries.[9] More than a quarter of a million fled into China's Guangxi province.[10]

Unlike America's disaster in Vietnam, the rest of the world has almost forgotten this inglorious escapade. But 1979 carries a multitude of warnings for Asia's future. There remains a widespread assumption, both in China and overseas, that China's huge population translates into huge military strength. Many territorial disputes remain unsolved between China, the 14 countries it borders, and even those it does not. Russia remains a potential rival. Prejudice against Chinese ethnic minorities is widespread across Southeast Asia. And most worryingly of all, the military-industrial complex is showing signs of twisting China's national interests to its own destructive ends.

CHINA TODAY

We have seen how the US military-industrial complex acts as a corporate parasite on the public purse, uniting thousands of businesses and millions of workers in the pursuit of common financial interest. We have also seen how Western Europe's former colonial powers uses their military-industrial complex to insulate themselves against accusations that they conspire with dictators to extract cheap resources from under-developed countries. The European Union is only the world's 13th largest producer of oil[11] (the US is its 3rd), and its aggressively extractive foreign policy reflects this handicap.

The purpose of China's military-industrial complex is the exact opposite to that of Europe's. Europe sells arms to dictators to ensure that they supply it with cheap, unrefined commodities. China, on the other hand, is still a poor country in many areas. It does not view its economic future as a resource bank for the rich world, or even as a supplier of low-end manufactured products. China's goal is to strip the West of its monopoly on advanced, high-value production. It has a 'catching up' strategy designed for just this purpose.

The growth of China's military budget reflects the fundamental role played by the military-industrial complex in China's development strategy. As we saw in Chapter 2, the acquisition of foreign technology is led by China's military intelligence establishment. China's 2010 military budget was 7.5 per cent higher than the previous year, with its 2011 budget 12.7 per cent higher than 2010, at $92 billion.[12] Although still a small proportion of America's defence spending, such huge annual hikes have led Japan to describe China's military spending as a 'global threat'.[13]

The size and reach of the Chinese military-industrial complex is growing accordingly. According to Richard Bitzinger, a professor at the University of Hawaii's Asia-Pacific Center for Security Studies, 'China possesses one of the oldest, largest, and most diversified military-industrial complexes in the developing world'. He describes the sector as containing around 1,000 enterprises employing some three million workers, many of whom are engineers and technicians.[14] China is one of the few countries to produce the full range of weapons, from small arms to nuclear missiles.

For its 'catching up' strategy to work, China needed to find its own spheres of influence, its own pliable resource banks. Much has been made of China's activities in Africa, so much so that there is no need to add to the literature. A more useful example of China's neo-colonial model is its dealings with the resource rich nations closer to home. In Central Asia, a handful of post-Soviet despotisms ensure the uninterrupted extraction of mineral wealth in return for their leaders' personal gain. China is a primary beneficiary of this process.

INLAND EMPIRE

The Central Asia 'stans' were until 20 years ago part of the Soviet Empire. Sparsely populated, Turkish-speaking and overwhelmingly Muslim, the steppes of Central Asia have for centuries proven a battle ground between empires. Now, their vast surplus of mineral wealth has become a vital input to China's economy. Two pipelines, one to Turkmenistan for natural gas and one to Kazakhstan for oil, have become strategic assets that place China's future in the hands of its western neighbours.

This future is by no means secure. In 2005 the Central Asian republic of Kyrgyzstan rose up in what became known as the Tulip Revolution. This unforeseen revolt forced the departure of the president and installed the pro-Western Bakiyev government. The revolution quickly spread to nearby Uzbekistan, where it was only halted by the massacre of hundreds of demonstrators at Andijan.[15] A domino effect threatened to bring down all the compliant post-Soviet governments that were proving so useful to China and Russia.

Russia and China blamed the revolutions on the US Central Intelligence Agency (CIA) and its British equivalent, MI6. The West, they claimed, was trying to destabilise the region for its own geopolitical ends. There was a fair amount of evidence in support of this allegation. At the time of the revolts, pro-democracy 'NGOs' such as the US National Endowment for Democracy, the International Republican Institute and Britain's Westminster Foundation for Democracy were engaging with opposition movements in the region.[16]

In 2011 a former Turkish intelligence official disclosed how hundreds of CIA agents infiltrated the moderate Islamist Gulen movement in Kyrgyzstan and Uzbekistan.[17] Another Islamist movement active in Central Asia was Hizb ut-Tahrir (HuT), headquartered in London. Although banned in many countries, this revolutionary organisation had a chain of schools paid for by the British taxpayer.[18] Before his election in May 2010, the British prime minister, David Cameron, swore repeatedly that he would ban HuT. Yet a year later, no signs of a ban had emerged.

Protecting pro-Chinese regimes in Central Asia has become a major objective of Beijing's foreign policy. With Russia, the Chinese government has led the creation of the Shanghai Cooperation Organisation (SCO), described by Western officials as an 'evil NATO'. This unites China, Russia and the 'stans' in a security pact intended to crush 'terrorism, separatism and extremism'.[19] In other words, China has no intention of allowing the West to sponsor political change in its own, despotic backyard.

The SCO's effectiveness largely relies on China and Russia acting in concert in the mutual neo-colonial exploitation of Central Asia. Any split between the two would have serious consequences for regional stability. Yet, as was the case with Vietnam in 1979, there is much that continues to divide the two former communist giants. A great deal of Russia's own mineral wealth is concentrated in its sparsely populated far eastern territories. There, a massive influx of Chinese is threatening Russia's control over a vital energy crossroads.

THE POWER OF BILLIONS

We described in Chapter 4 how China is using its vast population to rapidly colonise Tibet and Xinjiang. Russia is concerned that a similar transformation is taking place in its Far East, a vast area that accounts for a third of Russian territory. As Russia's own population declines, the result of unhealthy lifestyles and a low birth-rate, China is threatening Moscow's grip on the region. Nor is it likely that mutual antagonism towards the West will be enough to paper over Russia's suspicions of China's objectives in the region.

'China does not have to populate the Far East and eastern Siberia to get wheat it needs: resources,' said Russia's leader Vladimir Putin when asked about the threat of Chinese immigration.[20] 'We have been neighbours for hundreds of years. We know how to respect each other.' As a veteran Cold Warrior, Putin must have been aware that this statement was disingenuous. In 1969 the Soviet and Chinese armies clashed at the far-eastern border after Chinese leader Mao Tse Tung claimed that Russia had stolen large parts of the Russian Far East from China. At the height of the tensions Soviet leader Leonid Brezhnev even considered a pre-emptive nuclear strike.[21]

Although the border disputes have since been formally resolved, there is no guarantee that Chinese resentment at Russia's expropriation of former Chinese territory will not resurface. Much of the Russian Far East was once Outer Manchuria, part of Qing Dynasty china, until China's defeat in the Opium Wars allowed European powers, Russia included, to dictate terms. The Baidu Encyclopedia, China's answer to Wikipedia, describes China as being 'forced to cede' the region to Russia under 'two unequal treaties' that led to the 'occupation of our territories'.[22]

A posting on China's military website (blog.chinamil.com.cn) notes that, until the 'unfair treaty' of 1860, China's largest island was not Taiwan but the resource-rich Sakhalin, now part of Russia's Far East, and had been so for thousands of years. The blog describes how Japan and Russia, 'imperialist powers', infiltrated and occupied the island.[23] Given the strict censorship the Chinese authorities exert over the internet, especially military websites, it seems that officials see little wrong with this view of events.

Russia therefore has reason to fear reports of a huge influx of Chinese migrants into the Far East. Although estimates of this migration vary wildly,[24] Russia's Federal Migration Service has estimated that the Chinese will become the 'dominant' ethnic group in the region within two or three decades.[25] Russian President Dmitry Medvedev has warned that unless Moscow devotes greater attention to the Far East then 'in the final analysis we can lose everything'.[26] A *South China Morning Post* article from January 2011 described how China's development has so outstripped that of border towns in the Russian Far East that many local Russians have opted to learn Chinese.[27] Given their troubled past, it is easy to see how this situation could result in inter-state violence. Russia has announced that it is now giving its military forces in the Far East its 'top-priority attention'. 'They're still worried that China will invade Siberia one day because of the resources,' Dmitry Gorenburg, a senior analyst at military and public sector think tank CNA, told Reuters.[28]

A GREATER TIBET

Russia is not the only major that feels threatened by China's newfound prosperity. India is also concerned that China is using its state-managed economic strategy for the purposes of irredentism. This is because China believes that a vast expanse of north-east India is actually part of Tibet – and therefore part of China. India has come to view the rapid modernisation of Chinese Tibet as a problem. It worries that China is using this gulf in prosperity to soften-up Indian Tibet towards eventual Chinese annexation.

China claims about 90,000 square kilometres of mountain territory in north-east India, and occupies around 38,000 square kilometres of Kashmir claimed by India. China captured this part of Kashmir in 1962 in a Vietnam-style military adventure, catching India completely off guard. Three thousand Indian soldiers were killed in China's land-grab. Part of the problem was that India had blown its defence budget on expensive, prestige items: 'The Indian Army is without equipment, it is being said, partly because resources have gone into [its] highly advertised supersonic and transport planes and other gadgets, none of which are available to soldiers on the frontline.'[29]

So wrote J.K. Galbraith, then US ambassador to India. Galbraith noted that a key goal of the Chinese invasion was the capture of the Aksai Chin plateau.[30] This plateau allowed China to build a road between Tibet and the province of Xinjiang, the only two regions controlled by Beijing in which the Han Chinese were a minority. As discussed in Chapter 4, ending this minority status is a strategic goal of the Chinese government. Once this objective was achieved and the Chinese army had seized what it viewed as an appropriate amount of Himalayan territory, the war ended, but relations between the neighbours were poisoned. They have never fully recovered.

There are other reasons for mutual suspicion. India hosts Tibet's government-in-exile led by the Dalai Lama, based in Dharamsala. China views the Buddhist leader as a subversive 'separatist', so his presence in India does nothing to heal relations. Nor did India's decision, after the border war, to allow the CIA to recruit, train and arm Tibetan rebels to fight against Chinese occupation. It was these Tibetan rebels who first discovered and exposed outside China the devastation wrought by Chairman Mao's Great Leap Forward,[31] which again did very little to endear the exiled Tibetans or India to the Chinese Communist Party.

China's response has been economic and demographic. Senior officials decided that the best way to erode the influence of the Dalai Lama was to develop Tibet as quickly as possible. Han Chinese flooded into Tibet in order to reduce the power of the local Tibetans and to oversee the urbanisation of the Himalayan economy. 'Tibet is now transforming from fast development to comprehensive development, from relative backwardness to total opening and from simple agriculture to a complex economy,' Chinese Premier Wen Jiabao said in January 2011. Although Tibet's Han Chinese are significantly richer than the local population, even the Tibetans are being drawn into increasingly modern lifestyles.

The pace of development has not gone unnoticed in India, where Tibetans continue to pursue traditional patterns of economic life and are relatively poor as a result. In 2008 a report in the *Hindustan Times* noted the growing number of Indian Tibetans lured across the border by the bright lights on the Chinese side.[32] Numbers are unknown but officials said the migration was a dribble rather than a torrent. Nevertheless, New Delhi was sufficiently worried to authorise a new development policy in the Himalayan province of Arunachal Pradesh in a belated effort to restore developmental parity.

Yet India realises that this is too little, too late. In 2006 China completed a railway linking Tibet's capital Lhasa to lowland China, an economic funnel that can also be used for rapid military mobilisation. India cannot hope to catch up in economic terms. So it has instead opted for military reinforcement. In March 2011 the Indian Air Force deployed a second squadron of Sukhoi SU-30 jets to the north-east.[33] The army has raised two new mountain divisions – 36,000 soldiers – to patrol the Chinese frontier.[34] Tibet, on both sides of the border, has become increasingly militarised. It is yet another potential flashpoint between China and a powerful neighbour.

Under the British Empire, India was much bigger than it is now. The parts that broke off to become new countries in the twentieth century have a much better relationship with China than does India proper. The Chinese help to underwrite the power of Pakistan's military.[35] In Pakistan, Bangladesh and Sri Lanka the Beijing government has provided generous aid and investment in infrastructure, particularly in power and port development. Nepal, though never part of British India, has offset its former reliance on Delhi by moving more into China's sphere of influence.

A BURMESE WARNING

Yet nowhere has the model presented by China's military-industrial economy translated more directly into abject disaster than in Burma, the easternmost part of British India. Known officially as 'Myanmar' by the brutal military junta that controls the country, Burma is effectively owned by its generals. Commercial activity is impossible without dividing the spoils with the military. In 2007 Burma was ranked as the world's most corrupt country, alongside Somalia.[36] The government spends between 30 and 50 per cent of its budget on the military, against 3 per cent spent on health and 8 per cent on education.[37]

All major businesses are operated by the military state or by powerful entrepreneurs with close ties to the generals. A spate of privatisation in 2010 was viewed by many analysts as simply a transfer of resources from the generals to their cronies ahead of carefully managed elections that year, in which parties close to the military won 80 per cent of seats.[38] Military conglomerates such as the Union of Myanmar Economic Holdings and the Myanmar Economic Corporation continue to dominate the economy, however. Their military status is an enormous competitive advantage. Both, for instance, were exempted from a new law against tax evasion, as were other military cronies.[39]

Burma's strongest foreign ally is China, the country directly to its north. China arms and trains the Burmese military, builds infrastructure, is a major trade partner and uses its position on the UN Security Council to shield the regime from too much international censure. The US and European Union have applied sanctions to Burma, meaning that China has little serious competition in the exploitation of the country's significant energy resources. Moreover, having such a ruthless dictatorship as a neighbour casts China's own authoritarian regime in a comparatively softer light.

In the past, the relationship was far less close. Burma is a multiethnic society that has experienced great violence between the majority Burman population, represented by General Than Shwe's regime, and the other third of the population, which is made up of smaller minorities. Some of these minorities are ethnically Chinese. For decades, these Chinese groups formed the bedrock of the Communist Party of Burma, which for decades fought against the Burman military from the east of the country.

A group associated with the communists, the United Wa State Army (UWSA), is heavily involved in the production and smuggling of heroin and crystal meth, known locally as *yaa baa*. The UWSA also acts as a front for Chinese arms sales. According to the *Jane's Intelligence Review*, the UWSA acts as a middleman between Chinese arms makers and terrorist groups across Asia.[40] These include Indian separatist militias that operate close to the disputed Himalayan border with China. Such trade is possible because of a ceasefire between the UWSA and the Burmese government.

It is possible that such dubious arrangements will come back to haunt China. In August 2009 the Burmese military launched one of its periodic purges against rebel forces in Kokang province. Some 10,000 ethnic Chinese refugees fled the violence by crossing over the border into southern China. 'China will not tolerate the Myanmar government chasing the refugees across the border,' Chinese media quoted He Shengda, vice president of the Yunnan Academy of Social Sciences, as saying.[41]

However, China has little option but to 'tolerate' such chaos. The Kokang incident showed the limitations of China's influence in Burma. As the world's second largest producer of heroin (after Afghanistan) and with major energy reserves, Burma's gangster state has a great deal of leverage in China. Any impairment of relations could jeopardise China's energy security and see the problem of drug addiction in China's Yunnan province become even more acute. More than 60,000 people registered as heroin addicts in Yunnan in 2009 alone, while 80,000 people in the province have been diagnosed with HIV/AIDS,[42] a direct result of the UWSA's activities. It may be that China realises too late that Burma is a transnational threat to peace – a fact noted by the Nobel laureates Vaclav Havel and Bishop Desmond Tutu in a 2005 UN dossier.[43]

A SUN RE-RISEN?

For now, there is only one near neighbour fretted over by China's military planners. Despite the chaos and bloodshed along its southern border, this neighbour is not Burma. Despite its vast military power and nuclear weapons, it is not India. Nuclear-armed Pakistan teeters towards state-failure, Afghanistan is already there, Central Asia risks catching the same disease, Russia seems unlikely to be a friend for long, and North Korea's deranged autocracy threatens to implode. But none of these countries keep Chinese generals awake at night.

Curiously, the neighbour the China views as its gravest threat is one of the world's most orderly and advanced nations. It has no nuclear weapons, a very small army, little in the way of a military-industrial complex, a constitutional commitment to refrain from foreign wars, and a population that is less than one tenth the size of China's. Moreover, as the only country ever to have been struck by nuclear weapons, its population has a more acute sense than most of the devastation of war. The country in question is Japan.

The problem for China is not what Japan is now, but what it was 70 years ago, and what China fears it might be again in the future. During the nineteenth century Japan underwent a period of rapid industrialisation and established itself as the only Asian nation with European levels of development. In the early twentieth century Japan captured parts of Manchuria which Russia had seized from China, thereby becoming the first Asian power to win a military victory against a European nation. At around the same time Japan occupied Korea and installed a samurai, Ito Hirobumi, as resident general.

Inspired by the example of Great Britain, which like Japan was an industrialised island-state but one with a globe-spanning empire, the Japanese set about building up their own imperial might. This process was greatly abetted by World War II, in which Japan was allied to Nazi Germany. In the 1930s Japan conquered the rest of Manchuria before invading China in 1937. This campaign included the infamous Rape of Nanking, in which examples of war crimes by Japanese soldiers included mass rape, the live burial of captives, the execution of prisoners of war, and other crimes so brutal and degrading that they defied comprehension.[44]

Japan's participation in the war was ended by imperial overreach. Its attack on Pearl Harbour brought the United States into the conflict, an intervention that led to the US Air Force dropping atomic bombs on the Japanese cities of Hiroshima and Nagasaki in 1945. These bombs, coupled with the Soviet invasion of Manchuria, persuaded Japan to capitulate. Under the terms of its surrender, Japan agreed to dismantle its empire and military-industrial might and devote itself to peaceful activity, under the protection of the US.

There is a strong suspicion in China that the Japanese refuse to accept the horrors of their twentieth-century imperialism. Japan's treatment of the historical record is often contrasted with that of Germany, which has gone to great lengths to repudiate its behaviour under Adolf Hitler. The Germans have made it a crime, for instance, to deny the historical fact of the Holocaust. Japan's attitude is very different.

Examples abound. For instance, China complains bitterly about visits made by senior Japanese politicians to the Yasukuni Shrine near Tokyo, which lists the names of over two million soldiers who died fighting for Imperial Japan. Among the names are those of war criminals whose behaviour during World War II was comparable to that of senior Nazis.[45] These include Hideki Tojo, who was variously prime minister, war minister, and home affairs minister from 1941 to 1944 and Iwane Matsui, the commanding officer of the force responsible for the Nanking atrocities.

China and Korea have condemned Japan for producing school textbooks that glorify Japan's role in World War II and gloss over the horrors of Nanking.[46] Japanese historians reject such criticisms and say foreign accounts are exaggerated. Japan's ambassador to the US described Iris Chang's 1997 work *The Rape of Nanking* as 'one-sided', leading one Western commentator to point out that this was like the German ambassador complaining that *Schindler's List* was 'one sided'[47] – an unimaginable intervention. The problem is not helped by the dynastic nature of Japan's democracy. Many politicians are the children and grandchildren of previous leaders. In March 2011 Japan, for instance, appointed a new foreign minister descended from Hirobumi, the samurai who ruled Korea during the colonial period.[48]

In China, Japan has become the target for heated nationalist rhetoric. The two countries' dispute over the ownership of the Senkaku/Diaoyu islands in the East China Sea has become an opportunity for military brinkmanship. In March 2011 the Japanese made a formal complaint to Beijing after a Chinese military helicopter 'buzzed' a Japanese destroyer near the islands, flying overhead at a height of 40 metres. Japan's Defence Minister Toshimi Kitazawa described the action as 'extremely dangerous'.[49]

Further aggravating the situation are attempts by the US to persuade Japan to re-militarise, despite Japan's apparent lack of contrition about its militaristic past. At the moment Japan's defence relies on US Marines based at Futenma and Camp Schwab in Okinawa. Their presence is deeply unpopular with Okinawans, however, especially given a number of highly publicised crimes committed by US servicemen.[50] This difficulty, Japan's status as a close and wealthy US ally, and the challenge posed by an aggressive North Korea and rising China, have led Washington to increase pressure on Japan to take more responsibility for its own defence.

This process is happening faster than many realise. In the words of Selig Harrison, one of America's most prominent Asian strategists:

> Japan is accelerating a formidable buildup of sophisticated conventional military forces in addition to the steady expansion of civilian nuclear and space programs that are readily convertible to military purposes ... despite the election of a Democratic Party government, the development of new weapons systems started by the Liberal Democrats continues unabated under the direction of the increasingly assertive Self-Defence Forces ... With a defence budget that reached $51.4 billion last year, Japan is one of the largest defence spender after the United States, United Kingdom, France, China.[51]

Assuming this trend continues, China will once again be confronted by a highly sophisticated rival to its north-east. A rival that does not share China's view of their mutual history and which views China not as an intimidating giant, but as a weak and chaotic former colony. Japan is unlikely to accept Chinese regional leadership or allow itself to be bullied by strength of numbers. The potential for conflict is clear.

Nor is Japan the only neighbour with reason to doubt China's military prowess. To bring the story full circle, Vietnam may once again assume its historical role as a rival to China. The events of 1979 showed the country that it had little to fear from the giant to its north. Vietnam is unlikely to back down over its territorial disputes with China, especially as it grows wealthier. Like China, it is enjoying rapid export-led growth and development.

VIETNAM AND SOUTHEAST ASIA

Due east of Vietnam are two groups of islands which go by many names. The northern group are known in English as the Paracel Islands, but are known as the Hoàng Sa in Vietnamese and the Xisha in China and Taiwan. The southern group of islands is known in English as the Spratlys but as Nansha Islands to the Chinese and the Truong Sa Archipelago to the Vietnamese. In neither case are any of these obscure islands inhabited on a permanent basis. Yet this has not become a flashpoint between China and the other states – Taiwan, Vietnam, the Philippines, Malaysia and Brunei – who claim them as part of their territory. The islands are believed to sit atop deposits of oil and natural gas. They also straddle crucial shipping lanes, adding to their strategic value.

China is trying to use its new military might to scare the other claimants into submission. In February 2011 the Chinese navy conducted a show of strength near the islands, prompting a formal protest from Vietnam. Vietnamese and Chinese ships have clashed over the islands in the past, and all the parties to the dispute have raced against each other to establish military encampments on the islands. China won control of the Paracels in 1974 after using planes and ships to bomb Vietnamese troops out of their positions on the islands.

Vietnam is not the only Southeast Asian country to worry that China might use similar tactics to resolve the Spratly dispute. As in 1979, however, the real victims of such aggression could end up being the Chinese diaspora in its smaller neighbours. Malaysia, for instance, is home to a large Chinese minority – so large that the government has legalised economic discrimination against the Chinese and in favour of indigenous Malays. Ethnic Chinese make up between 3–4 per cent of Indonesia's 240 million people and a similar proportion in the Philippines. Lee Kuan Yew, the former leader of Chinese-majority Singapore, noted in 2006 the discrimination already faced by the Chinese in those countries. 'Our neighbours both have problems with their Chinese,' Lee said at a 2006 IMF-World Bank meeting. 'They are successful. They are hard-working and, therefore, they are systematically marginalised.'[52] This marginalisation could easily become more acute, rather than less so, if China tries to exert regional dominance.

Of course, there also is the issue of Taiwan. A vast amount of focus is already dedicated to the dangers surrounding this dispute, touched on in elsewhere in this book, and as the purpose of this chapter is to highlight lesser-known dangers it is needless to add to the literature. Suffice to say that any move by Taiwan towards formal independence from China would very possibly trigger a devastating war, quite possibly triggering US intervention.

THE FUTURE

China is a country haunted by the past. Its past is not a 'glorious' record of military domination and empire, but rather one of military defeat and subjugation by smaller nations, of humiliations still felt to this day. Western accounts of the 'rising China' rarely touch upon this element of the national psyche, but this sense of dispossession is crucial to how China views its neighbourhood. It is also driving China towards a new future which Beijing is determined will be very different to the past. Wealth will underwrite China's newfound power and prestige. 'To be rich is glorious,' said Deng Xiaoping, the leader who in the late 1970s oversaw China's transition from communism to capitalism, and also the bungled invasion of Vietnam.

But China's economic rise depends on the ability of its military-industrial complex to manage China's relationship with its neighbours, allowing China to access the resources it needs to fuel continued growth. This process is not going well. At every turn, China's attempts to secure energy supplies in Central Asia, in Burma, in the Russian Far East, even in the Spratly Islands, find it dealing with either ruthless and unreliable allies or with longstanding foes and rivals. This conclusion can be drawn without even mentioning Taiwan, the 'alternative China' founded by the defeated nationalist forces following World War II, which China has vowed to repatriate by fair means or force.

China's 1979 foray into Vietnam holds many lessons for why it must refrain from relying on a militarised version of growth. Only by securing resources on equitable terms, by rejecting neo-colonial support for tyranny and by resolving ancient territorial questions at a political level can China's prosperity be assured. Attempts to bully its neighbours into accepting China as Asia's hegemon will have a constricting effect on economic activity, as well as starting new wars in which the stakes are higher than ever before.

9
The Emerging Conflicts – Other Future Fault-lines of the World

The wars of the future will be alarming in several ways. They will be cripplingly expensive. They will involve nuclear weapons. And they will extend into both outer space and cyber space. A new arms race has begun, which combines the horror of nuclear weapons with the randomness of unconventional warfare. In this chapter we assess the likely cost of two imminent conflicts and the innovations that could make them even more devastating.

NEAR TERM WARS

Iran is bordered to the east and to the west by the consequences of US invasion. The 2001 invasion of Afghanistan removed the Taliban from power in Kabul, replacing the Sunni extremists with a government much more sympathetic to Iran's Shia theocracy. Two years later, the US-led invasion of Iraq toppled Saddam Hussein, Iran's mortal enemy for 30 years. In both cases Iran was quick to capitalise on the change of regime by bolstering its political influence in these countries. Given that the US considers Iran to be a rogue state, a member of an 'axis of evil', this progression of events appeared a poor return on American expenditure.

Estimates of this expenditure differ, but they have one thing in common: the figures involved are astronomical. In September 2010 a report for the US Congressional Research Service suggested that since the al-Qaeda attack on New York in September 2001, Congress has authorised $1.121 trillion for the three operations initiated since 9/11: the invasions of Iraq and Afghanistan and Operation Noble Eagle, a drive to improve the security of US military bases.[1] Earlier that year the National Priorities Project, described by Reuters as a 'nonpartisan budget research group', put the cost to the US taxpayer slightly lower, at $1.05 trillion.[2] In 2008 the Nobel Prize-winning economist Joseph Stiglitz, a vocal critic of the invasions, argued that the eventual financial cost to the US of the wars in Iraq and Afghanistan would amount to $3 trillion.[3]

There was some suggestion that the US would exploit its position as Iraq's occupier to award Iraqi oil contracts to US-based extractors, and then recoup its military costs via corporate taxation. This has not proved the case: the international tenders for the development of Iraq's oil fields have in most cases been awarded to companies from nations who opposed the invasion, including China.[4,5] It is therefore unlikely that the US will be able to replenish its coffers in this way. Moreover, some have linked the invasion of Iraq to the soaring oil prices which followed it, a shock that imposed unquantified – but presumably very substantial – costs on the US and global economy.[6]

If one accepts the lowest estimate of around $1 trillion, the cost of the two wars to Iran's east and west exceeded the annual gross domestic product of all but twelve of the world's economies.[7] This gives some idea of the wars' opportunity cost and the extent to which the $1 trillion could have been used to achieve humanitarian goals elsewhere. There are reasons to believe that an invasion of Iran could cost as much as the first two wars combined. These reasons are as follows.

THE COST OF AN INVASION OF IRAN TO THE US ECONOMY

There is a military consensus that air strikes could only delay, not destroy, Iran's nuclear programme. This has been the conclusion even of leaked US documents arguing in favour of military action.[8] In order to guarantee the end of the nuclear programme, which Iran claims is for purely civilian purposes, a ground invasion would be needed to secure and systematically destroy the nuclear facilities, entailing 'regime change' in the process.

With over 70 million people, Iran's population is larger than Iraq's and Afghanistan's combined. Whereas Iraq's armed forces were crippled by their defeat in Kuwait in 1991, and whereas the Taliban in Afghanistan were irregular fighters without sophisticated weapons, Iran's armed forces are led by veterans of the Iran–Iraq war. They have access to modern weapons from Russia and China and they have had plenty of opportunity to prepare for an invasion – especially for the kind of asymmetric tactics that extended the war in Iraq well beyond Saddam Hussein's defeat in 2003. The US alleges that Iran sponsors hostile militant groups in both Iraq and Afghanistan. If this is true, then Iran has the potential to escalate the conflicts in the both neighbours, increasing the military costs to the US on two other fronts.

Around 25 per cent of the world's oil supply flows though the Arabian/Persian Gulf, the body of water that divides Iran from peninsular Arabia. At its narrowest point, the Strait of Hormuz, the Gulf is just 30 nautical miles wide. Iran has stated that if it is attacked it will target shipping through the Strait, just as it did during the Iran–Iraq 'tanker war' of the 1980s.[9] The United Arab Emirates has already begun building a port to the east of the Strait in anticipation of such an event.[10] The shock to the global economy resulting from closure of the Strait, even a brief one, would be enormous.

In 2007 the conservative Heritage Foundation teamed with IHS Global Insight to simulate the likely impact of Iran disrupting Gulf oil supplies for two successive quarters. It found that the price of West Texas Intermediate crude oil would spike by $85 to $150 a barrel; that real US GDP would be cut by $161 billion over the calendar year; that real disposable personal incomes would decline by $260 billion; and that within six months private non-farm employment in the US would fall by one million jobs. The Foundation claimed that such ill-effects could be avoided if Washington pursued a laundry list of right-wing demands such as energy deregulation (including a mandate for oil drilling in Alaska) and increased military spending, because this would not only fund military operations against Iran but 'would stimulate the U.S. economy'.[11]

The cost to the rest of the world would be even greater. Whereas the US is able to source crude from its own oilfields and from those of Canada, the Gulf of Mexico and the Caribbean basin, the economies of China and Japan rely on Middle Eastern energy, not least from Iran itself.[12,13] An oil shock would drive up the input costs of manufacturing, costs that would eventually be passed to consumers, spreading inflation and hardship around the globe. The effect on Iran's economy would be catastrophic, without question.

Supply disruption of two months was the Foundation's 'worst-case' scenario, but it is possible that it was unduly optimistic. The force charged with keeping the Gulf open is the US Fifth Fleet, based in Bahrain. The fleet is undoubtedly a fearsome expression of conventional naval might. However, Iran has recognised that it would not be able to defeat the US in a conventional conflict and has instead sought unconventional means for disrupting shipping in the channel.

Iran has built up a fleet of thousands of lightweight, manoeuvrable speedboats of the type that threatened a suicide attack on US naval vessels in 2008.[14] Even large US vessels can be vulnerable to suicide ramming by small craft, as demonstrated by al-Qaeda's attack on the USS *Cole* in 2000. Iran has also unveiled three squadrons of lightly armed 'flying boats'.[15] Although it is possible that such tactics would prove ineffective – since the *Cole* attack the US has fitted its ships with weapons designed to counter small craft – there is a chance that this unconventional approach could prolong a conflict well beyond the Heritage estimates, especially if these tactics were also deployed against civilian oil tankers. Somali pirates in the Gulf of Aden have proven how effective small speedboats can be when it comes to hijacking giant vessels.

THE COST OF INACTION?

Assuming that the US is correct to accuse Iran of nuclear militarisation – a generous assumption given its failure to find weapons of mass destruction in Iraq – it is questionable whether a multi-trillion-dollar war is the logical response. The restrained US reaction to the development of nuclear weapons in India and Pakistan provided a springboard from which US diplomats have managed to preserve cooperative relations with both countries. Similar restraint in Iran's case would also have benefits.

The charges levelled against Iran are that it is a radical theocracy, that it seeks the destruction of one of its neighbours (Israel), that it sponsors terrorist groups, and that its acquisition of nuclear weapons would begin an arms race in the Middle East. Some argue that once Iran has obtained a doomsday weapon it would be able to commission the kind of oil crises described above with impunity. In other words, Iran would become an even greater threat to the status quo than it currently poses.

Most of these accusations require further qualification. Iran is an Islamist theocracy, but it is also one which permits elections (however limited),[16] public protests,[17] high-level dissent,[18] and in some cases a surprisingly free media.[19] Unlike Saudi Arabia – a US ally – Iran allows women to drive cars[20] and to uncover their faces in public. Iran is also a major bulwark against the exportation of Afghan heroin to Europe, a key funding stream for the Taliban.[21] By the standards of the region, Iran is not the most anti-democratic or the most ultra-orthodox country in the Middle East. Both those dubious prizes are won by Washington's Saudi allies.

Indeed, Iran has little choice but to manage its elections very carefully. The US funnels millions of dollars to its preferred opposition partners in Iran.[22] The amounts it donates are comparable to those raised by US presidential candidates – election war-chests which are viewed as critical to election victory in the US. Were Iran a free democracy, the US would be able to purchase the result of elections and install its preferred leaders, as it has arguably done through its manipulation of neighbouring Pakistan.

Iran is vocally opposed to the state of Israel, but it is not clear that it advocates Israel's military destruction. In interviews, Iran's President Mahmoud Ahmadinejad has tended to compare Israel's eventual demise with that of apartheid South Africa or the Soviet Union, neither of which were destroyed by war.[23] The consequences for Iran of either a direct or indirect (via its stooges in Hamas or Hezbollah) nuclear attack on Israel would be devastating, given that Israel possesses a second-strike nuclear capability.[24] Similarly, given that Iran is dependent on the flow of oil through the Persian Gulf, it is unlikely to impose blockades on oil traffic except in cases of extreme emergency, such as foreign invasion.

A military adventure against Iran's nuclear programme would never justify the cost to the US taxpayer. To destroy the nuclear sites permanently, this price tag would inevitably be above $1 trillion and could easily reach $2 trillion given an effective insurgency movement such as seen in Iraq. Few dispute the very real complications that Iran's foreign policy brings to Middle Eastern politics. However, the fact that Iran's civil society and political system are more inclusive than many of its neighbours should allow diplomats greater leverage to restrain Iran from provocative behaviour without recourse to the kind of attack that devastated Iraq and Afghanistan.

CRISIS II: THE KOREAN PENINSULA

North and South Korea stand forever on the brink of war. In March 2010 North Korea's seemingly unprovoked decision to sink the South Korean warship *Cheonan*,[25] followed by its shelling of the inhabited island of Yeonpyeon and its announcement of a uranium-based weapons programme,[26] led South Korea to warn that it will respond with air strikes to future acts of Northern aggression. Adding to the tension, the South has undertaken major military exercises near its border with the North.[27]

It is incorrect to describe North Korea as anything other than a threat to world peace. Its ruling family maintains its position via a personality cult, the suppression of human rights, and a brutal police state. The regime has ignored the significant hardships endured by its population to indulge in a reckless and extravagant pursuit of nuclear weapons. Its official newswire, one of the very few North Korean outlets to the wider world, gives the impression of a government that is paranoid, warlike, and highly erratic.[28]

The main financial cost of any war between the Koreas would not be damage caused by the North's nuclear weapons, which are yet to be fully weaponised, but by the damage inflicted to the South's capital Seoul by the 11,000 artillery pieces and rocket launchers the North has ranged against the city.[29] Seoul's proximity to the de facto border between the two Koreas has persuaded many South Koreans of the need to relocate their capital further south.[30,31]

Seoul is a city of 10 million people, more than 200,000 of them foreign nationals, and it is one of Asia's major economic hubs. Its GDP in 2006 was $194 billion. Seoul is proud of its advanced infrastructure – the city has the highest broadband internet penetration in the world. Representing a quarter of South Korea's population, the city is fundamental to national prosperity. And South Korea's economy is performing well, with the government forecasting GDP growth of 6.1 per cent in 2010 and 5 per cent in 2011.

An artillery bombardment by North Korea would force the evacuation of Seoul and would cause billions of dollars of damage to infrastructure. It was this prospect that forced the South's President Lee Myung-bak to convene a meeting of policymakers in November 2010 to discuss ways to limit the economic impact of such a barrage.[32] The press release from this meeting praised the public for its lack of panic-buying after recent North Korean attacks but said: 'The Government will not lower its guard and will closely monitor the developments in the financial markets around the clock. If necessary, it will employ pre-emptive measures.'

The financial burden for the US of involving itself in a new Korean war would be heavy. US commanders have predicted that such a conflict would cost the US upwards of $100 billion; that the cost to the countries involved and their immediate neighbours would run to $1 trillion; and that the conflict could cost a million lives.[33] North Korea's standing army totals more than one million soldiers, two-thirds of whom are stationed near the de-militarised zone which forms the de facto border between the Koreas. While there is little doubt that South Korean and US armed forces would eventually prove victorious, the experience from Iraq and Afghanistan indicates that the financial cost would soar far beyond the estimated $100 billion.

There is a worst-case scenario in which the costs of a Korean conflict would spiral dramatically. China is North Korea's only reliable ally and it has frequently shielded the North from censure at the UN Security Council.[34] China has consistently refused to criticise Kim Jong-il's regime in public and has set much store by the six-party negotiations process favoured by the administration of US President George W. Bush. That administration viewed two-way talks, preferred by the North Korean regime, as a means by which the North could solicit aid and other 'bribes' from Washington.

Despite China's record of support for the government in Pyongyang, there is a complacent assumption in many quarters that China will refuse to involve itself militarily should a new Korean War break out. If this assumption proves to be incorrect, the consequences are so grave as to be almost unimaginable. It would pit the two existing superpowers against each other in a war that would immediately halt the world's most significant trading relationship. It would be like a re-run of the first Korean War, which the US military estimates cost the Treasury $320 billion[35] at a time when global trade was far less developed.

Even if China merely imposed some kind of trade embargo, rather than sending in troops, the costs to the countries involved would be immense. The US, suddenly deprived of cheap Chinese consumer goods, would see the prices of many products suddenly soar. China would face the opposite problem. Its vast surplus of unsold inventory would depress prices, while unemployment would soar. Both countries would experience severe financial turbulence as markets tried to exploit the sudden cessation of trade. The ensuing recession would add many billions, if not trillions, to the cost of the war.

To some extent, the pending conflicts in North Korea and Iran express tension between China and America and their competing models of progress. One reason the US has failed to impose an oil embargo on Iran – the only economic sanction likely to prove effective – is because China desires Iran's oil. North Korea's deranged regime relies on aid from a Chinese government that continues to see some utility in having a rogue state as a neighbour. However, these tensions are minor when compared to the stresses generated by China's 'catching up' strategy – its quest to obtain the secrets of the US and European military-industrial complex.

THE NEW RESOURCES

The wars of tomorrow will not be fought over the commodities of today. The world is moving, however slowly, towards a post-oil economy. Many politicians in the West have realised the true cost of trade with Middle Eastern dictatorships. But resources remain finite and material desires unlimited – at least for some. The end of the oil economy will not mean an end to struggles over key resources. China and the US are racing to secure access to the minerals of tomorrow. Today we speak of petroleum, diesel, liquefied natural gas, coal. Tomorrow it will be lithium, uranium, thorium, coltan and the rare earth elements.

The future will be electric, electronic and battery-powered. The early twenty-first century saw an explosion in the number of devices using rechargeable batteries. These devices are becoming ever larger. Between 1997 and 2011 Toyota alone sold more than three million electric hybrid cars.[36] Towards the end of this period companies began to market cars powered exclusively by electric motors drawing on power stored in large batteries. The turmoil in the oil-producing Middle East caused first by the Iraq war and then by the uprisings of 2011 forced up petroleum prices, making electric vehicles a much more viable option.

A host of minerals are required to make these batteries. The first generation of electric cars, the Toyota Prius and Honda Insight, ran on a nickel-metal-hydride battery pack. The newer Chevrolet Volt and Nissan LEAD use lithium-ion batteries, the kind found in much smaller electronic gadgets. Toyota has said that in the future it expects its cars to use magnesium batteries, which can store more energy.[37] Mercedes-Benz, on the other hand, has opted against the electric route and instead sees the future in hydrogen fuel cells.[38]

Batteries are not the only electronic components that rely on 'new' resources. Violence in the war-torn Democratic Republic of Congo (DRC), formerly known as Zaire, is being driven by demand for colombo-tantalite ore, or coltan. This ore is used to make mobile telephones and other electronic devices. Coltan mines in the eastern DRC are fought over by rival militias seeking control over the revenue stream. The rare ore, which can be mined by hand, sells for hundreds of dollars per kilogram.[39] It is not the only exotic mineral implicated in the violence. A 2001 UN report noted that also fuelling the civil war were struggles over the supply of pyrochlore and niobium. Congolese miners are responsible for killing thousands of gorillas and elephants, as well as the rare and mysterious Bili ape.[40]

In four years, between 2003 and 2007, industrial demand for lithium doubled.[41] The largest reserves of lithium are buried beneath the salt flats of Bolivia, a poor and landlocked South American country prone to political unrest. 'We will not repeat the historical experience since the fifteenth century: raw materials exported for the industrialisation of the west that has left us poor,' Bolivia's mining minister, Luis Alberto Echazu, told the BBC in 2008.[42] Other nations have been less able to resist exploitation. Tibet, long subjugated by the People's Republic of China, is now seeing its salt flats mined for lithium by Chinese colonists, aided by investment from wealthy American investors such as Warren Buffett.[43,44] Such cooperation is unlikely to be the norm. As described in Chapter 1, the supply of rare earth elements is already a source of friction between the US and China.

TITAN RAIN

Of course, securing access to such resources is only one challenge when trying to produce advanced electronics. Knowing how to make the equipment is another difficulty. As explained in the first chapter, the US has done its best to prevent China legally purchasing companies with hi-tech manufacturing capability. China's response has been to launch a war on the US – a war not for tangible natural resources, but for *in*tangible intellectual goods. This war has largely gone unnoticed by the wider world, but its consequences could be very grave.

'Cyber warfare' refers to a conflict in which military hackers penetrate and alter the computer systems of an enemy state. Speaking at a seminar in early 2011, the former head of the US Central Intelligence Agency revealed an uncomfortable truth about this form of war: 'The advantage goes to the attacker in cyber space,' General Michael Hayden told his audience.[45] Hayden was speaking from first-hand experience. US computer systems have been besieged by hackers employed by the Chinese military to steal information and test for weaknesses.

China's electronic warfare is conducted by the Fourth Department, General Staff, of the People's Liberation Army. This department recruits some of China's most brilliant young mathematicians to train as computer programmers and hackers. In June 2010 the Chinese military unveiled a dedicated cyber-warfare base, with responsibility for both cyber-attack and defence.[46] A year earlier the US Strategic Command had established its own cyber-warfare base at Ford Meade, Maryland on the orders of the Defense Secretary.

This was a response to a series of high-profile cyber attacks on targets in the US and its allies. According to McAfee, a company which specialises in computer security, these attacks, which began in 2003, have stolen information from the US equivalent to the entire contents of the Library of Congress. Among the victims were NASA, Northrop Grumman, and Lockheed Martin and its subsidiaries, including Sandia National Laboratories. Sandia develops components for nuclear weapons. In 2009 the attackers stole terabytes of data on the F-35 Joint Strike Fighter.[47] Two years later the Chinese unveiled a similar-looking aircraft.[48]

The cyber-attacks were highly sophisticated, leaving few traces and conducted without the keystroke errors associated with amateur hackers. US officials gave the sequence of attacks a name – 'Titan Rain'. 'The United States is fighting a cyber-war today, and we are losing,' wrote Admiral Mike McConnell, a former US director of national intelligence, in 2010.[49] US officials say that the Chinese military has already hidden malware in US systems that could potentially shut down the US electrical grid, and everything that runs off it.[50]

Europe is also under cyber-siege. In 2007 the chancellor of Germany, Angela Merkel, complained about the attacks to China's Premier Wen Jiabao.[51] Wen replied that China was also targeted by professional hackers, presumably employed by Western intelligence agencies. Four years later, evidence emerged that Germany was itself a possible culprit. As victorious Egyptian demonstrators ransacked the building that housed their country's detested state security services, they found a contract signed with a German company to supply cyberwar software to the Egyptian regime.[52]

OUTER SPACE

The war in cyber-space is an information war. It is intimately connected to another war for information: the war in outer space. Satellites are crucial strategic assets. They capture images of enemy states, relay information from country to country, give pinpoint geographical positions to people on the ground and can bypass systems designed to limit freedom of speech, such as the so-called 'Great Firewall of China'. Both cyber-war and space-war are designed to control information. The ability to destroy satellites has become a crucial military objective.

In 2008 Russia and China proposed a ban on weapons in space. The fact the US rejected this treaty caused anger in China, according to diplomatic cables obtained by WikiLeaks, anger that led China to conduct an anti-satellite test.[53] In 2007 China used a rocket to shoot down a satellite, in what its foreign ministry described as an example of China's 'peaceful development of outer space'. Another WikiLeaks cable showed quite how seriously the US took the Chinese anti-satellite launch.[54] If a country can shoot down a satellite, it can also potentially shoot down a nuclear missile, and the US has sold advanced anti-missile systems to countries surrounding China.[55] The Chinese launch was another example of its attempt to keep pace with US military technology.

There is a large degree of overlap between anti-missile technology and anti-satellite technology. The issue of US missile defence, particularly its deployment in Eastern Europe, has vexed Russia, which sees the 'military balance' being disrupted. The US justifies its anti-missile systems with reference to Iran and North Korea, but this is a smokescreen: its real concerns are the vast nuclear arsenals of Russia and China. US criticism of its anti-satellite weapon prompted China to accuse the US of having developed a laser capable of shooting down missiles, a project that Northrop Grumman has been working on for years.[56] The US company Raytheon has even developed a laser that can shoot down enemy planes.[57]

The patterns of China's hacking activity indicate that anti-missile systems are not its only worry: it is also concerned about Washington's use of pilotless drones. In 2009 the Titan Rain hackers broke into South Korea's defence network and stole documents about secret US plans to sell Global Hawk drones to its Korean allies.[58] These particular drones were for reconnaissance, but China is reported to be alarmed by America's ever-increasing use of these pilotless planes in combat missions, and has worked to develop its own drone capability in response.[59]

Even US allies are becoming worried. In 2011 the British Ministry of Defence issued a report that asked whether the world had embarked upon 'an incremental and involuntary journey towards a Terminator-like reality'. It said that in future drones would acquire their targets automatically rather than being guided by a ground operator. Moreover, it warned that 'Western nations face significant challenges to their economic and industrial supremacy from the emerging Asian economies' and that to stay ahead in the drone race, 'the UK will need to address fundamental questions about its defence technological and industrial base'. Corporations will take the lead as they see drones as 'a future growth industry and a key source of future business'.[60]

The two strands of drones and militarisation of space flow into one in the new US space shuttle, the 37B. The new, unmanned shuttle has migrated from being NASA's responsibility to being that of the air force. The space plane, which is built by Boeing, undertook its second mission in March 2011. The military shrouded the launch in secrecy and refused to discuss its payload.[61] The shuttle's first mission in 2010 was equally secretive. Curiously, after the shuttle landed, photographs showed workers at Vandenberg Air Force Base approaching it wearing hazmat suits.[62] These suits, which were not worn by NASA ground staff,[63] indicated the presence of some sort of biological hazard.

THE WESTERN HEMISPHERE

The US is now using drones to further the 'war on drugs' in its southern neighbour Mexico.[64] Currently the drones are unarmed and are being used for surveillance, but they are a sign of the creeping militarisation of a problem that once fell squarely in the province of law and order. As with the militarisation of the response to terrorism, this development obviously benefits the military-industrial companies. They make far more money from military endeavours than they do from police ones.

The militarisation of law and order is a trend particularly noticeable in Latin America, where politicians have reached for heavy-handed responses to the increasingly brutal cocaine gangs. In recent years a number of independent 'Bolivarian' governments have come to power who have refused to place Western military-industrial interests ahead of the welfare of their own populations. Bolivia's drive to preserve its lithium wealth is one example of this kind of defiance. The US has reacted to this trend by building up its forces in Colombia, one of Washington's few strong allies in the region. The military escalation appears to be mainly targeted at Venezuela, a major oil supplier to the US whose government, under President Hugo Chavez, has worked against US influence in the region.

In October 2009 the US signed a deal with Colombia giving its forces access to seven Colombian military bases for a decade. A dossier compiled by the Venezuela Solidarity Campaign noted that the US forces would not be limited to anti-narcotics activity, but provides an opportunity for 'conducting full spectrum operations throughout South America'.[65] US forces operating from the bases have complete immunity from local law. Negotiations around the deal were shrouded in secrecy, with neither the US nor Colombian congresses informed.

The dossier went on to show that the US military now operates 37 facilities in Latin America. It noted that in April 2008 the US revived its 4th Fleet, dormant since 1950. The fleet will be based in Miami, Florida with a remit to patrol the Latin American shoreline. Brazil's leaders, including President Lula de Silva and Defence Minister Nelson Jobim, linked the surprise US decision to re-commission the 4th Fleet to Brazil's discovery of major oil fields.[66] Brazil responded by conducting naval drills to demonstrate that it would protect its oil against any US designs.[67]

Some might accuse the Brazilians of paranoia; after all, the Brazilian army conducts threat exercises based on the possibility of the EU invading Brazil to protect the Amazon from deforestation. However, President Lula, though a liberal, is no Bolivarian. He enjoyed reasonably cordial relationships with the Bush and Obama administrations and his leadership was praised globally. The fact that Lula's first reaction to the news of the US 4th Fleet was to assume it meant a US resource-grab gives some idea of how the northern states of the Americas are viewed in the southern part of the hemisphere. Clearly, Latin American governments believe they must prepare to defend their natural resources by force.

US anti-drugs efforts look like a pretext for the massive expansion of the US military presence in the region. Certainly, US admirals and generals seem to be far less interested in the thousands of tonnes of high-strength cannabis that enter the US from Canada each year.[68] Latin America has been steadily entangled in the militarised swamp of the 'war on drugs', which like the 'war on terror' is a vague and open-ended conflict that can never be proven to be definitively won or lost. For the military-industrial complex, this is the perfect kind of war.

The consequence of all this is that wars will never again follow a predictable pattern. Just as the 'turkey shoot' that the US envisaged in Iraq turned into a mixture of civil war, Islamist insurgency, and sectarian ethnic-cleansing, future military adventures in Iran and North Korea, in space and in cyber-space, will have wildly unforeseen consequences. The ability of some states to shoot down satellites, ram oil tankers with speedboats, hijack computer networks and deploy thousands of robot planes has not made the world a safer place. On the contrary, it guarantees that theoretical calculations of 'military balance' are worthless. In warfare the unconventional has become the conventional.

Part IV

A New Vision, a New Beginning in a New Millennium – A Practical Way of Reducing Arms, Armies and Wars for the Survival of Humanity

10
Averting Disaster – What Type of Global Security Architecture Fits in Today's World?

In his State of the Union speech in 2011, US President Barack Obama said that his country faced a 'Sputnik moment'. The analogy referred to America's response to the Soviet Union's success in launching the first orbital satellite in 1957. Obama, however, was referring to the rise of China, the country which he noted possessed both the world's fastest supercomputer and its largest solar power plant. The US must respond, said Obama, by investing in biomedical research, information technology, and clean energy. 'With more research and incentives, we can break our dependence on oil with biofuels, and become the first country to have a million electric vehicles on the road by 2015,' the president said.

Keen observers of State of the Union speeches experienced a sense of déjà vu. Five years earlier Obama's unpopular predecessor, George W. Bush, had used the same occasion to make exactly the same points. Bush warned that 'America is addicted to oil, which is often imported from unstable parts of the world'. Like Obama, Bush advocated the development of clean energy sources to meet this goal. He set a target to replace more than 75 per cent of US oil imports from the Middle East by 2025. Bush pledged to 'make our dependence on Middle Eastern oil a thing of the past'.

Crude oil is the one foreign import that the giant US economy cannot function without. Maintaining control over the oil supply route is a major reason for the heavy US military presence in the Arabian Gulf. Oil is a crucial justification for arming Arab regimes allied to Washington, such as those in Saudi Arabia and Jordan. And, as we saw in the previous chapter, these big-ticket arms sales are how the US pays for the oil that it imports from the Gulf kingdoms.

A curious trend has emerged. As the military-industrial complex has expanded, the ability of the US to win wars has actually dwindled. Since World War II, the US has not emerged wholly victorious from a single major conflict. The Korean War was a

Pyrrhic victory, one that preserved capitalism in South Korea but at a cost of over 50,000 American lives. Vietnam was a disastrous defeat. The first Gulf War 'freed' Kuwait back to its previous form of dictatorship but allowed the Iraqi aggressor, Saddam Hussein, to remain in power and massacre tens of thousands of his countrymen. The second Iraq War ousted Saddam, but triggered a civil war in which thousands of US soldiers and hundreds of thousands of civilians were killed, at a financial cost of trillions of dollars to the US taxpayer.

The US military-industrial complex is not providing value for money, it seems. Part of the problem is that the sophistication of the US armoury makes it ever easier to start wars, but no quicker to end them. In 2011 the US and Europe began air strikes on Libya, allegedly to protect one side in a civil war from the aggression of the other. (In the case of France and Britain, the campaign was transparently to protect oil investments.) Once the campaign started, it became clear that the US had blundered into the conflict with few clear goals in mind and incognisant of whether its Libyan allies were even worth fighting for.

CHINA'S RISE

By refusing to give China access to its military-industrial sector, its hi-tech weapons and dual-use items, the US has destabilised global trade. Minus the usual mechanism the US uses to balance its books with the developing world – big-ticket arms sales – the world's largest economy is falling ever more in debt to its greatest strategic rival. China, meanwhile, is trying to circumvent the US hi-tech embargo by employing an ever larger network of spies and hackers to close the technological divide. It may only be a matter of decades before the world's most sophisticated jet-fighters are built not by Lockheed Martin but by Chengdu Aircraft.

As China's military-industrial complex rapidly expands, it is beginning to acquire the same critical mass as its US and European equivalents. As the complex feeds off tax revenue, it will become ever more adept at permanently capturing those revenue streams, aided by political connections, a large dependent workforce, military-balance theory and other types of scare-mongering, and the intrinsic political power of men with guns. Before long the complex will be able to override China's national interest in favour of its own interest – war, and the re-supply of military equipment.

China's periphery holds immense potential for conflict. Its borders are still a matter for negotiation with several neighbours, and China's national history is replete with grudges. China is central to global trade, so isolationism is no longer an option. To become an industrial power, China needs reliable foreign partners to provide its industry with cheap raw materials for processing. It is not in China's interests for poorer countries to copy its own industrialisation, because then raw materials will be absorbed locally. So China must acquire puppet regimes and prevent them from being toppled by the agents of rival powers, as China is already trying to do in Central Asia and Africa.

EUROPE'S DEMISE

Then there is the European Union. This large group of wealthy nations is claimed by its admirers to represent a peaceable, humane alternative to the war-mongering of the US and the dictatorship of the Chinese Communist Parties. European nations are portrayed as standard bearers for liberal values, generous donors of development aid, seekers of diplomatic resolution to conflict, and of demilitarisation.

The US is endowed with vast natural resources of its own and has a low population density, which means that it can supply its own industries with raw materials. Europe, on the other hand, is densely populated. Its climate does not support much in the way of plantation agriculture. The world's top two producers of cotton are China and the US. Europe, on the other hand, produces just 2 per cent of the world's supply.[1] China and the US both feature in the world's top 10 producers of copper, whereas only one European state, Poland, sneaks into the top 20. Europeans are leading consumers of coffee, but they do not produce it.

Europe relies on importing raw materials from its former colonies. The continent is famed for its chocolate companies, but the cocoa beans are grown in West Africa, where child labour keeps costs low.[2] The tobacco plant is not grown in Great Britain, where for health reasons the sale and consumption of cigarettes is heavily discouraged, yet two of the world's five largest tobacco companies are British (BAT and Imperial). The French Total group is one of the world's largest oil companies, yet France pumps no oil of its own. Instead, Total operates in rogue states such as Burma[3] and Libya.

In order to balance its trade, Europe must swap value-added goods for raw materials. In the 1920s and 30s the Indian independence movement drew attention to Great Britain's habit of shipping cotton from India to Manchester, where the cotton would be milled into garments, and then shipped back to India to be sold to Indians. These terms of trade kept the 'value added', and therefore the wealth, in Great Britain. Once India obtained independence in 1947 it started to substitute imports with domestic manufacturing and is today one of the world's leading exporters of garments and textiles.[4]

SOLUTIONS TO POVERTY

Import substitution is not a 'magic bullet' for poverty – at least not on its own. Much of India remains desperately poor, and progress towards changing this state of affairs is slow. To cure poverty on a massive scale, it is necessary to follow the example set by China. China's strategy lifted 600 million people out of absolute poverty between 1981 and 2005.[5] The World Bank, which is headquartered in Washington, claims that China's success was based on 'openness to markets and competition, focus on private initiative and market mechanisms'.[6] This is not true, however.

The World Bank's own *Doing Business* report says that China is still a very difficult place for foreign companies to operate.[7] China's private sector employs 160 million people,[8] less than a third of the Chinese workforce. According to Reuters, private Chinese companies are 'compelled to sell stakes to state firms or priced out of bidding for assets by government-backed players'.[9] State firms, on the other hand, receive subsidies and tax breaks unavailable to the private sector. If the Chinese government wishes to stop a Western company taking over a Chinese one, it simply does so, as Coca-Cola discovered in 2009.[10]

This reality is the opposite of the Chinese free-market paradise described by the World Bank. China's rise has been entirely state-managed. The country has a centralised 'catching-up' strategy designed to strip the West of its technological edge – the 'value added' that transforms base metals into priceless electronics and machinery. To quote a report by the consultancy Accenture:

China is keen to increase its influence in emerging industry sectors at the top of the value chain as a means of laying the foundation for a dominant market position in the future. Just as the US government invested in semiconductors for a number of years before the sector began to produce returns, Beijing is doing the same in such fields as biotechnology, nanotechnology and renewable energy.[11]

This is what China's military-industrial complex exists to do: lead the technological race and capture the value-added. It is also why the military component is necessary. Europe and the US are militantly opposed to poor countries 'climbing the value chain'. They prefer the fiction that these countries can become wealthy simply by opening their doors to Western corporations to do as they please, with minimal regulation. Europe and the US do not apply this standard to themselves, of course – both strictly protect and subsidise their agricultural sectors, for instance.

A congressional US report on China's approach to 'intellectual property' gave a strong flavour of Western distaste for China's remarkable success in reducing poverty. China's 'indigenous innovation policies', the report says, are viewed by 'US and foreign firms' as 'potentially reducing business opportunities'.[12] The 'overriding concern' for US firms is that their products 'are effectively priced out of markets in China and other countries by low-cost imitations'. In China 'trade secrets' are stolen by 'employees, business partners, computer hackers, and regulatory agencies'. China is creating 'state champion' companies by favouring them in government procurement contracts and providing government funding,[13] the report complains, despite the US doing precisely the same in its own military-industrial sector.

The US is evidently more concerned about protecting its own advantages than in reducing poverty overseas, even on the colossal scale achieved by China. This curious set of priorities should not really come as a surprise. The West has also tried to stop poor countries from manufacturing cheap copies of anti-AIDS drugs developed by pharmaceutical multinationals. Having failed to stop their manufacture at source, the EU now tries to prevent the delivery of such cheap imitations by impounding shipments en route to their destination, despite the drugs' potential to prolong millions of lives.[14]

REPEATING CHINA'S MIRACLE

China's catching-up strategy works because China is big. It is so big that US and European companies cannot afford to boycott the Chinese market, even if engaging with it means transferring technology to their future Chinese competitors. Smaller countries can be isolated and bullied. In December 2010 the US and EU led a group of 'like-minded countries' to agree an Anti-Counterfeiting Trade Agreement.[15] India's government has voiced its concern at this so-called 'plurilateral' initiative, which will be used to coerce smaller countries into protecting the West's technological lead.[16]

To emulate China, smaller countries need to unite into disciplined regional blocs capable of resisting Euro-American pressure. India, China and Brazil have all benefited from the independence afforded by their size. All three countries are too large to be governed by a self-enriching clique that can be bought off by overseas interests and ignore the demands of the domestic population. Their governments can only survive by fostering development. This is true even of China, where the ruling Communist Party, though hardly democratic, counts 73 million members.[17]

There are plenty of regional blocs, but none have attained the necessary level of cohesion to begin a Chinese-style programme of 'catching up'. Groups such as the Association for Southeast Asian Nations (ASEAN), the African Union, the Arab League, the Organisation of Islamic Conferences (OIC), the South Asian Association of Regional Cooperation (SAARC) and Union of South American Nations (UNASUR) have the potential to shrug off the West's insistence that its 'intellectual property', often the product of state-subsidised research, is somehow more precious than the lives of the poor. Were these groups to pool sovereignty in a disciplined fashion, they would be able to climb the 'value chain' in the same way as has China. Instead, many countries within these blocs are controlled by leaders who cater to the interests of the rich world in exchange for the false security of European luxuries, offshore bank accounts and imported weapons.

Multilateralism brings a second advantage. When applied effectively, it can defuse nationalistic tensions that otherwise end in armed conflict. The fact that Great Britain and the Republic of Ireland were members of the EU helped to defuse tensions over the national status of Northern Ireland. Whether they viewed themselves as British or Irish, the inhabitants of the six counties shared a trans-national EU identity that blurred national divisions and reduced the scope for violence. Similar regional integration could downgrade the dispute between Pakistan and India over Kashmir, for instance, or Bolivia's tussles with Chile over access to the Pacific.

Right-wing elements in the US are vehemently opposed to the upwards induction of national sovereignty to multinational institutions. They condemn the United Nations as a 'world government' seeking to redistribute American wealth along socialist lines.[18,19] What these commentators fail to realise is that the US is unusual. In most countries, ethnicity and nationality do not neatly align, as they do in North America, but spread messily over national borders: Kurds in the Middle East, Pashtuns in South Asia, Basques in France and Spain, are all examples of cross-border ethnic 'messiness' that often ends in violence, because the nation-state is poorly equipped to deal with them. Trans-nationalism is a way of defusing the tensions associated with these sub-national groups.

Multilateral bodies are also well-placed to set minimum standards for the development. The Millennium Development Goals (MDGs) set by the UN are measurable, realistic targets for creating a world in which minimum standards of human security can be widely achieved. In the absence of such benchmarks, those who wish to do so can downplay absolute poverty as the inevitable condition of the poor world, making it yet another facet of the 'few bad apples' theory.

In the rich world, the basic requirements are easily catered for, and have been for centuries. One recent study discovered that the inhabitants of medieval England were considerably wealthier than people living in many poor countries today.[20] Aided by a benign climate and diverse agricultural production, Englishmen in the late Middle Ages enjoyed an average income per head of around $1,000 a year, adjusted for prices. This put them on a par with the modern inhabitants of India, Cambodia and Ghana. The MDGs aim to provide a similar standard of personal security to the inhabitants of the modern world, but there are nonetheless those who claim even these minimum standards as unattainable. According to the UN, US$300 billion a year would lift everyone on the planet above the extreme poverty line of $1 a day – that's just a third of each year's global military budget.

The UN faces challenges and needs some reform. In some cases, groups of powerful countries such as the G8 and G20 have splintered off to form their own conclaves, frustrated by having to accede to the demands of smaller and poorer nations in the UN setting. Other such groups have worked to capture institutions within the UN such as the Human Rights Council, where nations belonging to the Organisation of Islamic Conferences have targeted the council's work at Israel's treatment of the Palestinians, to the exclusion of other issues elsewhere in the world.

Peacekeeping is also a vexed topic, with small and under-resourced UN deployments struggling to contain some of the world's most vicious conflicts, such as those in Darfur and Congo. It is vital the oversight of peacekeeping operations is increased to ensure that resources match requirements and that the mission is performing as intended. The UN Security Council contains no permanent members from the southern hemisphere, meaning that only major northern powers have the power to authorise or veto military action on behalf of the body. This situation is not acceptable to Brazil, Nigeria, India and many other southern hemisphere countries. Changing this component of the UN is crucial if the organisation is to retain its moral authority and its ability to intervene in crisis situations in an impartial manner.

STATE CHAMPIONS

Developing nations must also ignore demands to open their markets fully to multinationals. Successful catching-up strategies require governments to support the creation of 'state champion' businesses that can grow large enough to compete with established European and American conglomerates. In Japan these state champions were known as *zaibatsu*. Often family owned, they included the Mitsubishi and Mitsui corporations. In South Korea the state champions were called *chaebol*, and included companies such as Samsung, Hyundai and LG. India's state champions also tend to be vertically integrated family-owned conglomerates, such as the Tata, Mittal and Reliance groups, which were sheltered by India's policy of trade protectionism and import-substitution. In the early stage of their development, the state can insulate such giants against commercial pressures, as China has done.[21] It is also possible to foster successful national oil companies, as Brazil showed with Petrobras and Malaysia with Petronas.

A degree of planned development is essential. India's wealth is overwhelmingly concentrated in coastal cities with maritime access to foreign markets. Inland, the country remains very poor. Changing this situation will require the state champions to be taxed and the revenues spent on improving electrification, education, roads, railways, and communications in the hinterland. As agricultural technology improves, so does productivity, but demand for rural labour declines with mechanisation, so urban centres must prepare to accommodate economic migrants.

All this entails what one might call an 'industrial complex' – the state working to establish major corporations that can generate a stream of tax revenue. Problems occur when this entity mutates into a military-industrial complex, a *lusus naturae* that thrives on warfare and promotes abusive trading relationships with poorer countries. Such a mutation is not inevitable. After World War II Japan and South Korea developed industrial complexes without excessive militarisation, although it should be said that both relied on the US security umbrella against their hostile communist neighbours.

The end of the oil economy is the best hope for dismantling the military-industrial complex. For decades, the US and Europe have believed that the 'stability' offered by friendly dictatorships was preferable to the uncertainty of political reform, particularly in the oil-producing Middle East. The military-industrial complex has emerged to balance Western trade with those regimes, to arm them against their own oppressed populations, and most of all to ensure the uninterrupted flow of crude oil through the Arabian Gulf.

The political might of the military-industrial complex has been such that whenever instability has struck the region, US and European military action has been the first response, not the last resort. 'We recognize the strategic challenges posed by a dependence on foreign oil,' said Lockheed Martin's Chief Technology Officer, Dr Ray O. Johnson, ahead of an energy conference sponsored by the company in London.[22]

Now, two successive presidents have signalled that they wish to end US dependence on imported oil. Bush's preferred solution was biofuels. Obama's is electricity, generated from new nuclear power-plants,[23] a solution that has also convinced European governments.[24] These solutions are hardly ideal from either an environmental or a security perspective, but they at least point to the eventual demotion of oil as the world's major energy source, a development that would do much to end the pattern of extractive warfare.

Similarly, it is dawning on Western societies that over the long-term, even 'friendly' dictatorships are damaging to their interests. Where democratic rights are suppressed, the result is frustrated politicians who organise violence. In Northern Ireland and Sri Lanka, minority groups were permanently frozen out of power by the majority, leading to conflict. Across the Muslim world, the West has armed and financed dictators from North Africa to Pakistan. The result has been al-Qaeda, 9/11, 7/7, and a failed state in Afghanistan where rebels from countless other countries have gathered in revolt.

The self-interested cliques in charge of those countries 'invested' their country's wealth in limousines and jet fighters, instead of the Chinese-style industrial and human development that might have created jobs for the unemployed youth. In 2011, it was these same millions of jobless youngsters who gathered to eject the regimes of Hosni Mubarak in Egypt and others across the region. They demanded leaders whose first priority was not to amass a personal fortune but to foster prosperity for their fellow citizens.

More broadly, the West needs to realise that its beggar-thy-neighbour attitude to development is not an effective means of preserving its own prosperity. Jealously hoarding 'intellectual property' will not make the world safer or more prosperous. Britain did not become poor when India began to manufacture its own garments, any more than the US will be impoverished by China 'stealing' its research. Rather, by sharing its advances with developing nations, the West will find itself inhabiting a far friendlier and less radicalised planet.

This is not to argue that the US should hand its military technology to China, which would be self-defeating. Dismantling the US military-industrial complex would drain much of the impetus from China's equivalent, which justifies its own expansion in reference to America's defence spending.[25] However, this would be politically difficult. A more workable solution would be to agree bilateral or multilateral reductions in military expenditure, the way that treaties between Russia and the US have reduced the size of the nuclear arsenal. This would allow for a vast reduction in military expenditure, sharp tax cuts, and a rise in disposable income.

By rejecting the medium-term outlook that infects many policy decisions and looking instead to the long-term interests of both West and East, these reforms would create a more prosperous, more stable planet for its inhabitants. This is not a utopian dream, but the product of bold policy. It requires leaders who can resist the empty arguments presented by the military-industrial lobby, arguments that have led to ever less security, a spate of unwinnable armed conflicts, and the poverty and hopelessness that wars bring with them. The economic system that has kept billions trapped in war, insurgency, starvation and ignorance can be re-balanced to confer the same prosperity on all countries that some already enjoy.

11
Replacing the Military-Industrial Complex – Making the Twenty-first Century the Century of Soft Power

The problems outlined in the previous chapters are by no means insuperable. Ordinary people in the US and Europe can do a great deal to embarrass their governments into replacing the military-industrial complex with a less harmful mode of international trade. By rejecting the false account of why some countries are wealthy and others poor, why wars are necessary and why arms sales are harmless, citizens can change the world for the better.

Security is a fundamental requirement for development. According to the 2011 Global Peace Index, violence cost the world economy $8.12 trillion in 2010. The Index noted that the main fountain of violence was no longer inter-state wars, but wars between repressive governments and the people they rule. Real security is produced by democratic governments which work for the interests of their own countrymen, ones that do not sell their services to wealthy foreigners; which invest in the broad human and industrial development of their country; and which do not blow their national resources on weapons and a giant military payroll. These three Ds of development, democracy and disarmament interact to produce the stability which is sadly lacking in vast swathes of the southern hemisphere.

In wealthy industrialised countries there is complacency over the course of life in the poor world. Many people simply assume that the situation will improve of its own accord. This is not the case. Speaking in October 2007, at the Annual Erskine Childers Lecture hosted by Uniting for Peace, Professor Sir Richard Jolly noted that 70 countries had suffered what he called catastrophic declines in per capita incomes in the 1980s and 1990s, and that nearly 20 countries were poorer than they had been 30 years earlier. Time and again, Western leaders meet for summits, grand photo opportunities in which they promise huge sums of aid to the developing world. Time and again, the money never actually materialises.[1,2]

One of the many unpleasant products that the industrialised countries have sold to their corrupted partners in the poor world is debt. By 2007 the debt of Liberia, at US4.9 billion, was eight times the country's gross domestic product.[3] The burden of paying the interest on such debts is immense. Between 1992 and 2006 Nigeria was paying out in debt repayments nearly six times the amount it received in aid from the West. President Olusegun Obasanjo said that the debt he had inherited from past military dictatorships was crippling his country's ability to invest in infrastructure, education and health care.[4]

Only by ending the era of militarised government can productive investment take place. If the loans to countries in Africa had been used to create a more benign social and economic environment, then the debt would not have been a problem. The economies would have grown swiftly and become sufficiently prosperous to pay off their debts. As it was, much of the debt amassed in Africa was funnelled into secret bank accounts held offshore, allowing Westerners to re-invest it for their own profit while demanding interest payments from Africa. Debt relief is necessary, but governmental reform is a prerequisite.

Reform is also necessary in the wealthy countries. There are those who would argue that the government cannot restructure free-market economies. The US, they would argue, is a capitalist society and capitalism is led by market forces. It is these forces that define the industries of the future and attempts by governments to 'pick winners' are futile. There is a market for US military products, and this market must be served. To do otherwise would be to set the US on a very different philosophical and economic philosophy from that which it championed throughout the Cold War and beyond. This is the view of the US Chamber of Commerce, for example: 'Whenever government tries to pick winners and losers, whether through burdensome regulations, central planning, or open-ended subsidies, it fails and taxpayers and consumers pay the price.'[5]

This argument ignores the overpowering presence of the government in the US weapons industry, and vice-versa. America's military-industrial complex bears little resemblance to a liberal economic market. Ironically, given that it was established to win the Cold War against Soviet Russia, the US military sector has much more in common with state socialism. Although they are theoretically independent companies, large US arms contractors are entirely reliant on government cooperation and resources, without which they would collapse. They are a 'winner' that has been 'picked' by the US government for three generations.

Industrialised nations need to replace their military-industrial complexes with ordinary industrial establishments. However, simply phasing out the arms manufacturers without replacing them with similarly advanced enterprises would create unemployment among the engineers and scientists currently employed to create deadly weapons. Thankfully, there is a new industry that could absorb their skills effectively – and more constructively.

The trade in crude oil is the centrepiece of military-industrial commerce. Now, however, governments are pouring billions into replacing oil with substances that are less harmful to the environment. The challenge is to discover new sources of energy which are cheap to produce and transport, and which can be used to power vehicles. This is an immense scientific and technical challenge which requires even more governmental support and investment that is currently wasted on the arms industry.

Dr Stuart Parkinson, in a presentation for Scientists for Global Responsibility in April 2011, demonstrated how Great Britain, which possess the world's largest arms company in BAE Systems and where 7 per cent of manufacturing workers are employed by the defence sector, could shift its emphasis to 'green collar' jobs. These include not only those in the renewable energy sector but also in waste management, pollution control, and carbon capture and storage.

Parkinson noted that the 'green collar' sector was growing rapidly and by 2010 employed nearly one million workers in the UK, depending on how the parameters of the sector were defined. He cited the *Jane's Defence & Security Intelligence Analysis 2011* to point out that while the defence market is worth one trillion US dollars annually, the energy and environmental market is worth at least eight times that amount. *Jane's,* the world's most respected defence analysts, conceded that while budgetary realities would see the defence market contract, the green sector is set to 'expand exponentially, especially in the renewable arena'. Parkinson noted that employment in the military and defence sector has already shrunk from 625,000 in 1985/86 to 410,000 in 1995/96.

The arms companies are already trying to re-invent themselves as providers of renewable energy. BAE Systems is using its engineering expertise to create wind farms and offshore turbines.[6] US companies are also getting involved, with Boeing supplying solar concentrator cells to solar energy projects designed to convert the sun's rays into electricity.[7]

Exporting these technologies to developing countries would help the West to balance its trade. At the same time it would provide poorer countries with the energy and ecological security needed to industrialise themselves, bypassing the 'smoke-stack' phase which contributes to climate change. Most promisingly, green exports from the US have the potential to close the trade imbalance with China. Between 2005 and 2010 the military-industrial company General Electric sold 1,400MW of wind turbine capacity to China, helped by US government subsidies for wind power of US$3 billion in the first half of 2010 alone.[8]

This would be a far more productive use of resources than current plans for big-ticket weapons expenditure. The US Department of Defense expects the new fleet of F-35 fighter jets to incur running costs of US$1 trillion during their 30-year life span.[9] Its 2009 budget allocated US$3.4 billion for a different new jet, Lockheed Martin's F-22 Raptor, to pay for just 20 of these aeroplanes, bringing the fleet up to 183 jets even before the F-35 comes on line. Another half-billion was allocated simply to keep the F-22 production line open.[10] Each of the new Zumwalt-class destroyers for the US Navy costs US$3.5 billion.[11] The UK's Trident nuclear weapons programme has cost some US$130 billion during its lifetime. The Stockholm International Peace Research Institute (SIPRI) estimates that US military spending has increased by 81 per cent since 2001, with global military spending reaching an all-time high in 2010[12] to the tune of $1.6 trillion. Moreover, by confronting the problem of climate change the spread of green energy offers hope of reversing climate change, which threatens to generate new conflicts over water and uncontaminated land in the twenty-first century.

The practicalities of winding down military expenditure were assessed by a panel of experts convened by the *New York Times* in May 2011.[13] One panellist, Professor Gordon Adams at the American University's School of International Service, argued that the US could cut 15 per cent from the defence budget, saving US$1 trillion, by laying off the 92,000 new defence personnel hired over the previous ten years and reducing the US presence in Asia and Europe, scaling back or terminating wasteful projects such as the F-35 fighter and the Virginia class submarine, and shrinking the bureaucracy at the Pentagon that consumes 40 per cent of its budget.

Other panellists suggested cutting the V-22 Osprey, which costs $100 million a plane; asking service personnel to pay more towards their healthcare benefits; replacing military trash collectors and fire prevention officers with lower-cost civilian workers; withdrawing from Iraq and Afghanistan; refraining from propping up 'venal' governments in chaotic states; letting rich allies defend themselves; and imposing a spending freeze on the Pentagon until it renders itself auditable and amenable to financial oversight. Although some of these factors are unique to the US, others could be adopted by other industrial nations with large military establishments.

CLOSING THE LOOPHOLES

A pressing requirement is to create mechanisms to prosecute those countries who act as fences and money-launderers for the despotic overseers of military-industrial trade. The wholesale theft of wealth from Africa, Central Asia, the Middle East, and Russia would be impossible were it not for this network of rogue dukedoms and pirate coves. When a European nation is discovered to have received billions of stolen dollars from an African or Middle Eastern dictator, that nation should be required to pay heavy compensation to the victim-state or face international sanctions, in the same way that individuals who launder stolen money or fence stolen goods are liable for prosecution.

Likewise, multinational bodies could take a lead in ordering the closure of the offshore havens through which these stolen funds are processed. 'How much safer would everybody's savings be if the whole world finally came together to outlaw shadow banking systems and offshore tax havens?' former British prime minister Gordon Brown asked the US Congress in an address in March 2009.[14] In 2009 Brown hosted a meeting of the G20 group of nations in London that was billed as the moment that the corrupt offshore system would be dismantled, with havens that failed to comply being placed on a 'blacklist'.

The result was sadly predictable. The 'blacklist' was compiled by the rich-countries' club known as the Organisation for Economic Co-operation and Development (OECD). It exonerated the tax havens protected by wealthy nations and – almost unbelievably – singled out for criticism Costa Rica, Uruguay, Malaysia and the Philippines.[15] For the rich world, it has been business as usual ever since. Changing this situation will require the victims of the offshore banking system to bypass self-interest groups such as the G20 and OECD and place real multilateral pressure on the West to close down its network of offshore havens.

The decision by the government of Great Britain to cancel the corruption investigation into BAE's al-Yamama arms deal with Saudi Arabia, in which Britain exchanged arms for 600,000 barrels of oil per day,[16] should have immediately triggered international sanctions against the UK, in exactly the same way that sanctions were levied against Iran for its nuclear programme. As devastating as nuclear weapons can be, tens of millions more people have been killed by the devastation wrought by military-industrial corruption. Millions of women, for instance, have died in childbirth due to the absence of roads and clinics that would have been constructed had the necessary funds not been diverted into the bank accounts of Western multinationals and their local bagmen. Millions of children have died from illnesses that decent sanitation would have prevented. Countries like the UK have shown that they cannot be trusted to investigate overseas corruption itself. Astonishingly, until 2009 the UK Serious Fraud Office had not managed to secure the prosecution of a single British company involved in overseas bribery.[17] Even more astonishing is the fact that the US Justice Department often leaves companies accused of overseas bribery to investigate themselves.[18]

Needless to say, the use of commission agents and re-sellers should also be outlawed on an international basis. The UN could help by establishing a body that adjudicates public tenders on behalf of developing countries, creating a barrier that prevents corrupt multinationals from bribing officials into purchasing goods and services their countries do not need, especially arms. When companies are caught employing such agents or offering bribes, any fines should be payable to the country in which the bribery took place, giving officials in those countries a greater incentive to expose malpractice.

For sanctions against fence-countries to become practically possible, activists and independent journalists need to challenge the narrative spun by the crony media. For too long state-champion multinationals have spoken through the media to blame Africans, Arabs and Asians for corruption, when it is these state-backed corporations that hire the local agents, pay the bribes, set up the offshore accounts, hide the fugitive capital, rig the internal investigations and sell the weapons that protect corrupt regimes from their own people. The real source of corruption lies not in the poor world but in the European and American military-industrial complex, which wilfully subverts the industrial development of poor nations in order to extract commodities and to prevent their industrialisation.

Changing the media is the simplest way that the grassroots can change the world. Bribery does not harm industrial development so long as the wealth stays in the country – China is highly corrupt[19] but it has achieved astonishing economic growth. It is when the fruits of corruption mysteriously find their way to the West that development grinds to a halt. Activists need to demand an explanation from their governments for why it is so easy for military-backed rulers to hide their wealth in Western jurisdictions. They need to ask their governments why they only 'discover' and 'freeze' such assets when these leaders are toppled. They need to ask why supposedly responsible industrialised countries maintain a network of secrecy jurisdictions through which corrupt payments can flow, and why conviction rates for overseas bribery are so pitifully low. They need to question why some of the world's largest oil and plantation companies, such as France's TotalFinaElf and Britain's Imperial Tobacco, hail from countries with no oil or plantations of their own. They need to ask why their governments and newspapers are so critical of some foreign regimes (China, Iran) and so silent about others (Saudi Arabia, Bahrain, Egypt under Mubarak, Uzbekistan).

Independent journalists also need to highlight those occasions when leaders tell the truth about the structure of global trade. Former President Horst Kohler of Germany was forced to resign in May 2010 for saying of the war in Afghanistan that: 'A country of our size, with its focus on exports and thus reliance on foreign trade, must be aware that military deployments are necessary in an emergency to protect our interests.'[20] It is not clear that ordinary Germans agree with militarised trade: 70 per cent of the German people opposed troops being sent to Afghanistan.

Challenging the suffocating respect for the military would also prove beneficial. Activists need to point out that whatever the individual valour of most US servicemen, the army has been implicated in a string of appalling scandals, from the Abu Ghraib prison photos in Iraq to the murderous 'Kill Team' that murdered innocent people for sport in Afghanistan. Civilians need a perspective on the military more akin to that of serving soldiers, who tend to have a more sceptical and realistic view of the chest-beating rhetoric attached to military service. In particular, the endless debate surrounding the military service of individual politicians in the US hampers policy discussions of military expenditure, to the benefit of weapons manufacturers.

Following the execution of Osama bin Laden, the fugitive leader of al-Qaeda, on 1 May 2011, during a special forces raid into Pakistan that was not authorised by that country's government, the US killed the most recent of a litany of 'faces of evil' that help to justify its wasteful military spending. In an attempt to glorify the operation, President Obama's counterterrorism adviser John Brennan claimed that bin Laden was armed, had used women as shields to prevent his death and that bin Laden's compound was a palace worth US$1 million. It emerged a day later that the 55-year-old bin Laden had offered no resistance, was unarmed, and that he had not used women as a shield – he was simply executed with two shots to the head and one to the chest. Nor was his dilapidated compound worth anything even close to US$1 million.

'Faces of evil' have often faced such embellishment by those seeking to transform them from men into demons. The sweep of history shows that today's 'face of evil' is often tomorrow's obscure and forgotten footnote. Younger generations are unable to comprehend why, for example, the pockmarked Nicaraguan dictator Manuel Noriega was held up by US officials in the 1980s as a Hitler-like threat. Zimbabwe's Robert Mugabe is no more unpleasant than many other leaders to have blighted Africa, but he is singled out in the West for Hitler-like comparisons because he dared to confiscate farmland from European settlers.

Activists in the US and worldwide must treat with great scepticism any attempt by military-industrial interests to create a 'new bin Laden', for instance out of the Yemen-based al-Qaeda figure Anwar al-Awlaki. 'Anwar al Awlaki: the new Osama bin Laden?' asked the pro-military *Daily Telegraph* in September 2010. 'Is Ilyas Kashmiri the New Bin Laden?' asked *Newsweek* a month later. One thing is certain: there will be 'a new bin Laden'. The military-industrial complex needs such figures. They allow it to present a good-versus-evil narrative that disguises inconvenient facts – for instance, that al-Qaeda was formed as a reaction to the tyrannical government of Saudi Arabia, a government funded and armed by the US and its allies to secure access to oil, after the Saudis had invited US forces to base themselves on its soil.

The developing world does not need handouts from industrialised nations. All it needs is a level playing field and leaders who place their country's interests over their own personal wealth. The military-industrial complex has worked to ensure that a level playing field never develops, that the poor world is always disadvantaged by war and ill-governance. Yet dictatorship spawns terrorism. The events of 11 September 2001 showed the costs of cultivating repressive regimes in far-flung places. The death of bin Laden changed nothing. Only by promoting democratisation, development and disarmament can the West ensure that this threat recedes, guaranteeing peace and security for a fraction of the price currently exacted by military-industrial interests.

Epilogue
The Path Ahead

Neo-classical economics is founded on some core assumptions about human nature. It assumes that human wants are potentially unlimited. It assumes that man is a rational consumer who endlessly seeks maximum value for himself. Economics is a discipline intended to solve these alleged problems in a world of limited resources.

The Scottish philosopher David Hume noted that humans have a tendency to transform descriptions of what 'is' the case into instructions for how they 'ought' to live. Hume argued that such a leap was logically indefensible, but his argument is by no means accepted by the majority of philosophers or indeed the wider human race.[1] Inspired by economics, some individuals continue to believe that one limousine is not enough; that you can never have too many swimming pools; that a house is no substitute for a palace.

The world has reached a fork in the road. In one direction lies a future in which the poor world discovers a new generation of leaders who are not beholden to foreign interests or pay-offs, whose greed is not unlimited. These leaders will be bound by the aspirations of their fellow citizens. For them, staying in power will not be a matter of buying machine guns and helicopters but of investing their country's resources in education, research and other forms of human development. Like China, these countries will devise a 'catching-up' strategy, broadening their economic base to include sophisticated manufacturing and service industries, even if this means 'stealing' techniques from the West. After all, the skills to transform raw materials are far more valuable than the materials themselves, but those skills can only be cultivated in an atmosphere of non-conflict and good governance.

The other path leads in a much darker direction. In this future, the rich world clings ever more tenaciously to its technological advantage and increases the punishments for those countries which attempt to catch-up. Its military industrial complexes place weapons and money in the hands of an ever-growing cast of puppet leaders, hiding their wealth, demonising their opponents, selling them luxuries and weapons, trading arms for raw materials harvested by impoverished farmers and miners. Conflict is inevitable in this version of the future, as the greediest 1 per cent uses their wealth and weaponry to fight over access to primary resources. The spread of atomic bombs from superpowers to minor regimes to non-state actors makes a nuclear attack more likely with every year that passes.

Which road the world follows depends largely on the actions of the US, which today retains easily the largest military-industrial complex but also has the internal resources to close down this establishment. America's options are clear. It can transfer its mostly deadly secrets to China in exchange for the avalanche of cheap consumer goods it buys from the Chinese, balancing its trade but accelerating the arms race. It can continue to arm the dictatorial monarchies of Gulf States in return for shipments of crude oil, despite the growing menace of Islamic terrorism which is funded and justified by exactly the same equation.[2] It can sink an ever-growing amount of tax revenue into the balance sheets of Lockheed Martin and other military-industrial giants, further damaging the incomes of ordinary US families whose living standards have stagnated for the past 30 years.[3]

There is an alternative, however, one that US policy-makers sometimes appear ready to consider. This would deny China the lethal technology it seeks, but also end the arms race by slashing America's own Cold War-levels of military spending. It would end America's reliance on imported oil, and its support for the regimes that supply it, by investing in new forms of energy that can be sourced closer to home and which generate less pollution. The US would support even potential competitors by helping them to nurture their own centres of technological excellence, not in a piecemeal effort to serve US trade interests but as an end in themselves.

OPTING FOR DOOM

At the present moment, it seems that the US has opted for the first, disastrous course. The last chapter noted that successive US governments have championed a reduction in crude oil imports and the use of cleaner energy. The net effect of these commitments has been less than invisible. The US imported more crude oil in the first few months of 2011 than it did during the entirety of 2010.[4] President Barack Obama's stated intention to cut oil imports by a third has been met with widespread and justifiable scepticism.[5]

Instead, the military-industrial complex appears to have emerged victorious. Yet again, its interests have trumped the national interests of the US. In 2010 Defence Secretary Robert Gates, in a speech to military-industrial executives, announced plans to tear up restrictions that impeded arms sales.[6] 'Stringent is not the same as effective,' Gates opined. Instead, the US would merely protect what Gates called America's 'Crown Jewels': those 'technologies and items that no foreign government or company can duplicate'. These items were, he said, 'the basis for maintaining our military technology advantage'.

Gates effectively conceded defeat to the military-industrial sector: 'Multinational companies can move production offshore, eroding our defence industrial base, undermining our control regimes in the process, not to mention losing American jobs.' On its website, one of these multinationals said it 'applauded' the administration's plans: 'Lockheed Martin has been a strong and consistent advocate for open markets, for a fair and level playing field for competition, and for a vastly-improved export control process that does not impede our international trade.'[7]

China was an early beneficiary of the new mindset in Washington. In January 2011 Obama stood with China's President Hu Jintao to sign a military-industrial deal that was unprecedented in its scale. Obama announced that the Chinese would invest US$45 billion in US hi-tech goods. According to a triumphant Chinese state media, China would invest in 'in US exports from agriculture, telecommunications and technology companies, including General Electric, Honeywell and Navistar'.[8] The two presidents chatted in the Oval Office before joining a group of businessmen that included the heads of Boeing, General Electric, Dow Chemical, Microsoft and Goldman Sachs. 'We want to sell you all kinds of stuff,' Obama told Hu during the press conference. 'We want to sell you planes, we want to sell you cars, we want to sell you software.'[9]

Soon afterwards Peter Lichtenbaum, a former US commerce secretary writing in *Defense News*, pointed out the security implications of such concessions. He noted that the US administration appeared so concerned with the trade imbalance that it 'appeared to disregard the continued national security rationale' for export controls. It noted that semiconductors, a leading US export, were on the control list because they could be weaponised by the Chinese military. He worried that Obama's stance would weaken the arms embargo against China operated by European states.[10]

Europe required little weakening. A year earlier the EU announced plans to 'review' the arms embargo against China.[11] France argued that selling European weapons to China might reduce China's ability to make its own arsenal, which would, apparently, be a good thing.[12] Chinese state propaganda has long petitioned for such an outcome, claiming that 'as China's defense development continues to gather momentum, the embargo will seem increasingly pathetic'.[13] This claim is untrue, as testified to by the fact China's aircraft industry continues to produce copies of obsolete Soviet fighter jets.[14]

Selling China the military technology it seeks is one way the US can get out of its financial hole. Another option is simply not to pay China back. America's foreign debt is denominated in dollars. The US Federal Reserve can reduce the value of these dollars simply by printing more of them. If the dollar loses 20 per cent of its value, then the amount the US owes to China also drops by 20 per cent. If it loses 50 per cent of its value, then the value of China's debt holdings are cut in half. China's exposure to US debt is so large – US\$1.2 trillion in October 2010, much of which is long-term debt[15] – that there is nowhere else it could rapidly invest its holdings. While smaller bond-holders could perhaps flee the devaluation, China is stuck.

This is exactly what the US is trying to do, according to many prominent experts. 'Historically, we have only ever got out of such situations with inflation,' said Henri Guaino, a senior adviser to France's President Nicolas Sarkozy, in October 2009. 'We can also get out with deflation, but it's much more painful politically, socially.' 'I'm advocating 6 per cent inflation for at least a couple of years,' said Harvard professor Kenneth Rogoff, a former chief economist at the International Monetary Fund.[16] 'It would ameliorate the debt bomb and help us work through the deleveraging process.' Following the 2008 financial crisis, the US Federal Reserve pumped over two trillion new dollars into the US economy.[17] It called this programme 'quantitative easing'.

How will China react to being swindled? Chinese state media called the US tactic 'self-centred' and leading to 'considerable spill-over effects in other parts of the world'.[18] 'In the long run the considerable depreciation of the dollar will help America to transfer its debts to others,' complained Li Xiangyang in the *People's Daily*. Because the Chinese currency is pegged to the dollar, inflation in the US would translate into inflation in China, with hugely unpredictable effects on its economy. If China removed the peg, the soaring value of its own currency against the dollar would make its exports to the US expensive and uncompetitive, risking hundreds of millions of Chinese jobs. Either way, the results threaten China's entire political and economic system. However, the issue cuts both ways. China views its holdings of US debt as a weapon. Senior Chinese generals have raised the possibility of 'dumping' US debt during any US-China conflict over Taiwan, to sew economic chaos in the US.[19]

The term 'currency war' has now entered the English lexicon.[20,21] It is a subset of the economic warfare that is the subject of this book. Currency war is simply one manifestation of the abusive system of state-managed military-industrial trade that has devastated much of the planet. It is a war over knowledge, the knowledge needed to make valuable machines, and over the raw materials and energy required to create those machines and keep them running. It is this knowledge and access which keeps the rich world rich, and these machines, modified for warfare, which keep the poor world so poor.

Not all Americans are willing to give up so easily, however. 'What could start a popular resurgence in this country against the abuses of concentrated, avaricious corporatism?' mused environmentalist and sometime-presidential candidate Ralph Nader in April 2011.[22] He noted that the wave of revolutions raging across the Middle East had been sparked by one man, a young fruit vendor sick of Tunisia's corrupt and dictatorial regime who had immolated himself in a town square. Other Arabs, equally sick of the Western-backed puppets who ruled them, took this as inspiration to risk their own lives in pursuit of change.

Across the world, the military-industrial system has wilfully handed power to that 1 per cent of humanity whose material desires can never be sated, who act as economic theory says they should – the leaders who murder, torture and steal in exchange for billions in a Swiss bank account, for a fourth yacht or a tenth palace. Such trappings are readily provided by Western corporations in exchange for unfettered access to the vast natural wealth of the developing world. Arms sales balance this trade and ensure that the avaricious kings and tyrants cannot be easily displaced, even by the violent insurgencies that pepper the poor world.

Tragically, the repercussions of co-opting foreign dictatorships to Western interests have been demonstrated by terrorist attacks on the West. However, millions are now realising that through collective action, unity and public awareness this system can be torn down peacefully. Grassroots activists are combining to confront the elite politicians, corporate executives, generals, and dictators who profit from the military-industrial economy while billions starve. Movements such as Fair Trade and micro-finance have challenged the prevailing corporate logic and improved the lives of millions. The internet is helping poorer countries to acquire the knowledge needed to upgrade their economies and end their status as 'resource banks'. The web has helped to deconstruct the false narratives spread by well-connected Western journalists just as it has also undermined the more formal types of censorship preferred by military-industrial dictators.

It is collective activity that offers the best hope for ending the military-industrial trading relations that have kept half the world in a state of war, misery and starvation. It is public unity that will divert tax revenues from the pockets of military companies into the human and economic development that provides lasting security. Knowledge and power ultimately cohere at the same point. As the diffusion of knowledge devolves power from the elite to the masses, the grip of the military-industrial complex will finally end, not in a bang but in the peaceful murmur of prosperity.

THE UNITED NATIONS AND NATO

'The [UN] Secretariat building in New York has 38 storeys. If it lost 10 storeys, it wouldn't make a bit of difference.' So said John Bolton, US President George W. Bush's ambassador to the UN, a leading advocate of US-orchestrated regime change not only in Iraq and Afghanistan but Iran, North Korea and any other state he views as a threat to American interests. Bolton represents the extreme end of hawkish opinion in the US, and his antipathy to the UN illustrates the organisation's role in obstructing war-makers even in the world's only superpower.

Of course, it is possible to criticise the UN rationally. Officials at the New York headquarters complain of the sluggishness and torpor, of a talking shop that is too slow, of delegates appointed because they are the relatives of powerful leaders. It is possible to point to the failure of peacekeeping missions in Rwanda and Yugoslavia, of the criminal behaviour of peacekeeping forces deployed in many parts of the world, and its failure to thwart warfare from breaking out in many other regions. A Security Council appointed from the ranks of World War Two victors, with two small European nations but which excludes the entire global South, is not a body which should have ultimate say over the use of military force.

These criticisms cannot simply be brushed aside. They are significant. Taken together, they give the impression of an expensive, impotent, amorphous creation that acts as a sinecure for the well connected, a bully pulpit for big or wealthy countries, a drain on the budgets of the countries that pay for it and a symbol of the fruitlessness of multilateralism. Such an image is a gift to those, like Bolton, who believe that countries such as the United States should be able to deploy force unfettered by the opinions of other nations.

However, individual UN programmes enjoy a much better reputation. The World Food Program, the United Nations Children's Fund (Unicef), the World Health Organisation and many others have completed what is widely acknowledged to be valuable work in developing countries. Even Bolton, albeit speaking of voluntarily-funded elements of the body, has said that 'many independent UN-affiliated funds, programs, and specialized agencies currently work well'.[23]

Reform is essential. A Security Council that better reflects the world, which includes representatives from Latin America, Africa and the Indian subcontinent, would address security issues in a way that is more credible than the current panel. More importantly, strengthening those parts of the UN which everyone agrees work effectively in the interests of the poor world will strengthen the moral legitimacy of the organisation as a whole.

Bolton's criticism of the UN could more justifiably be levelled at the North Atlantic Treaty Organisation (NATO). The UN, although often inefficient, addresses problems that no one denies exist: poverty, under-education, food shortages, even conflict situations. NATO, on the other, was built to contain a problem that is no longer extant: the Soviet Union. Today, NATO is a military alliance in search of an enemy – a dangerous prospect for the world.

To point this out is not to downplay the menace that Soviet communism once presented. The means by which the Soviet Union kept itself alive for 70 years were brutal and repressive. There was nothing improper about Western democracies clubbing together to defend themselves against the heavily armed Warsaw Pact. Nor was there any doubt that the egalitarian ideals that prompted the communist revolutions of the early twentieth century had long since curdled into Soviet stagnation and decline, with a KGB that would go to any means necessary to silence opponents.

Today, Russia under Vladmir Putin, formerly the KGB's chief, is not much more democratic than it was 30 years ago. But it does not pose an existential threat to NATO countries. Russia does not seek to impose a new economic system on the wider world and it has seized the opportunity to decommission its vast stockpile of nuclear weapons whenever the US has agreed to do the same. Many of the Soviet Union's former satellite nations are now ordinary eastern European democracies whose people live in relative freedom.

Why, then, has NATO not disbanded? Its raison d'être expired in the early 1990s. To justify its continuation the alliance has had to sniff around for new wars in which to entangle itself: Afghanistan, Libya, Kosovo. Understanding which conflicts the coalition sees within its purview, and which it does not, is no longer an easy task. A NATO that did not involve itself in the Falklands conflict in 1982, even at the height of the Cold War and even when Great Britain, one of its leading lights, was fighting to recover territory from a non-NATO state, now finds itself jumping into fights whose outcome, participants, and context are indistinct.

One remaining effect of NATO has been to sustain Cold War-levels of military spending. In June 2011, speaking in Brussels, the then US Defense Secretary Robert Gates berated European members of the alliance for failing to spend 2 per cent of their national wealth on weapons and the people to shoot them. He complained that some members' defence budgets had been 'chronically starved for adequate funding for a long time', saying that total European defence spending declined by nearly 15 per cent in the decade following 9/11. Today, he complained, just five of 28 allies – the US, the UK, France and Greece, along with Albania – spend more than NATO's agreed 2 per cent of GDP spending on defence.

Gates granted that this amount, which he saw as sadly inadequate, amounted to a sum of US$300 billion being spent every year on defence by the non-American members of NATO. This sum, which he claimed had 'short changed current operations', is 60 times larger than the 2010–11 budget of the UN. With the US contribution included, NATO defence spending was around 240 times the UN budget.

Throughout his speech, Gates castigated his country's European allies for relying on the US to defend them. Not once, however, did he explain what 'threat' the US was supposed to be defending them from. Gates did not seem to consider the possibility that European defence spending had stabilised because the threats facing the continent from the Soviet east had evaporated. Instead, his oratory was based on the assumption of a never ending supply of new wars for NATO to wage, in increasingly exotic locales.

With NATO reforming itself as a perpetual war-fighting machine zeroed-in on some internal conflicts, but not others, at the whim of member governments who distort the meaning of UN Resolutions to fit whatever objectives they set themselves, it is hardly surprising that states singled out by men like John Bolton have sought to arm themselves with what, to date, has proven the only failsafe against NATO 'intervention'.

Following the invasion of Iraq in 2003, Libya's dictator Muammar Gaddafi relinquished his country's nuclear programme. Within a decade his regime found itself under attack by NATO jets, after an apparent reconciliation with the alliance quickly turned sour amid 2011's Arab Spring. Had Gaddafi developed nuclear weapons and the missiles with which to deliver them to Europe, only a few hundred miles north across the Mediterranean, Gaddafi's regime would have been safe.

This lesson has been learned by the cruel dictatorship that governs North Korea. Shrugging off sanctions that have done little more than to impoverish the country's beleaguered population, the North Korean regime set its sights on obtaining the nuclear tools to deter NATO military action. Iran seems to be focused on the same goal, while Pakistan plays dubious games in Afghanistan safe in the knowledge that NATO cannot risk a nuclear attack from its arsenal of Hatf and Shaheen nuclear missiles. No matter how much NATO blows on defence expenditure, it only acts in countries that cannot retaliate with the atomic bomb. What greater incentive is there for threatened regimes to develop their own nuclear weapons?

The factors illustrate why the UN, for all its faults, offers a greater hope for preserving world peace than NATO or, indeed, any other combination of countries united against the rest. Improving the UN's ability to mediate and, yes, to deploy peacekeepers when required should be a far greater priority than re-arming NATO. Only then can a system develop in which military intervention is agreed on a democratic basis that does not give rogue regimes an incentive to develop doomsday weapons of mass destruction, which today, even after the end of the Cold War, remain the greatest threat to human civilisation and peace.

Appendix
List of Global Peace Organisations

Australia

Global Peace Index / Vision of
Humanity
P.O. Box 42
St Leonards NSW 1590
Sydney
+61 2 9901 8500
www.visionofhumanity.org

Peace Education Commission of
the International Peace Research
Association
c/o Toh Swee-Hin, Multi-Faith Centre
Griffith University
Kessels Road
Nathan
Qld 4111
+61 7 3735 7053
s.toh@griffith.edu.au

Austria

Europaisches Universitatszentrum fur
Friedensstudien
(European University Centre for Peace
Studies)
Friedenszentrum Burg Schlaining
7461 Stadtschlaining
Burg
+43 3355 2498
epu@epu.ac.at
www.epu.ac.at

European Union Agency for
Fundmantal Rights
Schwazenbergplatz 11
1040 Wien
+43 1 580 3060
information@fra.europa.eu
fra.europa.eu

Belgium

European Green Party Federation
Rue Wiertz 31
1050 Bruxelles
+32 2 626 0720
info@europeangreens.org
europeangreens.eu

European NGO Confederation for
Relief and Development
10 Sq Ambiorix
1000 Bruxelles
+32 2 743 8760
secretariat@concordeurope.org
www.concordeurope.org

Federation of Young European
Greens / Federation des Jeunes
Ecologistes Europeens
31 rue Wiertz
1050 Bruxelles
office@fyeg.org
www.fyeg.org

Friends of the Earth International –
Europe Office
Mundo-B Building
Rue d'Edimbourg 26
1050 Bruxelles
+32 2 893 1000
info@foeeurope.org
www.foeeurope.org

Groupe de Recherche et d'Information
sur la Paix et la Securite
rue de la Consolation 70
1030 Schaerbeek (Bruxelles)
+32 2 241 8420
admi@grip.org
www.grip.org

International Crisis Group
149 Ave Louise – Level 24
1050 Bruxelles
+32 2 502 9038
www.crisisgroup.org

Mayors for Peace 2020 Vision
Campaign
c/o Ieper Stadhuis
Grote Markt 34
8900 Ieper
+32 57 388957
2020visioncampaign@ieper.be
www.2020visioncampaign.org

Nonviolent Peaceforce
205 rue Belliard
1040 Bruxelles
+32 2 648 0076
europe@nonviolentpeaceforce.org
www.nonviolentpeaceforce.org

Pax Christi International
Rue du Vieux Marche aux Grains 21
1000 Bruxelles
+32 2 502 5550
hello@paxchristi.net
www.paxchristi.net

Peace Brigades International –
Colombia Project
11 rue de la Liniere
1060 Bruxelles
info@pbicolombia.org
www.peacebrigades.org/colombia.html

Quaker Council for European Affairs
Square Ambiorix 50
1000 Bruxelles
+32 2 230 4935
info@qcea.org
www.quaker.org/qcea

Search for Common Ground – Brussels
Office
Rue Belliard 205 – bte 13
1040 Bruxelles
+32 2 736 7262
brussels@sfcg.be
www.sfcg.org

Service Civil International –
International Office
St-Jacobsmarkt 82
2000 Antwerpen
+32 3 226 5727
info@sciint.org
www.sciint.org

SOLIDAR
Rue du Commerce 22
1000 Bruxelles
+32 2 500 1020
solidar@solidar.org
www.solidar.org

World Future Council – EU Office
Rue Marie-Therese 21
1000 Bruxelles
+32 2 210 1780
info.eu@worldfuturecouncil.org
www.worldfuturecouncil.org

Britain

4D for World Peace
97 Commercial Road
London E1 1RD
+44 20 7377 2111
vijay@vmpeace.org
www.4dworldpeace.org

Abolition 2000 UK
162 Holloway Road
London N7 8DQ
mail@abolition2000uk.org
www.abolition2000uk.org

The Acronym Institute for
Disarmament Diplomacy
24 Colvestone Crescent
London E8 2LH
+44 20 7503 8857
www.acronym.org.uk

Amnesty International
International Secretariat
Peter Benenson House
1 Easton Street
London WC1X 0DW
+44 20 7413 5500
amnestyis@amnesty.org
www.amnesty.org

Anglican Pacifist Fellowship
11 Weavers End
Hanslope
Milton Keynes MK19 7PA
enquires@anglicanpeacemaker.org.uk
www.anglicanpacifists.com

Arms Reduction Coalition
97 Commercial Road
London E1 1RD
vijay@vmpeace.org

Article 19 – Global Campaign for Free
Expression
Free Word Centre
60 Farringdon Road
London EC1R 3GA
+44 20 7324 2500
info@article19.org
www.article19.org

Bertrand Russell Peace Foundation
Russell House
Bulwell Lane
Nottingham NG6 0BT
+44 115 978 4504
elfeuro@compuserve.com
www.russfound.com

Bradford University Department of
Peace Studies
Bradford BD7 1DP
West Yorks
+44 1274 235235
r.day@bradford.ac.uk
www.brad.ac.uk/acad/peace/

British American Security Information
Council
The Grayston Centre
28 Charles Square
London N1 6HT
+44 20 7324 4680
kwaller@basicint.org
www.basicint.org

British Institute of Human Rights
School of Law
Queen Mary
University of London

Mile End Road
London E1 4NS
+44 20 7882 5850
info@bihr.org.uk
www.bihr.org.uk

British Overseas NGOs for
Development (BOND)
Regent's Wharf
8 All Saints Street
London N1 9RL
020 7837 8344
advocacy@bond.org.uk
www.bond.org.uk

Brahma Kumaris World Spiritual
University
Global Co-operation House
65 Pound Lane
London NW10 2HH
+44 20 8727 3350
www.bkwsu.org.uk

Campaign Against Arms Trade
11 Goodwin Street
Finsbury Park
London N4 3HQ
+44 20 7281 0297
enquiries@caat.org.uk
www.caat.org.uk

Campaign For Nuclear Disarmament
162 Holloway Road
London N7 8DQ
+44 207 700 2393
enquiries@cnduk.org
www.cnduk.org

Catholic Agency for Overseas
Development
Romero Close
Stockwell Road
London SW9 9TY
+44 20 7733 7900
cafod@cafod.org.uk
www.cafod.org.uk

The Royal Institute of International
Affairs
Chatham House

10 St James's Square
London SW1Y 4LE
+44 20 7957 5700
contact@chathamhouse.org
www.chathamhouse.org

Child Rights Information Network
c/o Save the Children UK
1 St John's Lane
London EC1M 4AR
+44 20 7012 6867
info@crin.org
www.crin.org

Christian Aid
35 Lower Marsh
Waterloo
London SE1 7RL
+44 20 7620 4444
info@christian-aid.org
www.christianaid.org.uk

CISV International
MEA House
Ellison Place
Newcastle-upon-Tyne NE1 8XS
+44 191 232 4998
international@cisv.org
www.cisv.org

Cluster Munition Coalition
5th Floor
Epworth House
25 City Road
London EC1Y 1AA
+44 20 7256 9500
info@stopclustermunitions.org
www.stopclustermunitions.org

Coalition to Stop the Use of Child
Soldiers – International Secretariat
4th Floor
9 Marshalsea Road
Borough
London SE1 1EP
+44 20 7367 4110
info@child-soldiers.org
www.child-soldiers.org

Concord Video & Film Council
Rosehill Centre
22 Hines Road
Ipswich
IP3 9BG
+44 1473 726012
sales@concordmedia.co.uk
www.bfi.org.uk

Conscience Taxes for Peace not War
Archway Resource Centre
1b Waterlow Road
London N19 5NJ
+44 20 7561 1061
info@conscienceonline.org.uk
www.conscienceonline.org.uk

Control Arms Campaign
c/o Amnesty International
1 Easton St
London WC1X 0DW
info@controlarms.org
www.controlarms.org

Crisis Action
48 Gray's Inn Road
London WC1X 8LT
+44 20 7269 9450
gemma.mortensen@crisisaction.org
crisisaction.org

Earthwatch Institute – Europe
Mayfield House
256 Banbury Road
Oxford OX2 7DE
+44 1865 318838
info@earthwatch.org.uk
www.earthwatch.org/europe

European Network for Peace and
Human Rights
c/o Bertrand Russell Peace Foundation
Russell House
Bulwell Lane
Nottingham NG6 0BT
+44 115 978 4504
elfeuro@compuserve.com
www.russfound.org

Forces Watch
www.forceswatch.net

Fortune Forum
97 Commercial Road
London E1 1RD
www.fortuneforum.org

Green Party
National Green Party office
56–64 Development House
Leonard Street
London EC2A 4LT
020 7549 0310
office@greenparty.org.uk
www.greenparty.org.uk

Greenpeace UK
Canonbury Villas
London N1 2PN
+44 20 7865 8100
info@uk.greenpeace.org
www.greenpeace.org.uk

Housmans Peace Resource Project
5 Caledonian Road
London N1 9DX
+44 20 7278 4474
worldpeace@gn.apc.org
www.housmans.info

International Action Network on Small
Arms
Development House
56–64 Leonard Street
London EC2A 4LT
+44 20 7065 0870
contact@iansa.org
www.iansa.org

International Alert
346 Clapham Road
London SW9 9AP
+44 20 7627 6800
general@international-alert.org
www.international-alert.org

International Coalition to Ban
Uranium Weapons
Bridge 5 Mill

22a Beswick Street
Ancoats
Manchester M4 7HR
+44 161 273 8293
info@bandepleteduranium.org
www.bandepleteduranium.org

International Humanist and Ethical
Union
1 Gower Street
London WC1 6HD
office-iheu@iheu.org
www.iheu.org

International Institute for Strategic
Studies
Arundel House
13–15 Arundel Street
London WC2R 3DX
+44 20 7379 7676
iiss@iiss.org
www.iiss.org

International Maritime Organization
4 Albert Embankment
London SE1 7SR
+44 20 7735 7611
info@imo.org
www.imo.org

International PEN
Brownlow House
50–51 High Holborn
London WC1V 6ER
+44 20 7405 0338
info@internationalpen.org.uk
www.internationalpen.org.uk

International Secretariat of
Nuclear-Free Local Authorities
c/o Nuclear-Free Local Authorities
Secretariat
Manchester City Council
Town Hall
Manchester M60 3NY
+44 161 234 3244
office@nuclearpolicy.info
www.nuclearpolicy.info

International Simultaneous Policy
Organisation
P.O. Box 26547
London SE3 7YT
+44 20 8464 4141
info@simpol.org
www.simpol.org

International Tibet Support Network
c/o Tibet Society UK
Unit 9, 139 Fonthill Road
London N4 3HF
itsn@tibetnetwork.org
www.tibetnetwork.org

International Vegetarian Union
c/o Vegetarian Society of the UK
Parkdale, Dunham Road
Altrincham WA14 4QG
www.ivu.org

Institute for Law Accountability and
Peace
c/o Vijay Mehta
97 Commercial Road
London E1 1RD
+44 20 7377 2111
vijay@vmpeace.org
www.inlap.freeuk.com

Islamic Human Rights Commission
P.O. Box 598
Wembley HA9 7XH
+44 20 8904 4222
info@ihrc.org
www.ihrc.org

Jubilee Debt Campaign
The Grayston Centre
28 Charles Sq
London N1 6HT
+44 20 7324 4722
info@jubileedebtcampaign.org.uk
www.jubileedebtcampaign.org.uk

Liberty – The National Council for
Civil Liberties
21 Tabard Street
London SE1 4LA
+44 20 7403 3888
www.liberty-human-rights.org.uk

Make Poverty History Coalition
c/o BOND
Regent's Wharf
8 All Saint's Street
London N1 9RL
webmaster@makepovertyhistory.org
www.makepovertyhistory.org

Medact
The Grayston Centre
28 Charles Square
London N1 6HT
+44 20 7324 4739
info@medact.org
www.medact.org

Mehta Centre
97 Commercial Road
London E1 1RD
+44 20 7377 2111
vijay@vmpeace.org
www.mehtacentre.org

Movement for the Abolition of War
11 Venetia Road
London N4 1EJ
+44 1908 511948
info@abolishwar.org.uk
www.abolishwar.org.uk

NATO Watch
17 Strath
Gairloch IV21 2BX
Ross-shire
+44 1445 712649
idavis@natowatch.org
www.natowatch.org

Network for Peace
5 Caledonian Road
London N1 9DX
+44 20 7278 0444
mail@networkforpeace.org.uk
www.networkforpeace.org.uk

New Economics Foundation
3 Jonathan Street
London SE11 5NH
+44 20 7820 6300
info@neweconomics.org
www.neweconomics.org

OneWorld International Foundation
2nd Floor, CAN Mezzanine
32–36 Loman Street
London SE1 0EH
+44 20 7922 7717
foundation@oneworld.net
uk.oneworld.net

Overseas Development Institute
111 Westminster Bridge Road
London SE1 7JD
+44 (0)20 7922 0300
odi@odi.org.uk
www.odi.org.uk

Oxfam International
Suite 20
266 Banbury Road
Oxford OX2 7DL
+44 1865 339100
information@oxfaminternational.org
www.oxfam.org

Oxford Research Group
Development House
56–64 Leonard Street
London EC2A 4LT
+44 20 7549 0298
org@oxfordresearchgroup.org.uk
www.oxfordresearchgroup.org.uk

Peace Brigades International
Brigadas Internacionales de Paz /
Brigades de Paix Internationales
Development House
56–64 Leonard Street
London EC2A 4LT
+44 20 7065 0775
admin@peacebrigades.org
www.peacebrigades.org

Peace Child International
The White House
46 High Street
Buntingford SG9 9AH
+44 1763 274459
info@peacechild.org
www.peacechild.org

Peace Direct
64 Leonard Street
London EC2A 4LT
+44 20 7549 0285
info@peacedirect.org
www.peacedirect.org

Peace Museum Office
Centenary Square
Bradford BD1 1HY
+44 1274 434009
peacemuseum@bradford.gov.uk
www.peacemuseum.org.uk

Peace News
5 Caledonian Road
London N1 9DY
+44 20 7278 3344
editorial@peacenews.info
www.peacenews.info

Peace One Day
St George's House
15 St George's Road
Richmond TW9 2LE
+44 20 8334 9900
info@peaceoneday.org
www.peaceoneday.org

Peace Pledge Union
1 Peace Passage
London N7 0BT
+44 20 7424 9444
www.ppu.org.uk

Pugwash Conferences on Science and
World Affairs
Ground Floor Flat
63A Great Russell Street
London WC1B 3BJ
+44 20 7405 6661
pugwash@mac.com
www.pugwash.org/uk

Quaker Peace & Disarmament
Programme
Friends House
175 Euston Road
London NW1 2BJ
+44 20 7663 1067
disarm@quaker.org.uk
www.quaker.org.uk

Religions for Peace – Europe
37 Grange Road
Bushey
Watford WD2 2LQ
+44 1923 211168
wcrp@btconnect.com
www.wcrp.org

Rights and Humanity
Royal Liver Building
Pier Head
Liverpool L3 1HU
+44 151 236 2426
office@rightsandhumanity.org
www.rightsandhumanity.org

Royal United Services Institute
Whitehall
London SW1A 2ET
+44 20 7747 2600
www.rusi.org

Saferworld
The Grayston Centre
28 Charles Square
London N1 6HT
+44 20 7324 4646
general@saferworld.org.uk
www.saferworld.org.uk

Scientists for Global Responsibility
Ingles Manor
Castle Hill Avenue
Folkestone CT20 2RD
+44 1303 851965
info@sgr.org.uk
www.sgr.org.uk

Schumacher Society
CREATE Environment Centre
Smeaton Road
Bristol BS1 6XN
+44 117 903 1081
admin@schumacher.org.uk
www.schumacher.org.uk

Scotland's for Peace
15 Barrland Street
Glasgow G41 1QH
+44 141 433 2821

info@scotland4peace.org
www.scotland4peace.org

Soroptimist International
87 Glisson Road
Cambridge CB1 2HG
+44 1223 311833
hq@soroptimistinternational.org
www.soroptimistinternational.org

Statewatch
P.O. Box 1516
London N16 0EW
+44 20 8802 1882
statewatch-off@geo2.poptel.org.uk
www.statewatch.org

Stop the War
231 Vauxhall Bridge
London SW1V 1EH
+44 20 7801 2768
office@stopwar.org.uk
www.stopwar.org.uk

Survival International
6 Charterhouse Buildings
London EC1M 7ET
+44 20 7687 8700
info@survivalinternational.org
www.survivalinternational.org

The Gandhi Foundation
Kingsley Hall
Powis Road
Bromley-by-Bow
London E3 3HJ
+44 845 313 8419
contact@gandhifoundation.org
gandhifoundation.org

The Peace Museum
Centenary Square
Bradford BD1 1HY
+44 1274 434009
peacemuseum@bradford.gov.uk
www.peacemuseum.org.uk

The Peace People
224 Lisburn Road
Belfast BT9 6GE

Northern Ireland
+44 2890 663465
bwccc@eircom.net
www.peacepeople.com

Trade Justice Movement
c/o Fairtrade Foundation
3rd Floor, Ibex House
42–47 Minories
London EC3N 1DY
+44 20 7440 8560
mail@tjm.org.uk
www.tjm.org.uk

United Nations Association of the UK
3 Whitehall Court
London SW1A 2EL
+44 20 7766 3454
membership@una.org.uk
www.una.org.uk

Uniting for Peace
97 Commercial Road
London E1 1RD
+44 207 377 2111
vijay@vmpeace.org
www.unitingforpeace.com

Vertic
Development House
56–64 Leonard Street
London EC2A 4LT
+44 20 7065 0880
unini.tobun@vertic.org
www.vertic.org

War Resisters' International
5 Caledonian Road
London N1 9DX
+44 20 7278 4040
info@wri-irg.org
wri-irg.org

War on Want
44–48 Shepherdess Walk
London N1 7JP
+44 20 7324 5040
support@waronwant.org
www.waronwant.org

Women's International League for
Peace and Freedom
Tindlemanor
52–54 Featherstone Street
London EC1Y 8RT
+44 20 7250 1968
office@ukwilpf.org.uk
www.ukwilpf.org.uk

Woodcraft Folk
Units 9/10
83 Crampton Street
London SE17 3BQ
+44 020 7703 4173
info@woodcraft.org.uk
www.woodcraft.org.uk

World Congress of Faiths
c/o London Inter Faith Centre
125 Salusbury Road
London NW6 6RG
+44 20 8959 3129
enquiries@worldfaiths.org
www.worldfaiths.org

World Court Project to Abolish
Nuclear Weapons
c/o George Farebrother
67 Summerheath Road
Hailsham BN27 3DR
+44 1323 844269
geowcpuk@gn.apc.org
www.peacebourne.serifweb.com/
WCPUK

World Development Movement
66 Offley Road
London SW9 0LS
+44 20 7820 4900
wdm@wdm.org.uk
www.wdm.org.uk

World Goodwill
Suite 54
3 Whitehall Court
London SW1A 2EF
+44 20 7839 4512
worldgoodwill.uk@lucistrust.org
www.worldgoodwill.org

World Orchestra for Peace
c/o 26 Lyndale Ave
London NW2 2QA
+44 20 7317 8433
ckconsult@compuserve.com
www.worldorchestraforpeace.com

Worldwide Consultative Association of
Retired Generals and Admirals
c/o 61 Sedlescombe Road
London SW6 1RE
+44 20 7385 6738
www.wcarga.org

Canada

International Education for Peace
Institute
101-1001 W Broadway – Suite 900
Vancouver
BC V6H 4E4
+1 604 639 7910
info@efpinternational.org
www.efpinternational.org

International Network for
Development Information Exchange
P.O. Box 8500
Ottawa, ON
K1G 3HG
indix@idrc.cd

Nobel Women's Initiative
1 Nicholas St – Suite 430
Ottawa, ON
K1N 7B7
+1 613 569 8400
info@nobelwomensinitiative.org
www.nobelwomensinitiative.org

Pacific Peace Working Group
c/o P Willis
3780 Lake Road
Denman Island, BC
V0R 1T0
+1 250 335 0351
info@pacificpeace.net
www.pacificpeace.net

Peace Brigades International / Brigade
Perdamaian Internasional – Indonesia
Project
Box 9
33 Boundary Trail
Clearwater, MB
R0K 0M0
+62 274 446 3996
coordinator@pbi-indonesia.org
www.peacebrigades.org

People's Global Action / Azione
Globale dei Popoli
c/o Canadian Union of Postal Workers
377 Bank Street
Ottawa, ON
K2P 1Y3
+1 613 236 7230
www.agp.org

Project Ploughshares
57 Erb Street West
Waterloo ON
N2L 6C2
+1 519 888 6541
www.ploughshares.ca

World Federalist Movement-Canada
207-145 Spruce Street
Ottawa, ON
K1R 6P1
+1 613 232 0647
wfcnat@web.ca
www.worldfederalistscanada.org

Costa Rica

University for Peace / Universidad para
la Paz / Universite pour la Paix
Apdo 138-6100
Ciudad Colon
+506 2205 9000
info@upeace.org
www.upeace.org

Czech Republic

Europe for Peace
c/o Czech Humanist Party
Dana Feminova
Na Slupi 5
12800 Praha 2
www.humanisteurope.org

Youth and Environment Europe
Kubatova 1/32
10200 Praha 10 – Hostivar
+420 2 7175 0643
info@yeenet.eu
www.yeenet.eu

Denmark

Climate Justice Action
c/o Anna Kollerup Nystrup
Solvgade 97 - 1 th
1307 Kobenhavn
info@climate-justice-action.org
www.climate-justice-action.org

Euro-Mediterranean Human Rights
Network / Reseau Euro-Mediterraneen
des Droits de l'Homme
Vestergade 16 - 2 sal
1456 Kobenhavn K
+45 3264 1700
msp@euromedrights.net
www.euromedrights.org

International Work Group for
Indigenous Affairs
Classensgade 11E
2100 Kobenhavn
+45 3527 0500
iwgia@iwgia.org
www.iwgia.org

France

Bibliotheque Internationale de la Paix
9–11 rue du Forst
57200 Sarreguemines
Moselle
+33 387 950018

Coordination Internationale pour la
Decennie / International Coalition for
the Decade
148 rue du Faubourg Saint Denis
75010 Paris
+33 14036 0660
secretariat@nvpdecade.org
www.nvpdecade.org

European Court of Human Rights
/ Cour europeenne des Droits de
l'Homme
Council of Europe
67075 Strasbourg Cedex
+33 388 412018

International Decade for a Culture of
Peace
UNESCO
7 Place de Fontenoy
75352 Paris 07 SP
+33 14568 0876
iycp@unesco.org
www.unesco.org/iycp

International Institute of Human
Rights / Institut International des
Droits de l'Homme
2 Allee Rene Cassin
67000 Strasbourg
+33 388 458445
administration@iidh.org
www.iidh.org

International Veterans for Peace
Liaison Committee
c/o ARAC
2 Pl du Meridien
94807 Villejuif
+33 14211 1111

Soldiers of Peace International
c/o 178 rue Garibaldi
69003 Lyon
+33 4 7895 4503
contact@aisp.fr
www.aisp.fr

Transcend Research Institute
7 rue du Cret de la Neige
01210 Versonnex
www.transcend.org/tri

UNESCO – Human Rights, Democracy
and Peace Division
1 rue Miollis
75732 Paris Cedex 15
+33 14568 1000
bpi@unesco.org
www.unesco.org

United Nations Educational, Scientific
and Cultural Organisation
7 Place de Fontenoy
75352 Paris
+33 14568 0580
www.unesco.org

World Citizen Registry
66 Bd Vincent Auriol
75013 Paris
+33 14586 0358
abc@recim.org
www.recim.org

Germany

Betterworld Links
norbert@betterworldlinks.org
www.betterworldlinks.org

European Network for Civil Peace
Services
c/o Helga Tempel
Foehrenstieg 8
22926 Ahrensburg
+49 4102 53337
helga.tempel@gmx.de
www.en-cps.org

European Plowshares Movement
c/o Wolfgang Sternstein
Hauptmannsreute 45
70192 Stuttgart
+49 711 293874
sternstein@uwi-eV.de
www.uwi-ev.de

Heidelberger Institut für Internationale
Konfliktforschung e.V.
Bergheimer Str. 58
69115 Heidelberg
+49.6221 54 3198
info@hiik.de
www.hiik.de

International Association of Lawyers
Against Nuclear Arms
Berlin Glinkasrtr 5–7
12437 Berlin
+49 30 2065 4857
jenny@ialana.de
www.ialana.net

International Network of Engineers
and Scientists for Global Responsibility
Schutzenstr 6a
10117 Berlin
+49 30 2065 3831
office@inesglobal.com
www.inesglobal.com

International Peace Exchange
c/o DFG-VK
Braunschweiger Str 22
44145 Dortmund
+49 231 818032
dfg-vk_bildungswerk_nrw@t-online.de
www.dfg-vk.de/bildungswerk-nrw

Internationale Gesellschaft fur
Menschenrechte / International Society
for Human Rights
Borsigallee 9
60388 Frankfurt/Main
+49 69 420 1080
info@ishr.org
www.ishr.org

United Nations Volunteers
Postfach 260111
53153 Bonn
+49 228 815 2000
hq@unv.org
www.unv.org

World Future Council Foundation
Mexikoring 29
22297 Hamburg
+49 40 3070 9140
info@worldfuturecouncil.org
www.worldfuturecouncil.org

World Peace Festival
Habichtweg 39
51429 Bergisch Gladbach
+49 2204 739424
www.worldpeacefestival.org

Ghana

West Africa Network for Peacebuilding
P.O. Box CT 4434
Cantonment-Accra

+233 21 775975
wanep@wanep.org
www.wanep.org

Greece

World Peace Council / Consejo
Mondial de la Paz
Othonos St 10
10557 Athinai
+30 210 3316 326
wpc@otenet.gr
www.wpc-in.org

Hong Kong

Asian Human Rights Commission
19/F, Go-Up Commercial Bldg
998 Canton Road
Mongkok
Kowloon
+852 2698 6339
ahrc@ahrc.asia
www.ahrchk.net

Hungary

World Federation of Democratic Youth
Frangepan utca 16
1139 Budapest
+36 1 350 2202
wfdy@wfdy.org
www.wfdy.org

India

Anuvrat Global Organisation
(ANUVIBHA)
Opp. Gaurav Tower
Malviya Nagar
Jaipur-302017 Rajasthan
+91 141 2722412
www.anuvibha.in

Indian Campaign for Nuclear
Disarmament
62 Bepin Behari Ganguly St.
1st Floor
Calcutta 700 012
West Bengal
+91 33 466 5659

Institute of Peace and Conflict Studies
B-7/3 Lower Ground Floor
Safdarjung Enclave
New Delhi 110029
+91 11 4100 1900
officemail@ipcs.org
www.ipcs.org

Nonviolent Peaceforce – Regional
Office for Asia
c/o Rajiv Vora
RW-20, Malibu Town
Sohna Road
Gurgaon 122018, Haryana
rvora@nonviolentpeaceforce.org
www.nonviolentpeaceforce.org

South Asia Peace Alliance
2/3A, Block A
Jangpura
New Delhi 110014
secretariat.sapa@gmail.com
www.southasiapeacealliance.org

Republic of Ireland

AFRI, Action from Ireland
134 Phibsborough Road
Dublin 7
+353 (0)1 882 7563/7581
admin@afri.ie
www.afri.ie

Concern Worldwide
52–55 Lower Camden Street
Dublin 2
+353 1 417 7700
www.concern.net

Front Line
International Foundation for the
Protection of Human Rights Defenders
81 Main Street
Blackrock
Co Dublin
+353 1 212 3750
info@frontlinedefenders.org
www.frontlinedefenders.org

Italy

Associazione per la Pace – Italian Peace
Association
Ufficio Nazionale
Via India 1
00196 Roma
+39 338 1357097
reforgassopace@gmail.com
www.assopace.org

Lama Gangchen World Peace
Foundation
Via Marco Polo 13
20124 Milano
+39 02 2901 0263
www.lgpt.net

Japan

Global Article 9 Campaign
c/o Peace Boat
3-14-3-2F Takadanobaba
Shinjuku-ku
Tokyo 169-0075
+81 3 3363 7561
article-9@peaceboat.gr.jp
www.article-9.org

International Association for Religious
Freedom
c/o Konko Church of Izuo
3-8-21 Sangenya-Nishi
Taisho-ku
Osaka 551-0001
+81 6 7503 5602
www.iarf.net

Japan Congress Against A- and
H-Bombs (GENSUIKIN)
5F Sohyo-kaikan
Kanda-Surugadai Chiyoda-ku
Tokyo 101-0062
+81 3 5289 8224
gensuikin@igc.apc.org
www.gensuikin.org

Mayors for Peace
c/o Hiroshima Peace Culture Foundation
1–5 Nakajima-cho
Naka-ku

Hiroshima 730-0811
+81 82 242 7821
mayorcon@pcf.city.hiroshima.jp
www.mayorsforpeace.org

Peace Boat
B1 - 3-13-1 - Takadanobaba
Shinjuku-ku
Tokyo 169-0075
+81 3 3363 8047
pbglobal@peaceboat.gr.jp
www.peaceboat.org

Kenya

Africa Peace Forum
P.O. Box 76621
Nairobi
+254 2 387 4092
apfo@amaniafrika.org
www.amaniafrika.org

Coalition for Peace in Africa
Coalition pour la Paix en Afrique
P.O. Box 13265
City Square GPO
00200 Nairobi
+254 20 273 6565
copa@copafrica.org
www.copafrica.org

Religions for Peace – Africa Office
P.O. Box 76398
00508 Nairobi
+254 20 386 2233
admin@wcrpafrica.org
www.wcrp.org

UNIFEM Regional Peace Project
c/o UNDP
P.O. Box 30218
Nairobi
+254 2 228776

United Nations Environment
Programme
P.O. Box 30552
00100 Nairobi
+254 20 762 1234
unepinfo@unep.org
www.unep.org

Liberia

Religions for Peace – West Africa
15th Street Sinkor
1000 Monrovia 10
+231 6 523789
lewisnyankoon@yahoo.com
www.wcrp.org

Malaysia

Third World Network
131 Jalan Macalister
10400 Penang
+60 4 226 6728
twnet@po.jaring.my
www.twnside.org.sg

Netherlands

Action for Solidarity, Equality,
Environment and Diversity – Europe
Plantage Doklaan 12a
1018 CM Amsterdam
+31 20 668 2236
info@aseed.net
www.aseed.net

Coalition for the International Criminal
Court – ICC Office
Bezuidenhoutseweg 99a
2594 AC Den Haag
+31 70 311 1080
cicc-hague@coalitionfortheicc.org
www.iccnow.org

Corporate Europe Observatory
De Wittenstr 25
1052 AK Amsterdam
+31 20 612 7023
ceo@corporateeurope.org
www.corporateeurope.org

European Network Against Arms
Trade
Anna Spenglerstr 71
1054 NH Amsterdam
+31 20 616 4684
info@stopwapenhandel.org
www.enaat.org

European Youth For Action
Minahassastr 1
1094 RS Amsterdam
+31 20 665 7743
eyfa@eyfa.org
www.eyfa.org

Global Anti-Nuclear Alliance
c/o Ak Malten
Fangmanweg 66
6862 EK Oosterbeek
+31 26 785 1473
www.cornnet.nl/~akmalten/gana1.html

Global Partnership for the Prevention
of Armed Conflict
c/o European Centre for
Conflict Prevention
Laan van Meerdervoort 70
2517 AN Den Haag
+31 70 311 0970
info@conflict-prevention.net
www.gppac.org

Greenpeace International
Ottho Heldringstraat 5
1066 AZ Amsterdam
The Netherlands
+31 20 718 2000
supporter.services.int@greenpeace.org
www.greenpeace.org

International Court of Justice
Peace Palace
Carnegieplein 2
2517 KJ The Hague
+31 0 70 302 23 23
www.icj-cij.org

International Criminal Court
P.O. Box 19519
2500 CM, The Hague
+31 0 70 515 8515
visits@icc-cpi.int
www.icc-cpi.int

International Network for the
Abolition of Foreign Military Bases
De Wittenstr 25
1052 AK Amsterdam

+31 20 662 6608
secretariat@no-bases.net
www.no-bases.org

International Network of Museums for
Peace
Laan van Meerdervoort 70
2517 AN Den Haag
+31 70 345 0202
secretariat@musuemsforpeace.org
www.museumsforpeace.org

Organisation for the Prohibition of
Chemical Weapons
Johan de Wittlaan 32
2517 JR Den Haag
+31 70 416 3300
mediabr@opcw.org
www.opcw.org

Transnational Institute
P.O. Box 14656
1001 LD Amsterdam
+31 20 662 6608
tni@tni.org
www.tni.org

United for Intercultural Action
Postbus 413
1000 AK Amsterdam
+31 20 683 4778
info@unitedagainstracism.org
www.unitedagainstracism.org

United Network of Young
Peacebuilders
Laan van Meerdenvoort 70
2517 AN Den Haag
+31 70 364 7799
info@unoy.org
www.unoy.org

World Federalist Movement – Institute
for Global Policy
Bezuidenhoutseweg 99A
2594 AC Den Haag
+31 70 363 4484
www.wfm-igp.org

New Zealand

International Peace Research
Association
c/o Kevin Clements, National Centre
for Peace and Conflict Studies
University of Otago, P.O. Box 56
Dunedin 9054
+64 3 479 9468
kevin.clements@otago.ac.nz
soc.kuleuven.be/iieb/ipraweb

Parliamentarians for Nuclear Non-
proliferation and Disarmament
P.O. Box 24-429
Manners Street
Wellington
+64 4 496 9629
pnnd@gsinstitute.org
www.gsinstitute.org/pnnd

Norway

Association of Human Rights Institutes
c/o Norwegian Centre for Human
Rights
P.O. Box 6706
St Olavs Plass
0130 Oslo
+47 2284 2001
www.humanrights.uio.no

International Peace Research Institute,
Oslo / Institutt for Fredsforskning
P.O. Box 9229
Gronland
0134 Oslo
+47 2254 7700
info@prio.no
www.prio.no

Portugal

European Centre for Global Interdependence and Solidarity – North-South
Centre
Av da Republica 15 - 4o
1050-185 Lisboa
+351 21 358 4030
nscinfo@coe.int
www.nscentre.org

Youth for Exchange and Understanding
Jardim da Alameda
P.O. Box 953
8001-911 Faro
+351 289 813061
sg@yeu-international.org
yeu-international.org

Puerto Rico

Alliance for a New Humanity
P.O. Box 10093
San Juan
Puerto Rico 00908
Info@anhglobal.org
www.anhglobal.org

Romania

Global Alliance for Ministries and
Departments of Peace
c/o PATRIR
Op 1 - CP 331
400110 Cluj-Napoca
+40 264 420298
corina.simon@patrir.ro
www.mfp-dop.org

Russia

International Crisis Group – Moscow
Office
Ul Belomorskaya 14-1
Entrance 7 – 1st Floor
125195 Moskva
+7 495 455 9897

Mezhdunarodnaya Assotsiatsiya
Fondov Mira / International Peace
Foundations' Association
Ul Prechistenka 10
119889 Moskva
+7 495 202 4236

Nonviolence International – CIS /
Mezhdunarodnoye Nyenasiliye
Samarkandskiy Bulvar 15 – korp 5 - kv
30
109507 Moskva
+7 495 291 1142
ninis@online.ru
www.policy.hu/kamenshikov/ninis

Senegal

School of Peace and Service
International Sufi School
Villa 111A
Sacre Coeur 3
Dakar
+221 33867 1435
sarsara@sentoo.sn
www.international-sufi-school.org

Slovenia

International Association of Peace
Messenger Cities
c/o Municipality of Slovenj Gradec
Solska ul 5
2380 Slovenj Gradec

South Africa

Institute for Security Studies / Institut
d'Etudes de Securite
P.O. Box 1787
Brooklyn Square
Tshwane (Pretoria) 0075
+27 12 346 9500
iss@issafrica.org
www.iss.co.za

Spain

Carta de la Paz / Letter of Peace
C/Modolell 41
08021 Barcelona
+34 93 414 5936
secretaria@cartadelapaz.org
www.letterofpeace.org

Fundació per la Pau
c/ Casp, 31
2n 1a A
08010 Barcelona
+34 93 302 51 29
info@fundacioperlapau.org
www.fundacioperlapau.org

Fundación Cultura de Paz
Calle Velázquez n.14, 3° dcha
28001 Madrid, Spain
+34 91 426 15 55
info@fund-culturadepaz.org
www.fund-culturadepaz.org

Peace Brigades International –
Guatemala Project
Romero 9
28720 Bustarviejo
Madrid
+34 91 848 2496
pbiguate@pangea.org
www.pbi-guatemala.org

Peace Brigades International – Mexico
Project
C/ Aribau 15-7-1a
08011 Barcelona
+34 93 451 1740
pbimep@skynet.be

Sri Lanka

WICPER
5/1, Roland Tower
Colombo 3
+94 11 2500229
info@wicper.org
www.wicper.org

Sweden

Dag Hammarskjöld Foundation
Övre Slottsgatan 2
SE-753 10 Uppsala
+46 18 410 10 00
secretariat@dhf.uu.se
www.dhf.uu.se

Parliamentary Forum on Small Arms
and Light Weapons
Box 612
10132 Stockholm
+46 8 653 2543
dybeck@parlforum.org
www.parlforum.org

Reconciliation Resource Network
c/o International IDEA
Stromsborg
10334 Stockholm
+46 8 698 3700
info@idea.int
www.idea.int/rrn

Stockholm International Peace
Research Institute
Signalistgatan 9
16970 Solna
+46 8 655 9700
sipri@sipri.org
www.sipri.org

Swedish Peace Council; Sveriges
Fredsrad
Fjällgatan 23 A
S-116 28 Stockholm
www.frednu.se

Switzerland

Association Mondiale pour l'Ecole
Instrument de Paix
5 rue du Simplon
1207 Geneve
+41 22 735 2422
eip-ge@vtxnet.ch
www.portail-eip.org

Commission of the Churches on
International Affairs
World Council of Churches
BP 2100
1211 Geneve 2
+41 22 791 6213
ccia@wcc-coe.org
www.oikoumene.org

Defence for Children International
CP 88
1211 Geneve 20
+41 22 734 0558
info@dci-is.org
www.defenceforchildren.org

Green Cross International
Rte de Florissant 160a
1231 Conches-Geneve
+41 22 789 1662
gcinternational@gci.ch
www.greencrossinternational.net

International Campaign to Ban
Landmines
9 rue de Cornavin

1201 Geneve
+41 22 920 0325
icbl@icbl.org
www.icbl.org

International Council of Voluntary
Agencies / Conseil International des
Agences Benevoles
26–28 ave Giuseppe Motta
1202 Geneve
+41 22 950 9600
seretariat@icva.ch
www.icva.ch

International Federation of Red Cross
and Red Crescent Societies
17 Chemin des Cretes
Petit-Saconnex
1211 Geneve 19
+41 22 730 4222
secretariat@ifrc.org
www.ifrc.org

International Olympic Truce
Foundation
c/o International Olympic Committee
Chateau de Vidy
1007 Lausanne
+41 21 621 6111
www.olympictruce.org

International Peace Bureau
Rue de Zurich 41
1201 Geneve
+41 22 731 6429
mailbox@ipb.org
www.ipb.org

NGO Committee for Disarmament –
Geneva
c/o IPB
Rue de Zurich 41
1201 Geneve
+41 22 731 6429
mailbox@ipb.org
www.ipb.org

Quaker UN Office – Geneva
13 Av du Mervelet
1209 Geneve
+41 22 748 4800
quno@quno.ch
www.quno.org

Servas International
Ceresstr 23
8008 Zurich
helpdesk@servas.org
www.servas.org

Service International pour les Droits de
l'Homme
International Service for Human Rights
CP 16
1211 Geneve 20
+41 22 733 5123

TRANSCEND: A Peace, Development
and Environment Network
c/o Dietrich Fischer
Magnolienpark 18
4052 Basel
+41 61 556 2369
fischer@transcend.org
www.transcend.org

UN Non-Governmental Liaison Service
(Geneva Office)
Palais des Nations
1211 Geneve 10
+41 22 917 2076
ngls@unctad.org
www.ngls.org

UNHCR Library & Visitors' Centre
P.O. Box 2500
1211 Geneve 2
+41 22 739 8488
library@unhcr.ch

United Nations – Office of the High
Commissioner for Human Rights
Palais des Nations
1211 Geneve 10
+41 22 917 1234
webadmin.hchr@unog.ch

United Nations High Commissioner for
Refugees
CP 2500
1211 Geneve 2
+41 22 739 8111
www.unhcr.org

United Nations Institute for
Disarmament Research
Palais des Nations
1211 Geneve 10
+41 22 917 3186
unidir@unog.ch
www.unidir.org

We the Peoples of the United Nations –
Global Registry
La Capucine
La Frasse
1660 Chateau-d'Oex
+41 26 924 6440

Women's International League for
Peace and Freedom
CP 28, 1 rue de Varembe
1211 Geneve 20
+41 22 919 7080
inforequest@wilpf.ch
www.wilpfinternational.org

World Council of Churches
P.O. Box 2100
150 route de Ferney
1211 Geneve 2
+41 22 791 6111
infowcc@wcc-coe.org
www.wcc-coe.org

World Economic Forum
World Economic Forum Switzerland
91–93 route de la Capite
CH-1223 Cologny/Geneva
+41 22 869 1212
contact@weforum.org
www.weforum.org

World Federation of United Nations
Associations / Federation Mondiale des
Associations pour les NU
c/o Palais des Nations – Room E4-2A

1211 Geneve 10
+41 22 917 3239
wfuna@unog.ch
www.wfuna.org

World Health Organisation
20 Av Appia
1211 Geneve 27
+41 22 791 2111
info@who.int
www.who.int

WWF International
Ave du Mont Blanc
1196 Gland
+41 22 364 9111
www.panda.org

Thailand

International Network of Engaged
Buddhists
666 Charoen Nakorn Road
Klong San
Bangkok 10600
+66 2860 2194
ineboffice@yahoo.com
www.inebnetwork.org

USA

American Friends Service Committee
1501 Cherry St.
Philadelphia, PA 19102
+1 215 241 7000
afsc.org

Arms Control Association
1313 L Street
NW, Suite 130
Washington, DC 20005
+1 202 463 8270
aca@armscontrol.org
www.armscontrol.org

Association of World Citizens
55 New Montgomery St – Suite 224
San Francisco
CA 94105
+1 415 541 9610
info@worldcitizens.org
www.worldcitizens.org

Carnegie Endowment for International
Peace
1779 Massachusetts Ave NW
Washington
DC 20036-2103
+1 202 483 7600
info@CarnegieEndowment.org
www.carnegieendowment.org

Center for Global Nonkilling
P.O. Box 12232
Honolulu
HI 96828
+1 808 551 4514
info@nonkilling.org
www.nonkilling.org

Clinton Global Initiative
1301 Avenue of the Americas
37th Floor
New York
NY 10019-6022
+1 212 397 2255
info@clintonglobalinitiative.org
www.clintonglobalinitiative.org

Coalition for the International Criminal
Court – UN Office
c/o WFM
708 Third Ave – 24th Floor
New York
NY 10017
+1 212 687 2863
cicc@coalitionfortheicc.org
www.iccnow.org

Coexistence International
Brandeis University – Mailstop 086
Waltham
MA 02545
+1 781 736 5017
coexistenceintl@brandeis.edu
www.coexistence.net

Culture of Peace Initiative –
International Secretariat
c/o Pathways to Peace
P.O. Box 1057
Larkspur
CA 94977

+1 415 461 0500
info@pathwaystopeace.org
www.cultureofpeace.org

EarthAction International
P.O. Box 63
Amherst
MA 01004
+1 413 549 8118
contact@earthaction.org
www.earthaction.org

Earthwatch Institute
3 Clock Tower Place – Suite 100
Box 75
Maynard
MA 01754
+1 978 461 0081
info@earthwatch.org
www.earthwatch.org

Global Action to Prevent War and
Armed Conflict
866 UN Plaza – Suite 4050
New York
NY 10017
+1 212 818 1815
coordinator@globalactionpw.org
www.globalactionpw.org

Global Campaign for Climate Action
700 46th St South
Birmingham
AL 35222
+1 514 287 9704
kate.karam@tcktcktck.org
gc-ca.org

Global Network Against Weapons and
Nuclear Power in Space
P.O. Box 652
Brunswick
ME 04011
+1 207 443 9502
globalnet@mindspring.com
www.space4peace.org

Global Security Institute
Middle Powers Initiative
866 UN Plaza

Suite 4050
New York
NY 10017
1 646 289 5170
mpi-ny@gsinstitute.org
www.gsinstitute.org

Human Rights Watch
Empire State Building – 34th Floor
350 5th Ave
New York
NY 10118-3299
+1 212 290 4700
newyork@hrw.org
www.hrw.org

IALANA
UN Office (Lawyers Committee on
Nuclear Policy)
866 UN Plaza, Suite 4050
New York
NY 10017-1936
+1 212 818 1861
johnburroughs@lcnp.org
ialana.net

International Association of Educators
for World Peace
P.O. Box 3282, Mastin Lake Station
Huntsville
AL 35810
+1 256 534 5501
mercieca@knology.net
www.iaewp.org

International Campaign to End Genocide
c/o Genocide Watch
P.O. Box 809
Washington
DC 20044
+1 703 448 0222
genocidewatch@aol.com
www.genocidewatch.org

International Committee for the Peace
Council
c/o Joseph Elder
1112 Grant Street
Madison
WI 53711
www.peacecouncil.org

International Crisis Group –
Washington Office
1629 K St NW – Suite 450
Washington
DC 20006
+1 202 785 1601

International Forum on Globalisation
1009 General Kennedy Ave – No 2
San Francisco
CA 94129
+1 415 561 7650
ifg@ifg.org
www.ifg.org

International Institute on Peace
Education
c/o Peace Education Center, Box 171
Teachers College, Columbia
University, 525 West 120th Street
New York
NY 10027
+1 212 678 8116

International Monetary Fund
700 19th Street N.W.
Washington
D.C. 20431
+ 1 202 623 7000
publicaffairs@imf.org
www.imf.org

International Nonviolent Initiatives
P.O. Box 540515
Waltham
MA 02454
+1 781 891 0814
monsky@brandeis.edu

International Peace Institute
777 United Nations Plaza
New York
NY 10017-3521
+1 212 687 4300
ipi@ipinst.org
www.ipacademy.org

International Philosophers for Peace
313 7th Ave
Radford
VA 24141
+1 540 639 2320

International Physicians for the
Prevention of Nuclear War
727 Massachusetts Ave
Cambridge
MA 02145
+1 617 868 5050
ippnwbos@ippnw.org
www.ippnw.org

Lawyers Without Borders
750 Main Street
Hartford
CT 06103
+1 860 541 2288
www.lawyerswithoutborders.org

Middle Powers Initiative
866 United Nations Plaza – Suite 4050
New York
NY 10017
+1 646 289 5170
mpi-ny@gsinstitute.org
www.middlepowers.org

Muslim Peace Fellowship / Ansar
as-Salam
P.O. Box 271
Nyack
NY 10960
+1 845 358 4601
mpf@forusa.org
www.mpfweb.org

NGO Committee on Disarmament,
Peace and Security
777 United Nations Plaza – Suite 3B
New York
NY 10017
+1 212 687 5340
ngocdps@ngocdps.org
disarm.igc.org

New York Metropolitan Martin Luther
King, Jr. Center for Nonviolence
576 East 165th Street
Bronx
NY 10456
+1 718 589 7858, ext 8
info@nymlkcenterfornonviolence.org
www.nymlkcenterfornonviolence.org

Nonviolence International
4000 Albermarle St – Suite 401
Washington
DC 20016
+1 202 244 0951
info@nonviolenceinternational.net
nonviolenceinternational.net

Nonviolent Peaceforce USA Office
425 Oak Grove Street
Minneapolis
MN 55403
+1 612 871 0005
information@nonviolentpeaceforce.org
www.nonviolentpeaceforce.org

Nuclear Age Peace Foundation
1187 Coast Village Road
Suite 1, PMB 121
Santa Barbara
CA 93108-2794
+ 1 805 965 3443
www.wagingpeace.org

Nuclear Threat Initiative
1747 Pennsylvania Ave NW – 7th Floor
Washington
DC 20006
+1 202 296 4810
contact@nti.org
www.nti.org

Parliamentarians for Global Action
211 E 43rd St – Suite 1604
New York
NY 10017
+1 212 687 7755
ParlGlobal@aol.com
www.PGAction.org

Parliamentarians for Nuclear Non-
proliferation and Disarmament – New
York Office
c/o Middle Powers Initiative
866 UN Plaza – Suite 4050
New York
NY 10017
+1 646 289 5170
mpi-ny@gsinstitute.org
www.gsinstitute.org/pnnd

Peace Movements Commission of
the International Peace Research
Association
c/o Carolyn Stephenson
Political Science Department
University of Hawaii
Honolulu
HI 96822-2281
+1 808 956 8195
cstephen@hawaii.edu

Peace Review
Peace & Justice Studies
University of San Francisco
2130 Fulton Street
San Francisco
CA 94117-1080
+1 415 422 2910
peacereview@usfca.edu
usf.usfca.edu/peacereview

Plowshares Network
c/o Jonah House
1301 Moreland Av
Baltimore
MD 21216
+1 410 233 6238
disarmnow@jonahhouse.org
www.jonahhouse.org

Quaker UN Office – New York
777 UN Plaza
New York
NY 10017
+1 212 682 2745
qunony@afsc.org
www.quno.org/newyork

Rainforest Action Network
221 Pine St – 5th Floor
San Francisco
CA 94104
+1 415 398 4404
answers@ran.org
www.ran.org

Reaching Critical Will
c/o WILPF UN Office
777 UN Plaza – 6th Floor
New York

NY 10017
+1 212 682 1265
info@reachingcriticalwill.org
www.reachingcriticalwill.org

Search for Common Ground –
Washington DC Office
1601 Conecticut Ave NW – Suite 200
Washington
DC 20009
+1 202 265 4300
search@sfcg.org
www.sfcg.org

Servicio Internacional Para la Paz /
International Service for Peace
P.O. Box 3584
Chico
CA 95927-3584
+1 530 892 0662
lpalmer@sipaz.org
sipaz.org

The Gandhi Worldwide Education
Institute
418 Lake Shore Blvd.
Wauconda
IL 60084-1522
questions@gandhiforchildren.org
www.gandhiforchildren.org

The World Bank Group
The World Bank
1818 H Street NW
Washington
DC 20433
+1 202 473 1000
www.worldbank.org

UN International Day of Peace – NGO
Committee
P.O. Box 340
Roosevelt
NJ 08555-0340
+1 609 462 9248
PforPeace@aol.com
www.InternationalDayOfPeace.org

UN Non-Governmental Liaison Service
(New York Office)
Room DC1-1106
United Nations
New York
NY 10017
+1 212-963 3125
ngls@un.org
www.un-ngls.org

UNICEF
3 United Nations Plaza
New York
NY 10017
+1 212 326 7000
aaltamirano@unicef.org
www.unicef.org

United Nations
UN Headquarters Building
New York
NY 10017
+1 212 963 1234

United Nations Department for
Disarmament Affairs
UN Headquarters Bldg (Rm DN25-12)
New York
NY 10017
+1 212 963 1570
www.un.org/disarmament

United Religions Initiative
P.O. Box 29242
San Francisco
CA 94129-0242
+1 415 561 2300
office@uri.org
www.uri.org

Universal Peace Federation
155 White Plains Road – Suite 222
Tarrytown
NY 10591
+1 914 631 1331
info@upf.org
upf.org

World Conference of Religions for
Peace
777 United Nations Plaza – 9th floor
New York
NY 10017
+1 212 687 2163
info@wcrp.org
www.wcrp.org

World Constitution and Parliament
Association
c/o Glen Martin
313 Seventh Ave
Radford
VA 24141
govt_rules@yahoo.com
www.wcpa.biz

World Federalist Movement
708 3rd Ave – 24th Floor
New York
NY 10017
+1 212 599 1320
pace@wfm-igp.org
www.wfm-igp.org

Notes

N.B. – URLs last accessed July 2011.

INTRODUCTION

1. www.federalreserve.gov/newsevents/speech/bernanke20100924a.htm
2. Verjee, Aly, 2011, 'A friendly little dictatorship in the Horn of Africa', *Foreign Policy,* 8 April, available here: www.foreignpolicy.com/articles/2011/04/08/a_friendly_little_dictatorship_in_the_horn_of_africa?page=0,0
3. MacAskill, Ewen and Branigan, Tania, 2011, 'Barack Obama risks China's ire with human rights remarks', *Guardian,* 19 January, available here: www.guardian.co.uk/world/2011/jan/19/barack-obama-china-human-rights
4. Kaplan, Fred, 2005, 'The idealist in the Bluebonnets', *Slate*, 26 April, available here: www.slate.com/id/2117517/
5. Unnamed reporter, 2009, 'Britain's lonely high-flier', *The Economist*, 8 January, available here: www.economist.com/node/12887368
6. Kosich, Dorothy, 2011, '"Booming" silver prices generate astounding demand – World Silver Survey', MineWeb, 7 April, available here: www.mineweb.com/mineweb/view/mineweb/en/page32?oid=124608&sn=Detail
7. 'Rolls-Royce facility of the future for Trent engines will be "Double First" for Singapore and Asia' www.rolls-royce.com/civil/news/2008/rr_facility_ofthefuture.jsp

CHAPTER 1

1. Morrison, Wayne M. and Labonte, Marc, 2009, 'China's holdings of U.S. securities: Implications for the U.S. economy', *CRS Report for Congress,* Congressional Research Service, 30 July, available here: www.fas.org/sgp/crs/row/RL34314.pdf
2. Schifferes, Steve, 2006, 'China's trillion dollar surplus', BBC News, 2 November, available here: http://news.bbc.co.uk/1/hi/business/6106280.stm
3. Kang Juan and Liang Chen, 2009, 'Fear swells over China's holding of US debt', *Global Times,* 8 May, available here: http://opinion.globaltimes.cn/Observer/2009-05/429718.html
4. www.census.gov/foreign-trade/balance/c5700.html#2009
5. R.A., 2010, 'A Chinese trade deficit', *The Economist,* 12 April, available here: www.economist.com/blogs/freeexchange/2010/04/china
6. Lui, Patricia, 2011, 'Yuan appreciation to slow in 2011, top forecasters predict: China credit', Bloomberg, 4 January, available here: www.bloomberg.com/news/2011-01-03/yuan-gain-to-slow-in-2011-top-forecasters-say.html
7. Wheatley, Alan, 2010, 'Case for yuan appreciation strong but not iron-clad', Reuters, 22 March, available here: www.reuters.com/article/2010/03/22/us-china-usa-yuan-lessons-analysis-sb-idUSTRE62L15F20100322

8. Cannato, Vincent J., 2011, 'The "Military-Industrial Complex" at 50', *National Review*, 17 January, available here: www.nationalreview.com/articles/257276/military-industrial-complex-50-vincent-j-cannato?page=2
9. Greenberg, David, 2011, 'Beware the military-industrial complex', *Slate*, 14 January, available here: www.slate.com/id/2281124/pagenum/2
10. Banusiewicz, John D., 2012, 'Lynn: U.S. must preserve its defence industrial base', American Forces Press Service, 12 May, available here: www.defense.gov/news/newsarticle.aspx?id=63913
11. Foster, Peter, 2011, 'Chinese man jailed for illegally exporting US military equipment', *Daily Telegraph*, 27 January, available here: www.telegraph.co.uk/news/worldnews/northamerica/usa/8285325/Chinese-man-jailed-for-illegally-exporting-US-military-equipment.html
12. Bowes, Peter, 2011, 'US engineer sold military secrets to China', BBC, 10 August, available here: www.bbc.co.uk/news/world-asia-pacific-10922531
13. Office of Public Affairs, 2009, 'Retired university professor sentenced to four years in prison for arms export violations involving citizen of China', US Department of Justice, 1 July, available here: www.justice.gov/opa/pr/2009/July/09-nsd-651.html
14. Warrick, Joby and Johnson, Carrie, 2008, 'Chinese spy "slept" in U.S. for 2 decades', *Washington Post*, 3 April, available here: www.washingtonpost.com/wp-dyn/content/article/2008/04/02/AR2008040203952.html
15. US China-Economic and Security Review Commission, 2009, 'Report to Congress', US Congress, November, available here: www.uscc.gov/annual_report/2009/annual_report_full_09.pdf
16. *Ibid.*, p.159.
17. *Ibid.*, p.148.
18. Agencies, 2010, 'US blocks China fibre optics deal over security', *China Daily*, 1 June, available here: www.chinadaily.com.cn/bizchina/2010-07/01/content_10044985.htm
19. Hambling, David, 2009, 'In the military, toxic tungsten is everywhere', *Wired*, 21 April, available here: www.wired.com/dangerroom/2009/04/toxic-tungste-1/
20. Reuters, 2010, 'Chinese miner backs out of US deal', *Financial Times*, 21 December, available here: www.ft.com/cms/s/0/0267d128-eea5-11de-944c-00144feab49a.html#axzz1CWk69OJc
21. Bartz, Diane, Prasad, Sakthi, and Lee, Melanie, 2010, 'US review of Huawei/3Leaf under way', Reuters, 28 January, available here: www.reuters.com/article/2011/01/28/us-huawei-idINTRE70R6K220110128
22. Blustein, Paul, 2005, 'Many oil experts unconcerned over China unocal bid', *Washington Post*, 1 July, available here: www.washingtonpost.com/wp-dyn/content/article/2005/06/30/AR2005063002081.html
23. Milmo, Cahal, 2010, 'Concern as China clamps down on rare earth exports', *Independent*, 2 January, available here: www.independent.co.uk/news/science/concern-as-china-clamps-down-on-rare-earth-exports-1855387.html
24. Tkacik, John Jr, 2008, 'Magnequench: CFIUS and China's thirst for U.S. defence technology', Heritage Foundation, 2 May, available here: www.heritage.org/research/reports/2008/05/magnequench-cfius-and-chinas-thirst-for-us-defense-technology
25. St. Clair, Jeffrey, 2006, 'Outsourcing US missile technology to China', *Counterpunch*, 7–9 April, available here: www.counterpunch.org/stclair04072006.html

26. Robison, Peter and Ratnam, Gopal, 2010, 'Pentagon loses control of bombs to China metal monopoly', Bloomberg, 29 September, available here: www.bloomberg.com/news/2010-09-29/pentagon-losing-control-of-afghanistan-bombs-to-china-s-neodymium-monopoly.html

27. Canadian Security and Intelligence Service, 2003, 'Weapons proliferation and the military-industrial complex of the PRC', Commentary No. 84, 27 August.

28. Giacomo, Carol, 2002, 'Israel second only to Russia in providing arms to China', Reuters, 31 August.

29. Urquhart, Conal, 'US acts over Israeli arms sales to China', *Guardian*, 13 June, available here: www.guardian.co.uk/world/2005/jun/13/usa.israel

30. BBC, 2001, 'China warns Israel over Awacs', BBC, 18 December, available here: http://news.bbc.co.uk/1/hi/world/middle_east/1717800.stm

31. Office of the US Secretary of Defense, 2010, *Military and Security Developments Involving the People's Republic of China 2010*, p.43, available here: www.defense.gov/pubs/pdfs/2010_CMPR_Final.pdf

32. SIPRI, 2009, *SIPRI Yearbook 2009*, Oxford University Press, p.308.

33. Scissors, Derek, 2010, '"Rebalancing" Chinese investment in the U.S.', Heritage Foundation, 13 July, available here: www.heritage.org/research/reports/2010/07/rebalancing-chinese-investment-in-the-us

34. O'Rourke, Ronald, 2010, 'Navy Ford (CVN-78) Class Aircraft Carrier Program: background and issues for Congress', Congressional Research Service, 24 August, available here: www.fas.org/sgp/crs/weapons/RS20643.pdf

35. Unnamed journalist, 2010, 'Documents confirm China's aircraft carrier plans', *Chosun Ilbo*, 17 December, available here: http://english.chosun.com/site/data/html_dir/2010/12/17/2010121700326.html

36. Xinhua, 2011, 'China, U.S. need cooperation to solve trade imbalance', China.ord.cn, 20 January, available here: www.china.org.cn/world/Hu_visit_us2011/2011-01/20/content_21785259.htm

37. *People's Daily*, 2010, 'US high-tech export curbs "cause of deficit"', 16 December, available here: http://english.peopledaily.com.cn/90001/90778/90861/7232491.html

38. Li, Jia, 2011, 'China eyes hi-tech imports', *People's Daily*, 18 March, available here: http://english.peopledaily.com.cn/90001/90778/7324727.html

39. Zhao, Zhihao, 2010, 'Sino–US trade war more about technology than money', *Global Times*, 6 January.

40. Steinbock, Dan, 2010, 'Time to lift Sino–US trade to new level', *China Daily*, 23 December, available here: www.chinadaily.com.cn/opinion/2010-12/23/content_11742742.htm

41. Wang, Yan, 2010, 'Ending restrictions key to Sino–US trade imbalance', *China Daily*, 30 April, available here: www.chinadaily.com.cn/china/2010-04/30/content_9794800.htm

42. *Ibid.*

43. www.census.gov/foreign-trade/Press-Release/current_press_release/exh15.pdf

44. Sahadi, Jeanne, 2009, '$4.8 trillion – interest on U.S. debt', CNN, 20 December, available here: http://money.cnn.com/2009/11/19/news/economy/debt_interest/index.htm

45. People's Daily Online, 2004, 'Official with Taiwan Affairs Office on the bottom line for use of force', *People's Daily*, 15 January, available here: http://english.peopledaily.com.cn/200401/15/eng20040115_132713.shtml

46. www.cfr.org/publication/8454/taiwan_relations_act.html

47. BBC, 2010, 'US says China's military has seen secret expansion', BBC News, 17 August, available here: www.bbc.co.uk/news/world-asia-pacific-10995111
48. Wines, Michael, 2011, 'U.S. Alarmed by harsh tone of China's military', *New York Times,* 11 October, available here: www.nytimes.com/2010/10/12/world/asia/12beijing.html
49. Watts, Jonathan, 2005, 'Rumsfeld warns China over military expansion', *Guardian,* 20 October, available here: www.guardian.co.uk/world/2005/oct/20/china.usa
50. Stewart, Phil, 2011, 'China's military advances challenge U.S. power: Gates', Reuters, 14 January, available here: www.reuters.com/article/2011/01/14/us-china-usa-idUSTRE70D0PQ20110114?pageNumber=2
51. SIPRI, 2009, p.309.

CHAPTER 2

1. http://countrystudies.us/russia/9.htm
2. Gattuso, James and Loris, Nicholas, 2008, 'The Detroit bailout: unsafe at any cost', Heritage Foundation, 16 November, available here: www.heritage.org/research/reports/2008/11/the-detroit-bailout-unsafe-at-any-cost
3. Ingrassia, Paul, 2010, 'Two cheers for the Detroit bailout', *Wall St Journal,* 2 August, available here: http://online.wsj.com/article/SB100014240527487039 99304575399670446387614.html
4. Wald, Matthew L., 2009, 'In Congress, a jump-start for clunkers', *New York Times,* 21 July, available here: www.nytimes.com/2009/08/01/business/01clunkers.html?pagewanted=1
5. World Bank, World Development Indicators.
6. Kyodo, 2010, '$170 billion eyed for Asia projects', *Japan Times,* 5 March, available here: http://search.japantimes.co.jp/cgi-bin/nb20100305a3.html
7. PTI, 2010, 'India's exports may cross $170 bn in 2009–10', *The Hindu,* 4 May, available here: www.thehindu.com/business/Economy/article421435.ece
8. Birchall, Jonathan, 2011, 'Walmart in global online sales expansion', *Financial Times,* 5 January, available here: www.ft.com/cms/s/0/4eb4bac2-18fd-11e0-9c12-00144feab49a.html#axzz1ChxolOeV
9. O'Doherty, John, 2011, 'Defence groups target US military spending', *Financial Times,* 24 January, available here: www.ft.com/cms/s/0/3825e908-27f7-11e0-8abc-00144feab49a.html#axzz1ChxolOeV
10. Peña, Vincent P., 2011, 'Pentagon cuts don't cut it. Want to really save money? Get a new security strategy', *Christian Science Monitor,* 2 November, available here: www.csmonitor.com/Commentary/Opinion/2011/0202/Pentagon-cuts-don-t-cut-it.-Want-to-really-save-money-Get-a-new-security-strategy
11. www.eia.doe.gov/energy_in_brief/foreign_oil_dependence.cfm
12. Hackett, James (ed.), 2010, *The Military Balance 2010*, International Institute for Strategic Studies.
13. Preble, Christopher and Friedman, Benjamin H., 2010, 'A U.S. defence budget worthy of its name', 18 November, available here: www.cato.org/pub_display.php?pub_id=12582
14. Press release, 2010, 'U.S. Government's 2010 financial report shows significant financial management and fiscal challenges', Government Accountability Office, 21 December, available here: www.gao.gov/press/financial_report_2010dec21.html

15. Novak, Lisa M., 2010, 'Military retirement system broken, board says', *Stars & Stripes,* 7 August, available here: www.stripes.com/news/military-retirement-system-broken-board-says-1.113754

16. SIPRI, 2009, 'World Nuclear Forces', *SIPRI Yearbook 2009,* Oxford University Press, p.347.

17. CNN Wire staff, 2011, 'Obama signs documents for new nuclear arms treaty with Russia', CNN, 3 February, available here: http://edition.cnn.com/2011/US/02/02/obama.start/?hpt=Sbin

18. Kaplan, Fred, 2011, 'Do we really need more submarines and aircraft carriers?', *Slate,* 14 February, available here: www.slate.com/id/2285080/

19. USGAO, 2010, , 'Actions needed to identify total costs of weapons complex infrastructure and research and production capabilities', *Report to the Subcommittee on Strategic Forces, Committee on Armed Services, House of Representatives,* June, available here: www.gao.gov/new.items/d10582.pdf

20. News release, 2010, 'DNI releases budget figure for 2010 national intelligence program', Office of the Director of National intelligence, 28 October, available here: www.dni.gov/press_releases/20101028_2010_NIP_release.pdf

21. Military OneSource Center, 2009, 'Report of the 2nd Quadrennial Quality of Life Review', Department of Defense, January, available here: http://cs.mhf.dod.mil/content/dav/mhf/QOL-Library/PDF/MHF/QOL%Resources/Reports/Quadrennial%Quality%of%Life%Review%202009.pdf

22. Foster, Mary, 2011, 'U.S. military purchases Gulf of Mexico seafood, boosting an industry battered by oil spill', *Washington Post,* 7 February, available here: www.washingtonpost.com/wp-dyn/content/article/2011/02/06/AR2011020603981.html

23. Dombey, David, 2009, 'US military supplier accused of prices fraud', *Financial Times,* 16 November, available here: www.ft.com/cms/s/0/3821ca18-d2f7-11de-af63-00144feabdc0.html#axzz1E7QceH92

24. Weiner, Tim, 2004, 'Lockheed and the future of warfare', *New York Times,* 28 November, available here: www.nytimes.com/2004/11/28/business/yourmoney/28lock.html?_r=1

25. Sahadi, Jeanne, 2009, '47 percent will pay no federal income tax', CNN, 3 October, available here: http://money.cnn.com/2009/09/30/pf/taxes/who_pays_taxes/index.htm

26. Maidment, Paul, 2006, 'America's best and worst paying jobs', *Forbes,* 23 May, available here: www.forbes.com/2006/05/20/best-paying-jobs_cx_pm_06work_0523jobs.html

27. CNN Fortune 500, available here: http://money.cnn.com/magazines/fortune/fortune500/2009/performers/industries/profits/

28. Weiner, 'Lockheed and the future of warfare'.

29. Associated Press, 2011, 'Lockheed CEO got $19.1m compensation in 2010', ABC News, 11 March, available here: http://abcnews.go.com/Business/wireStory?id=13118554

30. www.lockheedmartin.com/investor/corporate_governance/PoliticalDisclosures.html

31. www.campaignmoney.com/political/committees/lockheed-martin-employees-political-action-committee.asp?cycle=08

32. www.cma.army.mil/fndocumentviewer.aspx?docid=003676918

33. http://edition.cnn.com/SPECIALS/2001/trade.center/biochem.weapons/

34. www.lockheedmartin.com/aboutus/diversity/chairman.html

35. Johnson, Reuben F., 2010, 'Pork-barrel defence spending, russian-style', *National Review,* 29 April, available here: www.nationalreview.com/articles/229649/pork-barrel-defense-spending-russian-style/reuben-f-johnson

36. This economic argument, first mooted by Frédéric Bastiat in 1850, argues that breaking a window is economically beneficial. A glazier is paid to repair the window, and he spends his earnings on goods and services, thereby encouraging trade and the circulation of capital. The fallacy is that this fails to take into account that had the window not been broken its owner would have spent the money on something else – the opportunity cost.

37. Congressional Budget Justification, FY2011, Foreign Assistance, Summary tables, available here: www.state.gov/documents/organization/138174.pdf

38. Pfeffer, Anshel, 2010, 'Israel to purchase 20 Lockheed Martin F-35 fighter jets', *Haaretz,* 15 August, available here: www.haaretz.com/news/diplomacy-defense/israel-to-purchase-20-lockheed-martin-f-35-fighter-jets-1.308177

39. Gienger, Viola, 2011, 'Three decades with Egypt's military keep U.S. in loop', Bloomberg, 2 February, available here: www.bloomberg.com/news/2011-02-02/three-decades-of-missions-weapons-training-for-egypt-keep-u-s-in-loop.html

40. Article XXIII: Exceptions to the Agreement, www.wto.org/english/docs_e/legal_e/26-gats_01_e.htm

41. Trade Promotion Coordinating Committee, 2009, 'Export Programs Guide', US Department of Commerce,

42. McCormack, Richard, 2008, 'U.S. container exports still dominated by junk – scrap paper, scrap metal and bulk commodities', *Manufacturing & Technology News,* Volume 15, No. 14, 31 July, available here: www.manufacturingnews.com/news/08/0731/PIERS.html

43. Black, Ian, 2011, 'Barack Obama to authorise record $60bn Saudi arms sale', *Guardian*, 13 September, available here: www.guardian.co.uk/world/2010/sep/13/us-saudi-arabia-arms-deal

44. Bridgeman, Maggie, 2010, 'Obama seeks to expand arms exports by trimming approval process', McClatchy, 29 July, available here: www.mcclatchydc.com/2010/07/29/98337/obama-seeks-to-expand-arms-exports.html

45. *Ibid.*, pp.59–60.

46. www.export.gov

47. http://ecfr.gpoaccess.gov/cgi/t/text/text-idx?c=ecfr&sid=ba2d5996d28cc22033ea2bfb857555cc&rgn=div5&view=text&node=15:2.1.3.4.24&idno=15

48. Bureau of Industry and Security, US Department of Commerce, Chapter 3, Regional Stability (Section 742.6), available here: www.bis.doc.gov/policiesandregulations/05forpolcontrols/chap3_regstability.htm

49. http://ecfr.gpoaccess.gov/cgi/t/text/text-idx?c=ecfr&sid=ba2d5996d28cc22033ea2bfb857555cc&rgn=div5&view=text&node=15:2.1.3.4.24&idno=15#15:2.1.3.4.24.0.1.4

50. Baldwin, Tom and Prasad, Raekha, 2006, 'All work and no play makes Bush into a new partner', *The Times,* 1 March, available here: www.timesonline.co.uk/tol/news/world/asia/article736025.ece

51. DawnNews, 2010, 'Pakistan to get four F-16 tomorrow', *Dawn,* 25 June, available here: news.dawn.com/wps/wcm/connect/dawn-content-library/dawn/news/pakistan/16-pakistan+to+get+four+f-16+tomorrow-hs-04

52. Pandit, Rajat, 2010, 'Why does Pakistan need F-16 S to fight Taliban?', *Economic Times,* 17 January, available here: economictimes.indiatimes.com/news/politics/

nation/Why-does-Pakistan-need-F-16-S-to-fight-Taliban/articleshow/5454751.
cms

53. Banda, Sree Ram, 2010, 'Defence ties to dominate Obama's India visit', *International Business Times*, 1 November, available here: www.ibtimes.com/articles/77563/20101101/india-us-president-obama-visit-new-delhi-mumbai-g20-defense-boeing-lockheed-martin.htm

54. NDTV correspondent, 'Obama likely to push India to buy more US military hardware', NDTV Online, 8 November, available here: www.ndtv.com/article/india/obama-likely-to-push-india-to-buy-more-us-military-hardware-64903

55. Bull, Alister and Zengerle, Patricia, 2010, 'Obama wins India business', Reuters, 6 November, available here: www.reuters.com/article/idUSTRE6A24UN20101106

56. Unnamed reporter, 2011, 'India shortlists European firms, rejects US for $11bn jet order', *Economic Times*, 28 April, available here: http://articles.economictimes.indiatimes.com/2011-04-28/news/29482770_1_european-firms-strategic-ties-fighter-jet-contract

57. Dasgupta, Sunil and Cohen, Stephen P., 2011, 'Arms sales for India', *Foreign Policy*, March/April, p.22.

58. Unnamed reporter, 2005, 'Pakistan 'to receive F-16s soon', BBC, 31 July, available here: http://news.bbc.co.uk/1/hi/world/south_asia/4732637.stm

59. Unnamed reporter, 2010, 'US threat on Turkey arms sales', al-Jazeera, 17 August, available here: http://english.aljazeera.net/news/europe/2010/08/201 08164425178581.html

60. Special Correspondent, 2008, 'World Bank's new poverty norms find larger number of poor in India', *The Hindu*, 28 August, available here: www.hindu.com/2008/08/28/stories/2008082856061300.htm

61. BBC, 2010, '"More poor" in India than Africa', BBC News Online, 13 July, available here: www.bbc.co.uk/news/10609407

62. Lynch, Colum, 2005, 'Report finds combat deaths, armed conflicts on the decline', *Washington Post*, 18 October, available here: www.washingtonpost.com/wp-dyn/content/article/2005/10/17/AR2005101701768.html

63. Curtis, Mark, 2011, 'The great game: the reality of Britain's war in Afghanistan', War on Want, February.

64. Mosk, Matthew, 2010, 'Critics slam Obama administration for "hiding" massive Saudi arms deal', ABC News, 19 November, available here: abcnews.go.com/Blotter/critics-slam-obama-administration-hiding-massive-saudi-arms/story?id=12192558

65. Maclean, William, 2010, 'Saudi royal: punish WikiLeaks source "vigorously"', Reuters, 5 December, available here: www.reuters.com/article/idUSTRE6B41VA20101205

66. CNN wire staff, 2010, 'Saudi prince says Yemen is a security threat', CNN, 20 November, available here: edition.cnn.com/2010/WORLD/meast/11/19/saudi.arabia.yemen/index.html?eref=rss_latest&utm_source=feedburner&utm_medium=feed&utm_campaign=Feed:+rss/cnn_latest+(RSS:+Most+Recent)

67. United Nations Development Program, International Human Development Indicators 2010, available here: hdr.undp.org/en/statistics/

68. Shalal-Esa, Andrea, 2011, 'Cloudy outlook for U.S. arm sales to Mideast', Reuters, 2 February.

69. GAO, 2010, 'Persian Gulf: U.S. agencies need to improve licensing data and to document reviews of arms transfers for U.S. foreign policy and national

security goals', Report to Congressional Requesters, 28 September, available here: www.gao.gov/htext/d10918.html

70. Hawley, Susan, 2000, 'Exporting corruption: privatisation, multinationals and bribery', The Corner House, 30 June, available here: www.thecornerhouse.org. uk/resource/exporting-corruption-0#fn049

71. Lemer, Jeremy and Guerrera, Francesco, 2010, 'Third-party agents still used by GE', Financial Times, 29 July.

72. Office of Public Affairs, 2010, 'Twenty-two executives and employees of military and law enforcement products companies charged in foreign bribery scheme', US Department of Justice, 19 January, available here: washingtondc.fbi.gov/ dojpressrel/pressrel10/wfo011910.htm

73. Blitz, James, Gray, Alistair and Jenkins, Patrick, 2011, 'UK Treasury freezes Gaddafi assets of £1bn', Financial Times, 28 February, available here: www.ft.com/cms/s/0/0b31a390-437e-11e0-8f0d-00144feabdc0. html#axzz1KZAOxCCE

74. Baker , Richard and McKenzie, Nick, 2010, 'Sex, bribes in banknote deals', The Age, 24 March, available here: www.theage.com.au/business/sex-bribes-in-banknote-deals-20100523-w3yx.html

75. McKenzie, Nick and Baker, Richard, 2009, 'RBA gets "please explain" from Nigeria', The Age, 14 October, available here: www.theage.com.au/national/ rba-gets-please-explain-20091013-gvnq.html

76. McKenzie, Nick and Baker, Richard, 2010, 'Winnie Mandela enlisted to aid banknote deals', The Age, 6 August, available here: www.smh.com.au/national/ winnie-mandela-enlisted-to-aid-banknote-deals-20100805-11kqy.html

77. www.mintnigeria.com/structure.htm

78. McKenzie, Nick and Baker, Richard, 2009, 'RBA firm investigated over Nigerian deal', The Age, 2 October, available here: www.smh.com.au/business/rba-firm-investigated-over-nigerian-deal-20091001-gepl.html

79. Unnamed reporter, 2011, 'Who, What, Why: Why does the UK give aid to India?', BBC, 1 March, available here: www.bbc.co.uk/news/magazine-12607537

80. Pancevski, Bojan and MacDougall, Dan, 2011, 'Euro billions wasted on African failures', Sunday Times, 17 April.

81. Black, Ian and Chulov, Martin, 2011, 'Bahrain, Libya and Yemen try to crush protests with violence', Guardian, February 2011, available here: www. guardian.co.uk/world/2011/feb/18/bahrain-libya-yemen-protests-violence

CHAPTER 3

1. Jenkins, Sally, 2011, 'After a bloated Super Bowl in Dallas, it's time to rein in big game', Washington Post, 8 February, available here: www.washingtonpost. com/wp-dyn/content/article/2011/02/07/AR2011020705610.html?hpid=artslot

2. Mardell, Mark, 2010, 'How America sees the military: Is it due respect or reverence?', BBC, 28 August, available here: www.bbc.co.uk/blogs/thereporters/ markmardell/2010/08/how_america_sees_the_military.html

3. Sourced from WBIR, 2011, 'Blue Star Family license plates now available', Knoxville Times, 5 February, available here: http://story.knoxvilletimes.com/ index.php/ct/9/cid/a8d1772e8d5c87a8/id/42676175/ht/Update-Blue-Star-Fam-ily-license-plates-now-available/

4. Powers, Rod, 2011, 'The cost of war', US military guide, 1 February, available here: http://usmilitary.about.com/od/terrorism/a/iraqdeath1000.htm

5. Preston, Samuel H. and Buzzell, Emily, 2006, 'Mortality of American troops in Iraq', University of Pennsylvania Population Studies Center, 27 August.

6. News release, 2010, 'National census of fatal occupational injuries in 2009', US Department of Labor, 19 August, available here: www.bls.gov/news.release/pdf/cfoi.pdf

7. Carter, Phillip, 2003, 'Judicial deference to military may affect gay rights, war on terror', CNN, 15 July, available here: http://articles.cnn.com/2003-07-15/justice/findlaw.analysis.carter.security_1_judicial-branch-grant-letters-piracies-and-felonies?_s=PM:LAW

8. Unnamed reporter, 2010, 'Elena Kagan's military recruiting ban irks Republicans', BBC, 29 June, available here: www.bbc.co.uk/news/10456205

9. Montopoli, Brian, 2010, 'Glenn Beck, Sarah Palin to hold "restoring honor rally"', CBS News, 27 July, available here: www.cbsnews.com/8301-503544_162-20011688-503544.html

10. Romano, Lois, 2004, 'Bush's Guard service in question', *Washington Post,* 3 February, available here: www.washingtonpost.com/wp-dyn/articles/A7372-2004Feb2.html

11. Associated Press wire, 2004, '"Swift Boat" backer is major political financier', MSNBC, 27 August, available here: www.msnbc.msn.com/id/5844156/ns/politics/

12. Rove, Karl, 2010, *Courage and Consequence: My Life as a Conservative in the Fight,* Threshold Editions.

13. Transcript, 1971, 'Vietnam War veteran John Kerry's testimony before the Senate Foreign Relations Committee', 22 April.

14. www.youtube.com/watch?v=phqOuEhg9yE

15. News release, 2006, 'FEC collects $630,000 in civil penalties from three 527 organizations', Federal Election Commission, 23 December.

16. Borick, Chris, 2009, 'The Swift Boat ads in comparative context: an empirical examination of advertisement effectiveness', paper presented at the annual meeting of the American Association For Public Opinion Association, Fontainebleau Resort, Miami Beach.

17. Smith, Ben, 2008, 'Is McCain's war record fair game?', CBS News, 30 June, available here: www.cbsnews.com/stories/2008/06/30/politics/politico/main4218172.shtml?source=mostpop_story

18. Borger, Julian, 1999, 'Draft-dodge tale threatens Bush's run for presidency', *Guardian,* 29 September, available here: www.guardian.co.uk/world/1999/sep/29/uselections2000.usa

19. Conason, Joe, 1999, 'Selective service', *Salon,* 13 July, available here: www.salon.com/news/col/cona/1999/07/13/conason/print.html

20. Harnden, Toby, 2008, 'Barack Obama "wanted to join US military"', *Daily Telegraph,* 7 September, available here: www.telegraph.co.uk/news/worldnews/northamerica/usa/barackobama/2700555/Barack-Obama-wanted-to-join-the-US-military.html

21. Siddiqa, Ayesha, 2007, *Military Inc: Inside Pakistan's Military Economy*, Pluto Press, p.135.

22. *Ibid.,* p.127.

23. *Ibid.,* p.147.

24. Drury, Ian, 2011, '£1.3m cost of luxury homes for generals: huge rents for top brass as soldiers live in "slums"', *Daily Mail*, 18 February, available here: www.dailymail.co.uk/news/article-1358101/1-3m-cost-luxury-homes-generals-Huge-rents-brass-soldiers-live-slums.html. Read more: www.dailymail.co.uk/news/article-1358101/1-3m-cost-luxury-homes-generals-Huge-rents-brass-soldiers-live-slums.html#ixzz1EIhIBw8j

25. Newton Dunn, Tony, 2007, 'From Helmand to hellhole', *Sun*, 26 October, available here: www.thesun.co.uk/sol/homepage/news/387976/Army-unit-Return-to-England-Barracks-worse-than-jail.html

26. www.mod.uk/NR/rdonlyres/EAD1EABE-D86D-4EB4-B7A1-582E0F2ADCD0/0/200903002009DIN01058onFTRSreemploymentissues.pdf

27. Pyatt, Jamie, 2004, 'Mucky major a let-down', *Sun*, 12 February, available here: www.thesun.co.uk/sol/homepage/news/article153024.ece

28. *Ibid.*, pp.142–3.

29. Kirkup, James, 2010, 'Armed Forces' education allowance facing cuts' , *Telegraph*, 13 October, available here: www.telegraph.co.uk/news/newstopics/politics/defence/8061854/Armed-Forces-education-allowance-facing-cuts.html

30. *Ibid.*

31. Maddox, David, 2011, 'MoD under fire over inequality in school ranks', *Scotsman*, 9 January, available here: http://scotlandonsunday.scotsman.com/news/MoD-under-fire-over-inequality.6684287.jp

32. www.mod.uk/DefenceInternet/DefenceNews/DefencePolicyAndBusiness/ChangesToContinuityOfEducationAllowanceAnnounced.htm

33. Lampl, Sir Peter, 2007, 'University admissions by individual school', report for the Sutton Trust, 20 September.

34. Parrington, John, 2010, 'Oxbridge must not become the preserve of the wealthy', *Guardian*, 13 February, available here: www.guardian.co.uk/commentisfree/2011/feb/13/oxbridge-fee-increases

35. Rayment, Sean, 2010, 'SAS commander quits Army amid claims defence cuts have hit morale', *Telegraph*, 27 November, available here: www.telegraph.co.uk/news/newstopics/politics/defence/8164888/SAS-commander-quits-Army-amid-claims-defence-cuts-have-hit-morale.html

36. Harding, Thomas, 2008, 'Kit shortages put troops' lives at risk', *Telegraph*, 19 January, available here: www.telegraph.co.uk/news/uknews/1575995/Kit-shortages-put-troops-lives-at-risk.html

37. Kirkup, James, 2009, 'Gen Sir Richard Dannatt: "We need 24 hour surveillance in Afghanistan"', *Telegraph*, 19 August, available here: www.telegraph.co.uk/news/newstopics/politics/defence/6051666/Gen-Sir-Richard-Dannatt-We-need-24-hour-surveillance-in-Afghanistan.html

38. McSmith, Andy, 2009, 'Head of Army Dannatt takes vow of silence as army equipment row rages', Associated Press, 20 July.

39. Murphy, Joe, 2009, 'Ex-army chief Sir Richard Dannatt to be made Tory peer', *Evening Standard*, 7 October, available here: www.thisislondon.co.uk/standard/article-23753645-ex-army-sir-richard-dannatt-chief-falls-in-with-tories.do

40. Shipman, Tim, 2009, 'Dannatt is no "Tory stooge", insists Hague, after general enlists with the Conservatives', *Daily Mail*, 8 October, available here: www.dailymail.co.uk/news/article-1218763/Ex-Army-boss-Dannatt-unveiled-latest-Tory-recruit--just-days-attack-Brown-troop-numbers.html#ixzz1DZJVR4O1

41. Supplementary written evidence from Sir Sherard Cowper-Coles KCMG LVO, 'The UK's foreign policy towards Afghanistan and Pakistan', Foreign Affairs Select Committee, Session 2010–11, available here: www.publications. parliament.uk/pa/cm201011/cmselect/cmfaff/writev/afpak/afpak18.htm

42. Unnamed reporter, 2007, 'Democrats try to stifle calls to "defund" war', *Washington Times*, 14 February, available here: www.washingtontimes.com/ news/2007/feb/14/20070214-103208-7029r/

43. Hastings, Michael, 2011, 'Another runaway general: army deploys psy-ops on U.S. senators', *Rolling Stone*, 23 February, available here: www.rollingstone. com/politics/news/another-runaway-general-army-deploys-psy-ops-on-u-s-senators-20110223

44. Goddard, Peter; Robinson, Peter; and Parry, Katy, 2008, 'Patriotism meets plurality: reporting the 2003 Iraq War in the British press', *Media, War & Conflict*, 1: 9, p. 17, available here: http://mwc.sagepub.com/content/1/1/9. full.pdf

45. Townend, Judith, 2010, 'New survey shows media industry perceived as "cut-throat" and hard to break into', Online Journalism News, 17 July, available here: www.journalism.co.uk/news/new-survey-shows-media-industry-perceived-as--039-cut-throat-039-and-hard-to-break-into/s2/a539215/

46. Busfield, Steve, 2009, 'Alexander Lebedev: bringing the British press together?', *Guardian*, 27 February, available here: www.guardian.co.uk/media/ organgrinder/2009/feb/27/alexander-lebedev-london-evening-standard

47. Neil, Andrew, 2003, 'Fleet Street may be cut-throat but at least it's honest', *Evening Standard*, 14 May.

48. http://ibnlive.in.com/news/full-text-of-manmohan-singhs-speech-at-cms-meet/82035-3.html

49. Sivaswamy, Saisuresh, 2005, 'Advani puts Jinnah first', Rediff, 13 June, available here: www.rediff.com/news/2005/jun/13sai.htm

50. Gupta, Kachan, 2005, 'Advani's Jinnah never existed', *The Pioneer*, 7 June.

51. Staff writer, 2008, 'Advani blames media for Jinnah controversy', *Times of India*, 18 March.

52. Indo-Asian News Service (IANS), 2009, 'Advani went to Pakistan, praised Jinnah: Rahul Gandhi', reproduced in Sify News, 30 April, available here: www.sify.com/news/advani-went-to-pakistan-praised-jinnah-rahul-gandhi-news-national-je4uu0feijc.html

53. Q&A: Jaswant Singh, 2009, 'We needed to make a demon of Jinnah ... Let's learn from our mistakes', *Business Standard*, 17 August, available here: www. business-standard.com/india/news//we-needed-to-makedemonjinnah-let/s-learnour-mistakes//367190/

54. Allen, Nick, 2010, 'WikiLeaks: India "systematically torturing civilians in Kashmir"', *Telegraph*, 17 December, available here: www.telegraph.co.uk/ news/worldnews/wikileaks/8208084/WikiLeaks-India-systematically-torturing-civilians-in-Kashmir.html

55. RSF, 2011, 'Newspaper editor's murderers still at large two years later', Rapporteurs Sans Frontieres, 7 January, available here: http://en.rsf.org/sri-lanka-newspaper-editor-s-murderers-still-07-01-2011,39252.html

56. RSF, 2009, 'Open letter to His Excellency President Mahinda Rajapaksa', Rapporteurs Sans Frontieres, 16 July, available here: http://en.rsf.org/sri-lanka-open-letter-to-his-excellency-16-07-2009,33847.html

57. HRW, 2009, 'Sri Lanka: adopt international inquiry for aid worker killings', Human Rights Watch, 3 August, available here: www.hrw.org/en/news/2009/08/03/sri-lanka-adopt-international-inquiry-aid-worker-killings

58. BBC Online, 2010, 'Wikileaks: Sri Lanka's Rajapaksa blamed for killings', BBC, 2 December, available here: www.bbc.co.uk/news/world-south-asia-11897784

59. Presidential Media Unit, 2009.

60. Chamberlain, Gethin and Tran, Mark, 2009, '"More than 1,000 civilians killed" in attacks on Sri Lanka safe zone', *Guardian,* 3 August, available here: www.guardian.co.uk/world/2009/may/11/sri-lanka-civilian-deaths

61. Ethirajan, Anbarasan, 2009, 'UN images show Sri Lanka damage', BBC, 1 May, available here: http://news.bbc.co.uk/1/hi/world/south_asia/8028863.stm

62. Adler, Ben, 2011, 'Why Journalists Aren't Standing Up for WikiLeaks', *Newsweek,* 4 January, available here: www.newsweek.com/2011/01/04/why-journalists-aren-t-defending-julian-assange.html

CHAPTER 4

1. Martin, Daniel and Shipman, Tim, 2011, 'Hypocrisy goes on: Cameron takes arms dealers with him on Egypt visit to promote democracy', *Daily Mail,* 22 February, available here: www.dailymail.co.uk/news/article-1359316/Prime-Minister-David-Cameron-takes-arms-dealers-Egypt-promote-democracy.html

2. Kirkup, James, 2011, 'David Cameron: Britain has contributed to Middle East instability by backing autocratic regimes', *Telegraph,* 22 February, available here: www.telegraph.co.uk/news/newstopics/politics/david-cameron/8340068/David-Cameron-Britain-has-contributed-to-Middle-East-instability-by-backing-autocratic-regimes.html

3. Martin, Daniel, 2011, 'It is not wrong to sell arms, says David Cameron as he defends sale of weapons to Middle East', *Daily Mail,* 23 February, available here: www.dailymail.co.uk/news/article-1359712/David-Cameron-Its-wrong-sell-arms-Middle-East.html

4. Democracy index 2010, 'Democracy in retreat', Economist Intelligence Unit, available here: http://graphics.eiu.com/PDF/Democracy_Index_2010_web.pdf

5. Kampfner, John, 2011, 'When tyrants want tear gas, the UK has always been happy to oblige', *Guardian,* 20 February, available here: www.guardian.co.uk/commentisfree/2011/feb/20/teargas-for-tyrants

6. Peregin, Christian, 2011, 'Two Libyan fighter pilots defect to Malta', *Times of Malta,* 22 February, available here: www.timesofmalta.com/articles/view/20110222/local/two-libyan-fighter-pilots-defect-to-malta

7. Ganne, Antoine, 2007, 'Kadhafi entame une visite en France contestée par Rama Yade', Afrik.com, 9 December, available here: www.afrik.com/article13112.html

8. With agencies, 2011, 'Libye: Total et Vinci rapatrient leurs salariés', *Le Figaro,* 21 February, available here: http://marches.lefigaro.fr/news/societes.html?&ID_NEWS=179036785

9. Cretz, Ambassador Gene, 2009, 'French total-led consortiums accept lower production shares in Libya', Passed to the *Telegraph* by WikiLeaks, 4 June, available here: www.telegraph.co.uk/news/wikileaks-files/libya-wikileaks/8294570/french-total-led-consortiums-accept-lower-production-shares-in-libya.html

10. Lichtblau, Eric, Rohde, David and Risen, James, 2011, 'Shady dealings helped Qaddafi build fortune and regime', *New York Times*, 24 March, available here: www.nytimes.com/2011/03/24/world/africa/24qaddafi.html?pagewanted=1&_r=1

11. Fuhrmans, Vanessa, 2011, '"Golden Share" an Option for EADS', *Wall Street Journal*, 23 February, available here: http://online.wsj.com/article/SB10001424052748703775704576162080985105642.html

12. Allardyce, Jason, 2009, 'Tony Blair linked to arms trade with Libya', *Sunday Times*, 13 September, available here: www.timesonline.co.uk/tol/news/uk/scotland/article6832402.ece

13. Shipman, Tim, 2011, 'Blair's "dodgy deal" to arm Gaddafi: leaked paper shows how ex-PM agreed to supply military kit', *Daily Mail*, 1 March, available here: www.dailymail.co.uk/news/article-1361638/Libya-Tony-Blairs-dodgy-deal-arm-Gaddafi-leaked-paper-shows.html

14. Castle, Tim, 2011, 'Labour aided Libya over bomber release – report', *Telegraph*, 7 February, available here: http://uk.reuters.com/article/2011/02/07/uk-britain-libya-idUKTRE7163EW20110207

15. Ritter, Karl, 2011, 'Report: ex-minister says Gadhafi ordered Lockerbie', Associated Press, 23 February.

16. Kishtwari, Soraya, 2011, 'Prosecutor reveals how Britain let Gaddafi off', *The Times*, 25 February.

17. The UK's Special Representative for International Trade and Investment, Annual Review for the Financial Year Ending 31 March 2010, available here: www.thedukeofyork.org/DOYResources/PDFs/DOY_Pres_Aug.pdf

18. Fidler, Steven and Peel, Michael, 2007, 'Barter fund used to pay commissions to middlemen', *Financial Times*, 8 June, available here: www.ft.com/cms/s/0/579364ac-155c-11dc-b48a-000b5df10621.html#axzz1Enc7X9z4

19. Office of Public Affairs, 2010, 'BAE Systems PLC Pleads Guilty and Ordered to Pay $400 Million Criminal Fine', US Department of Justice, 1 March, available here: www.justice.gov/opa/pr/2010/March/10-crm-209.html

20. Booth, Jenny and agencies, 2007, 'Blair under pressure over al-Yamamah "bribes"', *The Times*, 7 June, available here: www.timesonline.co.uk/tol/news/uk/article1899076.ece

21. Leigh, David; Brooke, Heather; and Evan, Rob, 2010, 'WikiLeaks cables: "Rude" Prince Andrew shocks US ambassador', *Guardian*, 29 November, available here: www.guardian.co.uk/uk/2010/nov/29/wikileaks-cables-rude-prince-andrew

22. Dominiczak, Peter, 2009, 'Nigella gets new neighbours as squatters move in', *Evening Standard*, 24 November, available here: www.thisislondon.co.uk/standard/article-23774012-nigella-gets-some-new-neighbours-as-squatters-move-in.do

23. Inman, Philip, 2011, 'Mubarak family fortune could reach $70bn, say experts', *Guardian*, 4 February, available here: www.guardian.co.uk/world/2011/feb/04/hosni-mubarak-family-fortune

24. Foggo, Daniel and Swinford, Steven, 2008, 'Prince Andrew, his £15m home and the Kazakhstan connection', *The Times*, 27 July, available here: www.timesonline.co.uk/tol/news/uk/article4407240.ece

25. Hugeux, Vincent, 2010, 'Ali Bongo investit dans la pierre à Paris', *L'Express*, 27 May, available here: www.lexpress.fr/actualite/monde/afrique/ali-bongo-investit-dans-la-pierre-a-paris_895150.html

26. Diop, Boubacar Boris, 2010, 'Why is France still propping up Africa's dictators?', *Foreign Policy*, July/August, available here: www.foreignpolicy. com/articles/2010/06/21/la_vie_en

27. Peterson, Chris, 2011, 'Equatorial Guinea Head's Son Sought Luxury Yacht, Telegraph Says', Bloomberg, 1 March, available here: www.bloomberg.com/ news/2011-03-01/equatorial-guinea-head-s-son-sought-luxury-yacht-telegraph-says.html

28. Minority Staff of the Permanent Subcommittee on Investigations, 2004, 'Money laundering and foreign corruption: enforcement and effectiveness of the patriot act case study involving Riggs Bank', Committee on Governmental Affairs, 15 July.

29. Simonian, Hague, 2011, 'Swiss freeze Ben Ali and Gbagbo assets', *Financial Times*, 19 January, available here: www.ft.com/cms/s/0/a0ff7106-23e7-11e0-8bb1-00144feab49a.html#axzz1FG0EzjCr

30. Croft, Adrian, 2011, 'Britain Freezes Gaddafi Family's UK Assets', Reuters, 28 February, available here: http://uk.reuters.com/article/2011/02/27/uk-libya-britain-hague-idUKTRE71Q0UP20110227

31. Palmer, Brian, 2011, 'What happens to frozen assets?', *Slate*, 1 March, available here: www.slate.com/id/2286929/

32. News wires, 2010, 'Ex-dictator's assets frozen after bid to repatriate funds fails', France24, 3 February, available here: www.france24.com/en/20100203-ex-dictators-assets-frozen-after-bid-repatriate-funds-fails

33. AFP, 2011, 'Sweden freezes over a billion euros in Libyan assets', Zawya, 23 March.

34. Press release from Svenska Freds, 2011, 'Svenskar säljer mest vapen', Svenska Freds, 15 March, available here: www.svenskafreds.se/svenskar-saljer-mest-vapen

35. Hedgpeth, Dana, 2010, 'Daimler agrees to settle Justice Department charges of bribing foreign officials', *Washington Post*, 24 March, available here: www. washingtonpost.com/wp-dyn/content/article/2010/03/23/AR2010032302637. html

36. Tucson, Penelope (ed.), 'The creation of modern Saudi Arabia', India Office Political and Secret Files, c. 1914–39, Asia, Pacific and Africa Collections, British Library.

37. Walters, Simon, 2011, 'Cameron's F-word outburst at reporters over British Empire 'gaffe'', *Daily Mail*, 10 April, available here: www.dailymail.co.uk/ news/article-1375341/David-Camerons-F-word-outburst-reporters-British-Empire-gaffe.html. Read more: www.dailymail.co.uk/news/article-1375341/ David-Camerons-F-word-outburst-reporters-British-Empire-gaffe. html#ixzz1J6NWcEgD

38. Council of Foreign Relations transcript, 2009, 'Remarks by the President to the Ghanaian Parliament', 11 July, available here: www.cfr.org/ghana/remarks-president-ghanaian-parliament/p19789

39. www.qinetiq.com/global/about_us/our_history.html

40. Khalidi, Rashid, 'Peasant resistance to Zionism', included in *Blaming the Victims: Spurious Scholarship and the Palestinian Question*, Said, Edward and Hitchens, Christopher (eds), Verso, 1988, pp.214–15.

41. Abu-Lughod, Ibrahim, 'Territorially-based nationalism and the politics of negation', included in Said and Hitchens, pp.193–94.

42. Unnamed reporter, 2011, 'Yemeni president blames Israeli-U.S. plot amid massive anti-gov't protests', Xinhua, 1 March, available here: http://news. xinhuanet.com/english2010/world/2011-03/01/c_13756077.htm

43. Unnamed reporter, 2011, 'Rescuers find seven emaciated prisoners "buried alive in underground cell in Gaddafi's compound"', *Daily Mail,* 1 March, available here: www.dailymail.co.uk/news/article-1361555/Libya-protests-Rescuers-7-buried-alive-Gaddafis-compound-Benghazi.html#ixzz1FLVmKVnd

44. Unnamed reporter, 2009, 'Gaddafi refloats one-state idea after Gaza war', Reuters, 22 January, available here: http://in.reuters.com/article/2009/01/22/idINIndia-37599020090122

45. Shain, Michael, Kaplan, Don and Sheehy, Kate, 2011, 'CBS reporter's Cairo nightmare', *New York Post,* 16 February, available here: www.nypost.com/p/news/international/cbs_reporter_cairo_nightmare_pXiUVvhwIDdCrb-D95ybD5N

46. ASH/TG/HRF, 2011, 'Nasrallah exposes Israel's Egypt plot', Press TV, 8 February, available here: www.presstv.ir/detail/164239.html

47. Al-Mulhim, Abdulateef, 2011, 'An Israeli conspiracy that never existed', *Arab News,* 7 February, available here: http://arabnews.com/opinion/article253715.ece?comments=all

48. Cohen, Nick, 2011, 'Our absurd obsession with Israel is laid bare', *Guardian,* 27 February, available here: www.guardian.co.uk/commentisfree/2011/feb/27/nick-cohen-arab-middle-east-conflict

49. Gilligan, Andrew, 2010, 'Hizb ut Tahrir is not a gateway to terrorism, claims Whitehall report', *Daily Telegraph,* 25 July, available here: www.telegraph.co.uk/journalists/andrew-gilligan/7908262/Hizb-ut-Tahrir-is-not-a-gateway-to-terrorism-claims-Whitehall-report.html

50. Pipes, Daniel, 2011, 'My optimism on the new Arab revolt', *National Review,* 1 March, available here: www.nationalreview.com/articles/260923/new-arab-revolt-daniel-pipes

51. Mirsky, Georgiy, 2005, 'Syria and the birth of Pan-Arab extremism', Jamestown Foundation, 10 May, available here: www.jamestown.org/single/?no_cache=1&tx_ttnews[tt_news]=370

52. Telegram from the Embassy in Syria to the Department of State, 1958, *Foreign relations of the United States, 1958–1960,* 15 January, p.403, available here: http://digicoll.library.wisc.edu/cgi-bin/FRUS/FRUS-idx?type=turn&entity=FRUS.FRUS195860v13.p0437&id=FRUS.FRUS195860v13&isize=M

53. Haaretz Service, 2010, 'Turkish PM: Israel is the main threat to Mideast peace', *Haaretz,* 7 April, available here: www.haaretz.com/news/turkish-pm-israel-is-the-main-threat-to-mideast-peace-1.901

54. Barber, Tony, 2009, 'Turkey links gas pipeline to EU talks', *Financial Times,* 20 January, available here: www.ft.com/cms/s/0/73787212-e692-11dd-8e4f-0000779fd2ac.html#axzz1FN2TT25C

CHAPTER 5

1. UNCHR, see: www.un.org/News/Press/docs/2008/sgsm11643.doc.htm

2. UNHCR, see: www.unhcr.org/4ce5320a9.html

3. al-Ansary, Khalid, 2011, 'Iraqi religious heads call for Christians' protection', Reuters, 13 January.

4. Stewart, Phil and Birsel, Robert, 2009, 'Analysis – Under Obama, drone attacks on the rise in Pakistan', Reuters, 12 October, available here: www.reuters.com/article/idUSN11520882

5. Mujtaba, Haji, 2010, 'US drone strike kills 20 people in Pakistan', Reuters, 23 August.

6. Gall, Carlotta and Masood, Salman, 2009, 'Civilians flee as Pakistani forces hit resistance', New York Times, 29 April, available here: www.nytimes.com/2009/04/30/world/asia/30pstan.html

7. BBC, 2010, 'Karachi ethnic violence kills 12', BBC Online, 14 January, available here: www.bbc.co.uk/news/world-south-asia-12189055

8. Haider, Zeeshan, 2011, 'Q+A: Pakistan tries to survive another political crisis', Reuters, 5 January, available here: www.reuters.com/article/idUSTRE7041T920110105

9. Walsh, Declan, 2010, 'WikiLeaks cables: Pakistani army chief considered plan to oust president', Guardian, 30 November, available here: www.guardian.co.uk/world/2010/nov/30/wikileaks-cables-pakistani-leadership-wrangle

10. Caracol, 2010, 'Amenazas y agresiones denuncian líderes de mujeres desplazadas', Caracol Radio, 28 January, available here: www.caracol.com.co/nota.aspx?id=945437

11. Wire Staff, 2010, 'Female suicide bombers blamed in Moscow subway attacks', CNN, 29 March, available here: http://articles.cnn.com/2010-03-29/world/russia.subway.explosion_1_suicide-bombers-chechen-rebels-subway-stations?_s=PM:WORLD

12. Staff, 1999, 'Chechens targeted in Moscow and at home', Amnesty International, 22 December, available here: www.amnesty.org.uk/news_details.asp?NewsID=12967

13. BBC, 2007, 'Police evict Tamils from Colombo', BBC Online, 7 June, available here: http://news.bbc.co.uk/1/hi/world/south_asia/6729555.stm

14. IRIN, 2010, 'Bangladesh: Rohingya humanitarian crisis looms', Relief Web, 18 February, available here: www.reliefweb.int/rw/rwb.nsf/db900sid/SHIG-82SBWG?OpenDocument&query=rohingya

15. Biro, Peter, 2010, 'Life on the margins', Slate, 22 December, available here: www.slate.com/id/2278396/

16. Casciani, Dominic, 2004, 'Media linked to asylum violence', BBC News Online, 14 July, available here: http://news.bbc.co.uk/1/hi/uk/3890963.stm

17. Dix, Sarah, 2006, 'Urbanisation and the social protection of refugees in Nairobi', HumanExchange Magazine, Issue 35, Overseas Development Institute, available here: http://www.odihpn.org/report.asp?id=2841

18. Clemens, Michael A and Pettersson, Gunilla, 2008, 'New data on African health professionals abroad', Human Resources for Health, available here: www.human-resources-health.com/content/6/1/1

19. Peel, Quentin, 2005, 'A dynamic Europe needs immigrants', Financial Times, 3 March, available here: www.ft.com/cms/s/0/0db596e0-8b8c-11d9-89e5-00000e2511c8.html#axzz1J3tPbLeq

20. Creamer, Martin, 2010, 'South Africa down to only 500 mining engineers – Gold Fields', Mining Weekly, 2 December, available here: www.miningweekly.com/article/south-africa-down-to-staggeringly-low-500-mining-engineers-gold-fields-2010-12-02

21. Mutume, Gumisai, 2003, 'Reversing Africa's "brain drain"', *Africa Recovery,* July, available here: www.un.org/ecosocdev/geninfo/afrec/vol17no2/172brain. htm

22. 'M.S.', 2010, 'American politics: democracy in America: the political landscape: city v country', *The Economist,* 4 November, available here:www.economist. com/blogs/democracyinamerica/2010/11/political_landscape

23. Leyne, John, 2009, 'Political divide in the Iranian election', BBC, 9 June, available here: http://news.bbc.co.uk/1/hi/world/middle_east/8090577.stm

24. Spratt, Amanda, 2005, '*City versus country*: New Zealand's big political divide', *New Zealand Herald,* 25 September.

25. Higgins, Andante, 2008, 'McCain calls Obama's "bitter" comments "elitist"', CBS News, 14 April, available here: www.cbsnews.com/8301-502443_162-4013565-502443.html

26. Clarke, Natalie, 2009, 'Adultery, a Cameron cutie, the Turnip Taliban and a fight for the very soul of the Tory Party', *Daily Mail,* 4 November, available here: www.dailymail.co.uk/femail/article-1225099/Adultery-Cameron-cutie-Turnip-Taliban-fight-soul-Tory-Party.html

27. Peterson, Scott, 2007, 'Ahmadinejad: rock star in rural Iran', *Christian Science Monitor,* 7 December, available here: www.csmonitor.com/2007/1207/p01s07-wome.html

28. Farmer, Jon, 2010, 'Chávez receives warning shot but time is on his side', *Latin American Weekly Report,* 30 September.

29. Wilson, Scott, 2002, 'Clash of visions pushed Venezuela toward coup', *Washington Post,* 21 April.

30. Walker, Andrew, 2007, 'Beyond the rural betrayal: lessons from the Thaksin era for the Mekong region', Australian National University, paper presented at International Conference on Critical Transitions in the Mekong Region, Chiang Mai Grandview Hotel, 29–31 January.

31. BBC, 2010, 'Profile: Thailand's Reds and Yellows', BBC Online, 20 April, available here: http://news.bbc.co.uk/1/hi/8004306.stm

32. Unnamed reporter, 2006, 'Akbar Bugti's dead body found: ISPR', *Pakistan Tribune,* 1 September, available here: www.paktribune.com/news/index. shtml?152844

33. Mickleburgh, Rod, 2011, 'Former Pakistan ruler Musharraf seeks support for comeback in Canada', *Globe and Mail,* 21 January, available here: www. theglobeandmail.com/news/world/former-pakistan-ruler-musharraf-seeks-support-for-comeback-in-canada/article1878218/

34. Zelaya, Xiomara, 2009, 'My father has been punished for helping Honduras', *New Statesman,* 17 September, available here: www.newstatesman.com/inter-national-politics/2009/09/coup-regime-honduras-father

35. BBC, 2010, 'Honduras country profile', BBC Online, 29 January, available here: http://news.bbc.co.uk/1/hi/world/americas/country_profiles/1225416. stm#media

36. Lacey, Mark, 2009, 'Leader's ouster not a coup, says the Honduran military', *New York Times,* 1 July, available here; www.nytimes.com/2009/07/02/world/americas/02coup.html?_r=1

37. PRI, 2010, 'Manuel Zelaya, Honduras' former president in exile', *The World,* 15 July, available here: www.theworld.org/2010/07/15/manuel-zelaya-honduras%E2%80%99-president-in-exile/

38. Ramesh, Randeep, 2006, 'Nepal rejoices as peace deal ends civil war', *Guardian*, 23 November, available here: www.guardian.co.uk/world/2006/nov/23/nepal

39. Shah, Amir, 2010, 'Taliban stone couple to death for adultery', Associated Press, 16 August.

40. Rathje, W.J., 2001, 'Why the Taliban are destroying Buddhas', *USA Today*, 22 March, available here: www.usatoday.com/news/science/archaeology/2001-03-22-afghan-buddhas.htm

41. Islamabad, 2009, 'Taliban bans education for girls in Swat Valley', *Washington Times*, 5 January, available here: www.washingtontimes.com/news/2009/jan/05/taliban-bans-education-for-girls-in-pakistans-swat/

42. Subramanian, Nirupama, 2009, 'Sharia pact "swung public mood against Taliban"', *The Hindu*, 6 May, available here: www.hinduonnet.com/2009/05/06/stories/2009050655141100.htm

43. Sohail, Abdul Nasir, 2006, 'Religious organization TNSM re-emerges in Pakistan', Jamestown Foundation, 17 May.

44. Reuters, 2009, 'Xinjiang pipeline oils wheels', reported in *The Standard*, 14 December, available here: http://thestandard.com.hk/news_detail.asp?we_cat=2&art_id=91871&sid=26412058&con_type=1&d_str=20091214&fc=1

45. Anderlini, Jamil, 2008, 'Xinjiang oil boom fuels Uighur resentment', *Financial Times*, 28 August.

46. Sommerville, Quentin, 2005, 'China's grip on Xinjiang Muslims', BBC, 29 November, available here: http://news.bbc.co.uk/1/hi/world/asia-pacific/4482048.stm

47. Staff, 2009, 'Uighur ethnic identity under threat in China', Amnesty International, April, available here: www.amnesty.org/en/library/asset/ASA17/010/2009/en/e952496e-57bb-48eb-9741-e6b7fed2a7d4/asa170102009en.pdf

48. Wong, Edward, 2009, 'Clashes in China shed light on ethnic divide', *New York Times*, 7 July, available here: www.nytimes.com/2009/07/08/world/asia/08china.html

49. 'Banyan', 2009, 'Imperial instincts', *The Economist*, 7 July, available here: www.economist.com/blogs/banyan/2009/07/imperial_instincts

50. Staff, 2010, 'New testimonies reinforce call for China to investigate Xinjiang riots', Amnesty International, 1 July, available here: www.amnesty.org/en/news-and-updates/report/new-testimonies-reinforce-call-china-investigate-xinjiang-riots-2010-07-02

51. www.freetibet.org/about/migration

52. Grammaticas, Damian, 2010, 'Is development killing Tibet's way of life?', BBC, 16 July, available here: www.bbc.co.uk/news/world-asia-pacific-10638506

53. Pomfret, John, 1999, 'A less Tibetan Tibet; many residents fear Chinese migration will dilute culture', *Washington Post*, 31 October.

54. NDTV correspondent, 2009, 'Bal Thackeray attacks Sachin's India', NDTV, 16 November, available here: www.ndtv.com/news/india/bal_thackeray_attacks_sachins_india.php

CHAPTER 6

1. Rogers, David, 2008, 'Pelosi: "I'm trying to save the planet"', Politico, 29 July, available here: www.politico.com/news/stories/0708/12122.html

2. Starr, Penny, 2011, 'New study shows that offshore drilling could make Alaska the eighth largest oil producer in the World – ahead of Libya and Nigeria', CNS

News, 25 February, available here: www.cnsnews.com/news/article/new-study-shows-offshore-drilling-alaska

3. 2008, 'Petroleum, pollution and poverty in the Niger Delta', Amnesty International, p. 9, available here: www.amnesty.org/en/library/asset/AFR44/017/2009/en/e2415061-da5c-44f8-a73c-a7a4766ee21d/afr440172009en.pdf

4. *Ibid.*, p.11.

5. *Ibid.*, p.13.

6. Barnett, Antony, 2005, 'UK arms sales to Africa reach £1 billion mark', *Guardian,* 12 June, available here: www.guardian.co.uk/politics/2005/jun/12/uk.hearafrica05

7. sm/at/cb/oa, 2009, 'IRAQ: War remnants, pollution behind rise in cancer deaths?', IRIN, 14 October, available here: www.irinnews.org/Report.aspx?ReportID=86572

8. Unnamed reporter, 2009, 'Soldier died from exposure depleted uranium during Gulf War', *Daily Telegraph*, 10 September, available here: www.telegraph.co.uk/news/uknews/defence/6168039/Soldier-died-from-exposure-depleted-uranium-during-Gulf-War.html

9. Faruqi, Anwar, 2010, 'Iraq city with soaring child cancer gets new hospital', AFP, 22 October.

10. WuDunn, Sheryl, 1993, 'Nuclear dump reported in Tibet', *New York Times,* 19 April, available here: www.nytimes.com/1993/04/19/world/nuclear-dump-site-reported-in-tibet.html

11. Yeoman, Fran, 2010, 'Women at the deadly end of the cluster-bomb debate', *The Times,* 23 February.

12. Wiseman, Paul, 2003, 'Cluster bombs kill in Iraq, even after shooting ends', *USA Today,* 16 December, available here: www.usatoday.com/news/world/iraq/2003-12-10-cluster-bomb-cover_x.htm

13. Ed. Xiong Tong, 2011, 'Two killed, 11 wounded in bomb explosions in N Iraq', Xinhua, 17 March, available here: http://news.xinhuanet.com/english2010/world/2011-03/17/c_13784343.htm

14. Chivers, CJ, 2011, 'Qaddafi troops fire cluster bombs into civilian areas', *New York Times,* 15 April, available here: www.nytimes.com/2011/04/16/world/africa/16libya.html?_r=1&hp

15. Martorell, R., Kettel Khan, L. and Schroeder, D.G., 1994, 'Reversibility of stunting: epidemiological findings in children from developing countries', Centre for International Health, Emory University, School of Public Health.

16. *Ibid.*

17. UNICEF, 2010, 'Asia-Pacific regional workshop on the reduction of stunting through improvement of complementary feeding and maternal nutrition', available here: www.unicef.org/eapro/WorkshopReport_ReductionOfStunting_2010-06-07_FINAL.pdf

18. Akresh, Richard, Verwimp, Philip, and Bundervoet, Tom, 2009, 'Civil war, crop failure, and child stunting in Rwanda', University of Illinois at Urbana-Champaign, Department of Economics, available here: https://netfiles.uiuc.edu/akresh/www/Research/Akresh_RwandaChildHealth.pdf

19. Whitehall J., 2008, 'Anthropometry and renal size of children suffering under sustained conflict in Sri Lanka,' *Journal of Paediatrics and Child Health*, Volume 44, Issue 11, pp.656–60.

20. Milman, Anna, Frongillo, Edward A. and Hwang, Ji-Yun, 2005, 'Differential improvement among countries in child stunting is associated with long-term

development and specific interventions', *Journal of Nutrition*, Volume 135, June, pp.1415–22.

21. Ivanovic, Daniza M. et al, 2002, 'Nutritional status, brain development and scholastic achievement of Chilean high-school graduates from high and low intellectual quotient and socio-economic status', *British Journal of Nutrition*, Volume 87, Issue 1, September, pp.81–92.

22. Galler J.R., Ramsey F., 1989, 'A follow-up study of the influence of early malnutrition on development: behavior at home and at school', *Journal of the American Academy of Child and Adolescent Psychiatry*, 28: pp.254–61.

23. Bureau report, 2008, 'Govt speaks in two voices on Naxalism', Zee News, 23 November, available here: www.zeenews.com/news485858.html

24. UN Department of Social & Economic Affairs, 2010, *State of the World's Indigenous Peoples*, p.29, available here: www.un.org/esa/socdev/unpfii/documents/SOWIP_web.pdf

25. *Ibid.*, pp.225–6.

26. Kettle, Martin, 2000, 'President "ordered murder" of Congo leader', *Guardian*, 10 August, available here: www.guardian.co.uk/world/2000/aug/10/martinkettle

27. Ndikumana, Léonce and Boyce, James K., 2008, 'New estimates of capital flight from sub-Saharan African countries: linkages with external borrowing and policy options,' Political Economy Research Institute, University of Massachusetts Amherst, April, available here: www.peri.umass.edu/fileadmin/pdf/working_papers/working_papers_151-200/WP166.pdf

28. Heggstad, Carl and Fjeldstad, Odd-Helge, 2010, 'How banks assist capital flight from Africa: a literature review', Chr. Michelsen Institute, Commissioned by the Norwegian Agency for Development Cooperation, available here: www.taxjustice.net/cms/upload/pdf/CMI_1003_How_banks_assist_capital_flight_from_Africa.pdf

29. Transcript of speech given by President Barack Obama, 2009, published 27 March, available here: www.cfr.org/publication/18952/obamas_strategy_for_afghanistan_and_pakistan_march_2009.html

30. Silensky, Mark, 2010, 'An irony of war: human development as warfare in Afghanistan', *Colloquium*, Volume 3, Number 3 (October), available here: usacac.army.mil/blog/blogs/coin/archive/2010/10/11/an-irony-of-war.aspx

31. Garamone, Jim, 2010, 'Afghanistan now has forces, resources, Petraeus says', American Forces Press Service, 2 September, available here: www.defense.gov/news/newsarticle.aspx?id=60702

32. Cornwell, Susan, 2010, 'House approves money for Afghan surge', Reuters, 2 July, available here: www.reuters.com/article/idUSTRE6603UF20100702

33. Department of Economic and Social Affairs of the UN, 2010, 'The Millennium Development Goals Report', United Nations, 15 June, p.4, available here: www.un.org/millenniumgoals/pdf/MDG%Report%2010%En%r15%-low%res%20100615%-.pdf

34. *Ibid.*, p.14.

35. Svedberg, Peter, 2006, 'Declining child malnutrition: a reassessment', *International Journal of Epidemiology*, 22 August, available here: http://people.su.se/~svedb/DecliningChildMalnutr.pdf

36. 'The Millennium Development Goals Report', p.13.

37. *Ibid.*, p.15.

38. *Ibid.*, p.18.

39. Yumkella, Kandeh K., 2011, 'Response by Kandeh K. Yumkella Director-General to the Assessment of UNIDO conducted by The Department for International Development Under the Multilateral Aid Review', UNIDO, 22 February, available here: www.unido.org/fileadmin/user_media/News/2011/UNIDO_Response_DFID_final.pdf

40. Department of International Development, 2011, 'Multilateral Aid Review: ensuring maximum value for money for UK aid through multilateral organisations', March, available here: www.dfid.gov.uk/Documents/publications1/mar/multilateral_aid_review.pdf

CHAPTER 7

1. Bergen, Peter, 2009, 'Saudi investigation: would-be assassin hid bomb in underwear', CNN, 30 September, available here: http://edition.cnn.com/2009/WORLD/meast/09/30/saudi.arabia.attack/

2. Unnamed reporter, 2010, 'Profile: Al-Qaeda "bomb maker" Ibrahim al-Asiri', BBC, 13 October, available here: www.bbc.co.uk/news/world-middle-east-11662143

3. Schemm, Paul, 2010, 'Ibrahim Hassan al-Asiri, Yemen bombmaker, key suspect in terror plot', Huffington Post, 31 October, available here: www.huffingtonpost.com/2010/11/01/ibrahim-hassan-alasiri-ye_n_776842.html

4. Gully, Andrew, 2010, 'Saudi bombmaker is prime suspect in Yemen parcel plot', AFP, 31 October.

5. Jehl, Douglas, Kifner, John and Schmitt, Eric, 1996, 'Fatal lapses – A special report: how U.S. missteps and delay opened door to Saudi Blast', New York Times, 7 July, available here: www.nytimes.com/1996/07/07/world/fatal-lapses-special-report-us-missteps-delay-opened-door-saudi-blast.html

6. Porter, Gareth, 2009, 'US Officials leaked false story blaming Iran for Khobar attack', Antiwar.com, 25 June, available here: http://original.antiwar.com/porter/2009/06/24/us-officials-leaked-false-story-blaming-iran-for-khobar-at-tack/

7. Whitlock, Craig and Ladaa, Munir, 2006, 'Al-Qaeda's New Leadership', Washington Post, available here: www.washingtonpost.com/wp-srv/world/specials/terror/omar.html

8. Hambling, David, 2008, 'IRA historian: today's terrorists are "amateurs" – and still deadly', interview with Andy R. Oppenheimer, Wired, 11 December, available here: www.wired.com/dangerroom/2008/12/how-to-defeat-i/

9. Unnamed reporter, 2011, '7/7 inquests: "Pakistan calls to bomber" in days before', BBC, 2 February, available here: www.bbc.co.uk/news/uk-12345809

10. Wedeman, Ben, 2003, 'Najaf bombing kills Shiite leader, followers say', CNN, 30 August, available here: http://edition.cnn.com/2003/WORLD/meast/08/29/sprj.irq.najaf/

11. Unnamed reporter, 2007, 'Timeline: major bombings in Iraq since 2003', Reuters, 15 August, available here: www.reuters.com/article/2007/08/15/us-iraq-blasts-idUSL1585489520070815

12. Shachtman, Noah, 2007, 'Superbombs 101', Wired, 6 March, available here: www.wired.com/dangerroom/2007/03/efp_101_the_sup/

13. Spiegel, Peter, 2005, 'Insurgents bombs cause US death toll to rise', Financial Times, 18 August, available here: www.ft.com/cms/s/0/ff0bc180-0ffe-11da-bd5c-00000e2511c8.html#axzz1HFXQznnb

14. Moore, Solomon, 2008, 'U.S. bombs Iraqi insurgent hideouts', *New York Times*, 11 January, available here: www.nytimes.com/2008/01/11/world/middleeast/11iraq.html
15. Lando, Barry M., 2007, *Web of Deceit*, Other Press LLC, New York, p.79.
16. Grdovic, Mark, 2009, *A Leader's Handbook to Unconventional Warfare*, US Army John F. Kennedy Special Warfare Center and School, November, available here: www.soc.mil/swcs/swmag/Assets/SWCS%Publications/Leaders%Guide%Final.pdf
17. *Ibid.*, p.5.
18. *Ibid.*, p.14.
19. *Ibid.*, p.22.
20. *Ibid.*, p.12.
21. Kinzer, Stephen, 1987, 'Fighting expands in North Nicaragua', *New York Times*, 8 January.
22. Landmine & Cluster Monitor, Nicaragua, available here: www.the-monitor.org/index.php/publications/display?url=lm/2004/nicaragua.html#fnB4490
23. Jalal, Ayesha and Bose, Sugata, 1998, *Modern South Asia*, Routledge, London and New York, p.233.
24. Abramson, David M., 2010, 'Foreign religious education and the Central Asian Islamic revival: impact and prospects for stability', Central Asia-Caucasus Institute Silk Road Studies Program, Johns Hopkins University, March, available here: www.silkroadstudies.org/new/docs/silkroadpapers/1003Abramson.pdf
25. Interview with Pervez Musharraf, 2010, 'Pakistan is always seen as the rogue', *Der Spiegel*, 10 April, available here: www.spiegel.de/international/world/0,1518,721110,00.html
26. Loyd, Antony, 2010, 'Colonel Imam: "I have the Green Beret but the Taleban beret is better"', *Sunday Times*, 23 February, available here: www.timesonline.co.uk/tol/news/world/asia/article7036961.ece
27. Waraich, Omar, 2011, 'Taliban "godfather" dies while held by Islamist militants', *Independent,* 25 January, available here: www.independent.co.uk/news/world/asia/taliban-godfather-dies-while-held-by-islamist-militants-2193326.html
28. Perlez, Jane, 2011, 'Onetime Taliban handler dies in their hands', *New York Times,* 24 January, available here: www.nytimes.com/2011/01/25/world/asia/25pakistan.html
29. Dreazen, Yochi J., 2011, 'IED casualties up despite increased vigilance', *National Journal,* 3 March, available here: www.nationaljournal.com/nationalsecurity/ied-casualties-up-despite-increased-vigilance-20110303
30. Loyd, 'Colonel Imam: "I have the Green Beret..."'.
31. Staff Writers, 2009, 'Pentagon to focus on IED threat in Afghanistan: Gates', AFP, 12 November.
32. Interview with Jack Cloonan, 2005, 'When 9/11 happens, what was your history with Al Qaeda?', *Frontline,* PBS, 13 July, available here: www.pbs.org/wgbh/pages/frontline//////torture/interviews/cloonan.html
33. Defence Human Resources Activity, 'Ali Mohamed Case', available here: www.dhra.mil/perserec/adr/counterterrorism/mohamed.htm
34. Williams, Lance and McCormick, Erin, 2001, 'Al Qaeda terrorist worked with FBI / Ex-Silicon Valley resident plotted embassy attacks', *San Francisco Chronicle*, 4 November.

35. Tran, Mark, 2010, 'Manuel Noriega – from US friend to foe', *Guardian*, 27 April, available here: www.guardian.co.uk/world/2010/apr/27/manuel-noriega-us-friend-foe

36. Arsenault, Chris, 2010, 'US-trained cartel terrorises Mexico', al-Jazeera, 3 November, available here: http://english.aljazeera.net/indepth/features/2010/1 0/20101019212440609775.html

37. Short, Anthony, 1970, 'The Communist Party of Malaya: in search of revolutionary situations', *The World Today*, Volume 26, Number 12, December.

38. McGeown, Kate, 2010, 'Philippines and China to sign first military deal', BBC, 7 December, available here: www.bbc.co.uk/news/world-asia-pacific-11933849

39. Hensengerth, Oliver, 2005, 'The Burmese Communist Party in the state-to-state relations between China and Burma', Leeds East Asia Papers, No. 67.

40. Ware, John, 2003 'A licence to murder', *Panorama*, BBC 1, available here: http://news.bbc.co.uk/1/hi/programmes/panorama/2019301.stm

41. Human Rights Watch, 2004, Slovakia country report, available here: www. hrw.org/en/node/12175/section/1

42. Lévy, Bernard-Henry, 2004, *Who Killed Daniel Pearl?*, Duckworth Publishing, p.406.

43. Musharraf, Pervez, 2006, *In The Line Of Fire: A Memoir*, Simon & Schuster, pp.224–28.

44. Hassan, S. Raza, 2010, 'Plan to install cellphone jammers in jails hits snag', *Dawn*, 8 November, available here: www.dawn.com/2010/11/08/plan-to-install-cellphone-jammers-in-jails-hits-snag.html

45. Lévy, *Who Killed Daniel Pearl?*, pp.256–7.

46. Reuters, 2004, 'Who is Azahari Husin?', *Sydney Morning Herald*, 10 September, available here: www.smh.com.au/articles/2004/09/09/1094530774504.html

47. Griswold, Eliza, 2005, 'The next Islamist revolution?', *New York Times*, 23 January, available here: www.nytimes.com/2005/01/23/magazine/23BANG. html

48. Unnamed reporter, 2002, 'Atta "trained in Afghanistan"', BBC, 24 August, available here: http://news.bbc.co.uk/1/hi/world/americas/2213701.stm

49. Bradley, John R., 2005, 'Al Qaeda and the House of Saud: eternal enemies or secret bedfellows', *The Washington Quarterly*, The Center for Strategic and International Studies and the Massachusetts Institute of Technology, Autumn, pp.139–52, available here: www.twq.com/05autumn/docs/05autumn_bradley. pdf

50. Henderson, Simon, 2004, 'Bin Laden increases his challenge to the House of Saud', *The Times*, 31 March, available here: www.timesonline.co.uk/tol/news/ world/article436784.ece

51. Interview with Scott McLeod, 2003, 'Osama Bin Laden vs. the House of Saud', *Time*, 14 May, available here: www.time.com/time/world/article/0,8599,451935,00.html Read more: www.time.com/time/world/article/0,8599,451935,00. html#ixzz1HVz9aSps

52. Chairman: Paul Murphy, 2005, 'Report into the London terrorist attacks on 7 July 2005', Intelligence and Security Committee, May, p.12 available here: http://news.bbc.co.uk/1/shared/bsp/hi/pdfs/11_05_06_isc_london_attacks_ report.pdf

53. Walsh, Declan, 2009, 'Pakistan's ex-leader in exile: Pervez Musharraf's quiet new life in London', *Guardian*, 9 September, available here: www.guardian. co.uk/world/2009/sep/09/pakistan-pervez-musharraf-exile-london

54. Dawn.com, 2011, 'Education emergency Pakistan', *Dawn*, 9 March, available here: www.dawn.com/2011/03/09/education-emeregency-pakistan.html
55. Murphy, 'Report into the London terrorist attacks...', p.12.
56. *Ibid.*, p.4.
57. Maudoodi, Sayyed Abulala, 1955, *The Process of Islamic Revolution*, Lahore, Maktaba Jama'at-e-Islami, Pakistan.
58. Mawdudi, A. A. 1992, first published 1947, *The Economic Problem of Man and Its Islamic Solution*, Islamic Publications (Pvt.) Ltd, Lahore, p.4.
59. BBC, 1984, 'On this day', 12 October, available here: http://news.bbc.co.uk/onthisday/hi/dates/stories/october/12/newsid_2531000/2531583.stm
60. Finn, Peter, 2011, 'Peter King, IRA supporter and enthusiastic counter-terrorism advocate', *Washington Post*, 5 March, available here: www.washingtonpost.com/wp-dyn/content/article/2011/03/04/AR2011030406635.html
61. Massie, Alex, 2011, 'Did Obama ask Peter King to be his Ambassador to Ireland?', *The Spectator*, 8 March, available here: www.spectator.co.uk/alexmassie/6762590/did-obama-ask-peter-king-to-be-his-ambassador-to-ireland.thtml

CHAPTER 8

1. Linder, Rear Adml (Retd) James B. and Gregor, Dr A. James, 1981, 'The Chinese communist air force in the "punitive" war against Vietnam', *Air University Review*, September–October.
2. Elleman, Bruce, 1996, 'Sino-Soviet relations and the February 1979 Sino–Vietnamese Conflict', Vietnam Symposium, Texas Tech University, 18–20 April.
3. Federal Research Division of the Library of Congress, for U.S. Department of the Army, available here: http://countrystudies.us/vietnam/60.htm
4. Van der Kroef, Justus M., 1979, 'New patterns of strategic conflict in Southeast Asia', *Parameters: Journal of the US Army War College*, available here: www.carlisle.army.mil/usawc/parameters/Articles/1980/1980%van%der%kroef.pdf
5. Elleman, 'Sino-Soviet relations...'.
6. Bakshi, Col. G. D., 2000, 'The Sino-Vietnam War – 1979: Case studies in limited wars', *Indian Defence Review*, Volume 14 (2) July–September.
7. AFP, 2009, 'In China, war with Vietnam is forgotten history: ex-infantryman', *Gulf Times*, 18 February.
8. Interview with author.
9. News Stories, 2005, 'Last Vietnamese boat refugee leaves Malaysia', UNHCR, 30 August, available here: www.unhcr.org/43141e9d4.html
10. Lam, Tom, 2000, 'The Exodus of Hoa refugees from Vietnam and their settlement in Guangxi: China's refugee settlement strategies', *Journal of Refugee Studies*, 13 (4): pp.374–90.
11. CIA World Factbook, 2011, Country Comparison, Oil Production, available here: https://www.cia.gov/library/publications/the-world-factbook/rankorder/2173rank.html
12. Jackson, Guy, 2011, 'Chinese military "growing fast": think tank', AFP, 8 March.
13. Unnamed reporter, 2010, 'Japan defence review warns of China's military might', BBC, 17 December, available here: www.bbc.co.uk/news/world-asia-pacific-12015362

14. Bitzinger, Richard A., 2011, 'The PRC's defense industry: reform without improvement', Jamestown Foundation, 1 March, available here: www.jamestown.org/single/?no_cache=1&tx_ttnews%5Btt_news%5D=3726

15. Unnamed reporter, 2005, 'The blood-red revolution', *The Economist,* 19 May, available here: www.economist.com/node/3992111

16. www.ned.org/where-we-work/eurasia/kyrgyzstan

17. Stein, Jeff, 2011, 'Islamic group is CIA front, ex-Turkish intel chief says', SpyTalk blog, *Washington Post,* 5 January, available here: http://voices.washingtonpost.com/spy-talk/2011/01/islamic_group_is_cia_front_ex-.html?wprss=spy-talk

18. Unnamed reporter, 2009, 'Islamists who want to destroy the state get £100,000 funding', *Daily Telegraph,* 25 October, available here: www.telegraph.co.uk/news/uknews/6427369/Islamists-who-want-to-destroy-the-state-get-100000-funding.html

19. The Shanghai Convention on Combating Terrorism, Separatism and Extremism, 2009, available here: www.sectsco.org/EN/show.asp?id=68

20. Jiang Yi, 2010, 'Developing Russian Far East, rejuvenating northeast China', *People's Daily,* 10 September.

21. Blair, David, 2009, 'Why the restless Chinese are warming to Russia's frozen east', *Daily Telegraph,* 16 July, available here: www.telegraph.co.uk/comment/5845646/Why-the-restless-Chinese-are-warming-to-Russias-frozen-east.html

22. Baidu.com, '外满洲', available here: http://baike.baidu.com/view/1066615.htm

23. 'Aiven', '天南海北 > 文章列表', blog.chinamil.com.cn, 2009, available here: http://blog.chinamil.com.cn/group.asp?gid=15&pid=69816

24. Repnikova, Maria and Balzer, Harley, 2009, 'Chinese migration to Russia: missed opportunities', Woodrow Wilson Centre for International Scholars, available here: http://wilsoncenter.org/topics/pubs/No3_ChineseMigtoRussia.pdf

25. Zeihan, Peter, 'Analysis: Russia's Far East turning Chinese', ABC News, 14 July, available here: http://abcnews.go.com/International/story?id=82969&page=1

26. Kucera, Joshua, 2010, 'China's Russian invasion', *The Diplomat,* 19 February, available here: http://the-diplomat.com/2010/02/19/china%E2%80%99s-russian-invasion/

27. Eimer, David, 2011, 'Neighbouring Russian and Chinese cities face vastly different economic fortunes', *South China Morning Post,* 4 January, available here: http://topics.scmp.com/news/china-news-watch/article/Neighbouring-Russian-and-Chinese-cities-face-vastly-different-economic-fortunes

28. Grove, Thomas, 2011, 'Analysis: Russia turns military gaze east to counter China', Reuters, 1 March, available here: www.reuters.com/article/2011/03/01/us-russia-china-military-idUSTRE72027S20110301?pageNumber=2

29. Galbraith, John Kenneth, 1969, 'Border War 1', *Ambassador's Journal,* Paragon House, Tesoro Books, p.432.

30. *Ibid.,* p.435.

31. Unnamed reporter, 1974, 'ESPIONAGE: Trying to Expose the CIA', *Time,* 22 April.

32. Naqshbandi, Aurangzeb, 2008, 'Crossovers to China worry Arunachal', *Hindustan Times,* 13 November, available here: http://www.hindustantimes.com/News-Feed/newdelhi/Crossovers-to-China-worry-Arunachal/Article1-351058.aspx

33. IANS wire, 2011, 'IAF inducts second SU-30 squadron in northeast', Sify, 1 March.

34. TNN, 2011, 'Modernisation of Chinese armed forces a serious concern: Antony', *The Times of India,* 17 February, available here: http://articles.timesofindia. indiatimes.com/2011-02-17/india/28554655_1_modernisation-new-infantry-mountain-divisions-border-issue

35. Siddiqa, Ayesha, 2007, *Military Inc.: Inside Pakistan's Military Economy*, Pluto Press, London, p.66.

36. Corruption Perceptions Index 2007, Transparency International.

37. Havel, Vacláv and Tutu, Desmond, 2005, 'Threat to the peace: a call for the UN Security Council to act in Burma', 20 September, p.11, available here: www. unscburma.org/Docs/Threat%to%the%Peace.pdf

38. Corben, Roy, 2011, 'Burma's path to privatization keeps armed forces in economic control', Voice of America, 25 January, available here: www.voanews. com/english/news/Burmas-Path-to-Privatization-Keeps-Armed-Forces-in-Economic-Control-114568884.html

39. Wai Moe, 2011, 'Military firms excluded from tax evasion law', *Irrawaddy,* 7 January, available here: www.irrawaddy.org/article.php?art_id=20488

40. Pubby, Mannu, 2008, 'China emerging as main source of arms to N-E rebels: Jane's Review', *Indian Express,* 22 May, available here: www.indianexpress. com/news/china-emerging-as-main-source-of-arms-to-ne-rebels-janes-review/312894/

41. Qiu, Yongzheng and Guo, Qiang, 2009, 'Myanmar conflict puts China in dilemma', *Global Times,* 28 August, available here: http://china.globaltimes. cn/diplomacy/2009-08/461980.html

42. Wade, Francis, 2010, 'Burma fuelling China's heroin crisis', Democratic Voice of Burma, 12 March, available here: www.dvb.no/news/burma-fuelling-china%E2%80%99s-heroin-crisis/8103

43. Havel and Tutu, 'Threat to the peace'.

44. Chang, Iris, 1997, *The Rape of Nanking*, Penguin, London.

45. 'The 14 Class-A war criminals enshrined at Yasukuni', China.org, available here: www.china.org.cn/english/features/135371.htm

46. Unnamed reporter, 2005, 'Japan history texts anger E Asia', BBC, 5 April, available here: http://news.bbc.co.uk/1/hi/world/asia-pacific/4411771.stm

47. Hochschild, Adam, 1998, 'A year later, Chang's work still inspires', *Salon,* 11 January.

48. Unnamed reporter, 2011, 'Colonial Governor's descendant named Japan's new FM', *Chosun Ilbo,* 10 March, available here: http://english.chosun.com/site/ data/html_dir/2011/03/10/2011031000843.html

49. Brinsley, John and Harrington, Patrick, 2011, 'China naval spats in disputed waters draw mounting protests', Bloomberg, 9 March.

50. Unnamed reporter, 2008, '2 more Okinawa Marines arrested', *Stars & Stripes,* 20 February, available here: www.stripes.com/news/2-more-okinawa-marines-arrested-1.75211

51. Harrison, Selig H., 2011, 'On the remilitarization of Japan', *The Hankyoreh,* 3 February, available here: http://english.hani.co.kr/arti/english_edition/e_ opinion/402584.html

52. Guerin, Bill, 2006, 'Trials and travails of Indonesia's richest man', *Asia Times Online,* 14 October, available here: www.atimes.com/atimes/Southeast_Asia/ HJ14Ae01.html

CHAPTER 9

1. Belasco, Amy, 2010, 'The cost of Iraq, Afghanistan, and other global war on terror operations since 9/11', Congressional Research Service, September, available here: www.fas.org/sgp/crs/natsec/RL33110.pdf

2. Reuters, 2010, 'Q+A-Cost of Iraq, Afghanistan tops $1 trillion', Reuters, 14 January, available here: www.reuters.com/article/idUSN1415708320100114

3. Stiglitz, Joseph and Bilmes, Linda, 2008, 'The three trillion dollar war', *The Times,* 23 February, available here: www.timesonline.co.uk/tol/comment/columnists/guest_contributors/article3419840.ece

4. Hoyos, Carola, 2009, 'New breed strikes lucky at Iraq oil auction', *Financial Times,* 13 December, available here: www.ft.com/cms/s/0/1535ac84-e816-11de-8a02-00144feab49a.html#ixzz18NO2dhEV

5. BBC, 2009. 'Iraq oil development rights contracts awarded', BBC Online, 11 December, available here: news.bbc.co.uk/1/hi/8407274.stm

6. Landers, Jim, 2007, 'Iraq's troubles push oil costs up', *Dallas Morning News,* 10 November, available at: www.dallasnews.com/sharedcontent/dws/bus/stories/DN-IraqOil_10bus.ART.North.Edition1.42010ac.html

7. Staff reporter, 2010, 'Korean GDP "to reach $1 trillion next year"', *Chosun Ilbo,*17 December, available at: english.chosun.com/site/data/html_dir/2010/10/29/2010102901029.html

8. Whitell, Giles, 2010, 'Pentagon chief raises threat of attack as Iran taunts US with missile display', *The Times,* 19 April, available here: www.timesonline.co.uk/tol/news/world/us_and_americas/article7101161.ece

9. Sciolino, Elaine, 1987, 'From air and sea, Iran–Iraq "Tanker War" heats up', *New York Times,* 3 September.

10. Nayouf, Hayyan, 2009, 'UAE builds port to counter Iran threats', al-Arabiya.net, 3 March, available here: www.alarabiya.net/articles/2009/03/03/67650.html

11. Carofano, James; Beach, William; Cohen, Ariel; Curtis, Lisa; Foertsch, Tracy L.; Acosta Fraser, Alison; Lieberman, Ben; and Phillips, James, 2007, 'If Iran provokes an energy crisis: modeling the problem in a WarGame', Heritage Foundation, 25 July, available here: www.heritage.org/Research/Reports/2007/07/If-Iran-Provokes-an-Energy-Crisis-Modeling-the-Problem-in-a-War-Game

12. Hogg, Chris, 2010, 'China–Iran: old ties, modern dependency', BBC News, 26 July, available here: www.bbc.co.uk/news/world-asia-pacific-10730154

13. Rajendran, Raj, 2010, 'Japanese sanctions may cut Iran oil exports by 25 per cent, Nomura says', Bloomberg, 5 October, available here: www.businessweek.com/news/2010-10-05/japanese-sanctions-may-cut-iran-oil-exports-by-25-nomura-says.html

14. Theodoulou, Michael, 2008, 'Iran speedboats "threatened suicide attack on US" in Strait of Hormuz', *The Times,* 7 January, available here: www.timesonline.co.uk/tol/news/world/middle_east/article3147217.ece

15. Lendon, Brad, 2010, 'Iran unveils squadrons of flying boats', CNN, 28 September, available here: http://news.blogs.cnn.com/2010/09/28/iran-unveils-squadrons-of-flying-boats/

16. Ballen, Ken and Doherty, Patrick, 2009, 'The Iranian people speak', *Washington Post,* 15 June, available here: www.washingtonpost.com/wp-dyn/content/article/2009/06/14/AR2009061401757.html

17. Biouki, Kayvon, 2007, 'Students clash as President Mahmoud Ahmadinejad faces protest at campus speech', *The Times,* 9 October, available here: www.timesonline.co.uk/tol/news/world/middle_east/article2617562.ece

18. WikiLeaks, 2010, 'US embassy cables: opponents step up pressure on Mahmoud Ahmadinejad', *Guardian,* 28 November, available here: www.guardian.co.uk/world/us-embassy-cables-documents/203516

19. BBC, 2009, 'Iran TV plans Slumdog film boost', BBC Online, 18 March, available here: news.bbc.co.uk/1/hi/world/middle_east/7951015.stm

20. Leyne, John, 2008, 'Iran unveils plan for women's car', BBC News, 7 October, available here: news.bbc.co.uk/1/hi/7657810.stm

21. Brazier, James, 2008, 'The Iran–Saudi Cold War', *Diplomatic Courier,* 6 November, available here: www.diplomaticourier.org/kmitan/articleback.php?newsid=228

22. USAID/Washington/Middle East Bureau 2008, 2009, 'Annual Program Statement', USAID, 30 June, Agreement Officer: Khem Gurung, available here: www.usatoday.com/news/pdf/usaid.pdf

23. CNN Larry King Live, 2008, 'Interview with Iranian President Mahmoud Ahmadinejad', CNN, 23 September, available here: transcripts.cnn.com/TRANSCRIPTS/0809/23/lkl.01.html

24. Plushnick-Masti, Ramit, 2006, 'Israel buys 2 nuclear-capable submarines', Associated Press, 25 August.

25. Lim, Bomi, 2010, 'North Korea blamed for torpedo that sank South's ship', Bloomberg, 20 May, available here: www.bloomberg.com/news/2010-05-19/south-korea-to-accuse-north-of-torpedo-attack-in-march-sinking-of-warship.html

26. Sudworth, John, 2010, 'North Korean artillery hits South Korean island', BBC News, 23 November, available here: www.bbc.co.uk/news/world-asia-pacific-11818005

27. Kim, Do-gyun, 2010, 'North Korea says won't react to South drill', Reuters, 20 December, available here: www.reuters.com/article/idUSTOE6BG05Y20101220

28. www.kcna.co.jp

29. Demick, Barbara, 2003, 'Seoul's vulnerability is key to war scenarios', *Los Angeles Times,* 27 May.

30. Robinson, Colin and Baker, Rear Adm. (Rtd) Stephen H., 2003, 'Stand-off with North Korea: war scenarios and consequences', Center for Defence Information, available here: www.cdi.org/north-korea/north-korea-crisis.pdf

31. Kim, Jack, 2010, 'South Korea's MPs vote to strip Seoul of its capital status', *The Scotsman,* 23 June, available at: news.scotsman.com/world/South-Korea39s-MPs-vote-to.6377481.jp

32. Latest headlines, 2010, 'President presides over an emergency meeting on the nation's security and the economy', Office of the President, 25 November, available here: http://english.president.go.kr/pre_activity/latest/latest_view.php?uno=4382

33. Gen. Gary Luck, 1995, testimony before the Senate Armed Services Committee, 26 January, cited in Oberdorfer, Don, 1997, 'The Two Koreas: A Contemporary History,' Addison-Wesley, p.324.

34. Varner, Bill, 2010, 'China blocks UN censure for North Korean missile test', Bloomberg, 10 April, available here: www.bloomberg.com/apps/news?sid=aNndYudaUHzg&pid=newsarchive

35. See www.history.navy.mil/library/online/costs_of_major_us_wars.htm

36. Reprinted with permission from HybridCars, 2011, 'Toyota reaches 3 million global hybrid car sales', Reuters, 10 March, available here: www.reuters.com/article/2011/03/10/idUS409910782820110310

37. Ohnsman, Alan, 2011, 'Toyota studies magnesium battery as lithium alternate', Bloomberg, 12 January, available here: www.bloomberg.com/news/2011-01-10/toyota-developing-magnesium-battery-as-lithium-alternate.html

38. Fletcher, Graeme, 2011, 'Merc F-Cell is a glimpse of the future', *National Post,* 25 March, available here: www.nationalpost.com/opinion/columnists/Merc+Cell+glimpse+future/4500597/story.html

39. Totolo, Edoardo, 2009, 'Coltan and conflict in the DRC', *ISN Security Watch*, 11 February, available here: www.isn.ethz.ch/isn/Current-Affairs/Security-Watch/Detail/?lng=en&id=96390

40. Chadwick, Alex, 2001, 'Coltan mining and Eastern Congo's gorillas', NPR, 20 December, available here: www.npr.org/programs/re/archivesdate/2001/dec/20011220.coltan.html

41. Lewis, Leo, 2008, 'Grand plans for global energy are under threat – but from unexpected sources', *The Times*, 29 November, available here: http://business.timesonline.co.uk/tol/business/industry_sectors/technology/article5254564.ece

42. Kahya, Damian, 2008, 'Bolivia holds key to electric car future', BBC, 9 November, available here: http://news.bbc.co.uk/1/hi/business/7707847.stm

43. Dealbook, 2010, 'China's BYD in strategic move for Tibet miner', *New York Times,* 17 September, available here: http://dealbook.nytimes.com/2010/09/17/chinas-byd-in-strategic-move-for-tibet-miner/

44. http://english.peopledaily.com.cn/90001/90780/91342/6611914.html

45. Ricks, Thomas E., 2010, 'Six things that worry the former director of the CIA, Gen. Michael Hayden', *Foreign Policy,* 25 January, available here: http://ricks.foreignpolicy.com/posts/2011/01/25/six_things_that_worry_the_former_director_of_the_cia_gen_michael_hayden

46. Hsiao, L.C. Russell, 2010, 'China's cyber command?', *China Brief*, Jamestown, Vol X, Issue 15, 22 July, available here: www.jamestown.org/uploads/media/cb_010_74.pdf

47. Solution Brief, 2010, 'Advanced persistent threat', McAfee, available here: www.mcafee.com/us/resources/solution-briefs/sb-advanced-persistent-threats.pdf

48. Page, Jeremy, 2011, 'China stealth jet "leak" viewed as intentional', *Wall St Journal,* 8 January, available here: http://online.wsj.com/article/SB10001424052748704055204576067514151124434.html

49. McConnell, Mike, 2010, 'Mike McConnell on how to win the cyber-war we're losing', *Washington Post*, 28 February, available here: www.washingtonpost.com/wp-dyn/content/article/2010/02/25/AR2010022502493.html

50. Dilanian, Ken, 2011, 'Virtual war a real threat', *Los Angeles Times*, 28 March, available here: www.latimes.com/news/nationworld/nation/la-na-cyber-war-20110328,0,6416856.story

51. Xinhua newswire, 2007, 'Premier Wen told Merkel China opposes hackers', *China Daily*, 27 August, available here: www2.chinadaily.com.cn/china/2007-08/27/content_6059831.htm

52. Deibert, Ron and Rohozinski, Rafal, 2011, 'The new cyber military-industrial complex', *Globe & Mail*, 28 March, available here: www.theglobeandmail.com/news/opinions/opinion/the-new-cyber-military-industrial-complex/article1957159/

53. Classified By: DCM Daniel Piccutu, 2010, 'China's angst over U.S. satellite interception', obtained by WikiLeaks, available here: www.wikileaks.ch/cable/2008/02/08BEIJING647.html

54. Classified By: EAP DAS David Shear, 2010, 'Demarche following China's January 2010 intercept flight-test', obtained by WikiLeaks, available here: www.wikileaks.ch/cable/2010/01/10STATE2634.html

55. Li, Xiaokun, 2010, 'US report claims China shoots down its own satellite', *China Daily,* 19 July, available here: www.chinadaily.com.cn/world/2010-07/19/content_10121179.htm

56. Peplow, Mark, 2004, 'US tests antimissile laser', *Nature,* 15 November, available here: www.nature.com/news/2004/041115/full/news041115-1.html

57. Emery, Daniel, 2010, 'Anti-aircraft laser unveiled at Farnborough Airshow', BBC, 19 July, available here: www.bbc.co.uk/news/technology-10682693

58. Yonhap, 2011, 'Chinese hackers stole S. Korean documents on spy drones: lawmaker', Yonhap, 7 March, available here: http://english.yonhapnews.co.kr/national/2011/03/07/86/0301000000AEN20110307002200315F.HTML

59. Page, Jeremy, 2010, 'China's new drones raise eyebrows', *Wall Street Journal,* 18 November, available here: http://online.wsj.com/article/SB10001424052748703374304575622350604500556.html

60. MoD, 2011, 'The UK approach to unmanned aircraft systems', UK Ministry of Defence Joint Doctrine Note, 30 March, available here: www.mod.uk/NR/rdonlyres/DDE54504-AF8E-4A4C-8710-514C6FB66D67/0/20110401JDN211UASv1WebU.pdf

61. Halvorson, Todd, 2011, 'Air Force launches unmanned spacecraft', *USA Today,* 5 March, available here: www.usatoday.com/tech/science/space/2011-03-05-space-plane_N.htm

62. http://news.blogs.cnn.com/2010/12/03/air-force-robot-space-plane-returns/

63. http://dsc.discovery.com/videos/when-we-left-earth-first-shuttle-landing.html

64. Thompson, Ginger and Mazzetti, Mark, 2011, 'U.S. drones fight Mexican drug trade', *New York Times,* 15 March, available here: www.nytimes.com/2011/03/16/world/americas/16drug.html?_r=1&hp

65. Dominguez, Francisco, 2010, 'No to the militarization of Latin America: Venezuela under threat', Venezuela Solidarity Campaign, p.6.

66. *Ibid.,* pp.10–13.

67. Benson, Todd, 2008, 'New fleet may mean U.S. covets Brazil's oil: Lula', Reuters, 18 September, available here: www.reuters.com/article/2008/09/18/us-brazil-oil-usa-idUSN1827567620080918

68. Beaudan, Eric, 2002, 'Canada poised to ease pot laws', 3 October, available here: www.csmonitor.com/2002/1003/p06s01-woam.html

CHAPTER 10

1. Unnamed reporter, 2007, 'EU revises subsidy scheme for cotton production', Xinhua, 11 December.

2. Hawksley, Humphrey, 2001, 'Mali's children in chocolate slavery', BBC, 12 April, available here: http://news.bbc.co.uk/1/hi/world/africa/1272522.stm

3. http://burma.total.com/

4. PTI, 2011, 'Garment exports up 24 per cent in February', *Business Standard,* 31 March, available here: www.business-standard.com/india/news/garment-exports24-in-february/130822/on

5. Toh Han Shih, 2011, 'China proving to be saviour of the world's poorest people', *South China Morning Post*, 14 February, available here: http://topics. scmp.com/news/china-business-watch/article/China-proving-to-be-saviour-of-the-worlds-poorest-people

6. http://web.worldbank.org/WBSITE/EXTERNAL/TOPICS/EXTPOVERTY/0,,c ontentMDK:20195240~pagePK:148956~piPK:216618~theSitePK:336992,00. html

7. www.doingbusiness.org/rankings

8. Xinhua, 2011, 'China's private sector employs 160m people', *China Daily*, 5 February, available here: http://english.peopledaily.com. cn/90001/90776/90882/7280334.html

9. Kang Lim, Benjamin, 2011, 'China's state-owned enterprises urged to reform', Reuters, 2 March, available here: www.reuters.com/article/2011/03/02/china-enterprises-idUSTOE72103A20110302

10. Tucker, Sundeep, 2009, 'China blocks Coca-Cola bid for Huiyuan', *Financial Times,* 19 March, available here: www.ft.com/cms/s/0/5c645830-1391-11de-9e32-0000779fd2ac.html#axzz1IRz2g11v

11. Sleigh, Andrew and von Lewinski, Hans, 2006, 'China: moving up the value chain', Accenture, September, available here: www.accenture.com/us-en/ outlook/Pages/outlook-journal-2006-china-value-chain.aspx

12. U.S. International Trade Commission, 2010, 'China: intellectual property infringement, indigenous innovation policies, and frameworks for measuring the effects on the U.S. economy', Investigation No. 332–51, November, available here: www.usitc.gov/publications/332/pub4199.pdf

13. *Ibid.*, p.xxi,

14. Freedman, Jennifer M, 2010, 'India, Brazil complain at WTO over generic drug seizures by European Union', 12 May, available here: www.bloomberg.com/ news/2010-05-12/india-brazil-complain-at-wto-over-generic-drug-seizures-by-european-union.html

15. http://trade.ec.europa.eu/doclib/docs/2010/december/tradoc_147079.pdf

16. Press Information Bureau, 2011, 'Anand Sharma chairs consultative committee of Parliament on challenges in IPR – international and domestic', Government of India, 29 March: http://pib.nic.in/newsite/erelease.aspx?relid=71341

17. McGivering, Jill, 2007, 'Pros and cons of party membership', BBC, 15 October, available here: http://news.bbc.co.uk/1/hi/world/asia-pacific/7044594.stm

18. Schlafly, Phyllis, 2008, 'Obama's sovereignty giveaway plan', WorldNetDaily, 22 February, www.wnd.com/index.php?pageId=56959

19. Simpson, James, 2009, 'Obama to surrender US sovereignty at UN global warming conference', *Washington Examiner*, 19 October, available here: www. examiner.com/independent-in-washington-dc/obama-to-surrender-us-sover-eignty-at-un-global-warming-conference

20. Insley, Jill, 2010, 'Medieval Britons were richer than modern poor people, study finds', *Guardian*, 6 December, available here: www.guardian.co.uk/ money/2010/dec/06/medieval-britons-richer-than-modern-poor

21. Kang Lim, 'China's state-owned enterprises…'.

22. Press release, 2010, 'Lockheed Martin energizes new energy summit in London', available here: www.lockheedmartin.com/news/enr/2010/new-energy-summit. html

23. ABC News, 2010 'Obama: safe nuclear plants are a "necessity"', 16 February, available here: http://abcnews.go.com/Politics/video/obama-safe-nuclear-plants-necessity-9852906
24. Gray, Louise, 2011, 'New nuclear is "no brainer", says ex-government adviser', *Daily Telegraph*, 29 March, available here: www.telegraph.co.uk/earth/energy/8413600/New-nuclear-is-no-brainer-says-ex-government-adviser.html
25. Wu Zhong, 2011, 'PLA fires budget guns', *Asia Times Online*, 9 March, available here: www.atimes.com/atimes/China/MC09Ad01.html

CHAPTER 11

1. Unnamed reporter, 2006, 'Africa pledges "not materialised"', BBC, 11 March, available here: http://news.bbc.co.uk/1/hi/uk_politics/4795738.stm
2. Katz, Jonathan M, and Mendoza, Martha, 2010, 'Haiti still waiting for aid pledged by U.S., others', Associated Press, 4 October.
3. McClanahan, Paige, 2011, 'Africa's "Iron Lady" revitalizes Liberia', *Christian Science Monitor*, 12 April, available here: www.csmonitor.com/World/Africa/2011/0412/Africa-s-Iron-Lady-revitalizes-Liberia
4. Penketh, Anne, 2006, 'Nigeria is Africa's first nation to clear debt to the West', *Independent*, 22 April, available here: www.independent.co.uk/news/world/africa/nigeria-is-africas-first-nation-to-clear-debt-to-the-west-475127.html
5. Woellart, Lorraine, 2008, 'Obama embraces "green path" in economic stimulus plan', Bloomberg, 2 December, available here: www.bloomberg.com/apps/news?pid=newsarchive&sid=aGZs6vevDXyg
6. Dennehy, Mike, 2009, 'Wind of change could help government reach renewable target', BAE Systems news release, 13 January, available here: www.baesystems.com/Newsroom/NewsReleases/autoGen_10901314321.html
7. Garlick, Dave, 2006, 'Boeing wins contract to build solar cells for renewable energy', Boeing press release, 28 August, available here: www.boeing.com/news/releases/2006/q3/060828a_nr.html
8. Unnamed reporter, 2010, 'China–U.S. "green" trade row intensifies', UPI, 18 October, available here: www.upi.com/Science_News/Resource-Wars/2010/10/18/China-US-green-trade-row-intensifies/UPI-38051287419176/
9. Capaccio, Tony, 2011, 'Lockheed Martin F-35 Operating Costs May Reach $1 Trillion,' *Bloomberg*, April 21.
10. Sharp, Travis, 2009, 'Three weapons systems to watch in 2009', Center for Arms Control, 26 February, available here: http://armscontrolcenter.org/policy/securityspending/articles/022609_fy10_topline_systems_to_watch/
11. Sharp, David, 2011, 'Bath Iron Works shifts focus to new-style warship', *Business Week,* 9 May, available here: www.businessweek.com/ap/financialnews/D9N4593G0.htm
12. Ringstrom, Anna, 2011, 'Global military spending hits high but growth slows', *Reuters*, April 10.
13. Various authors, 2011, 'How to cut the military', *New York Times,* 8 May, available here: www.nytimes.com/roomfordebate/2011/05/08/how-to-cut-the-military?ref=opinion
14. Brown, Gordon, 2009, 'Gordon Brown's speech to US Congress', full text reproduced in the *Guardian,* 4 March, available here: www.guardian.co.uk/world/2009/mar/04/gordon-brown-speech-to-congress

15. OECD, 2009, 'A progress report on the jurisdictions surveyed by the OECD global forum in implementing the internationally agreed tax standard', progress made as at 2 April 2009, available here: www.oecd.org/dataoecd/38/14/42497950. pdf

16. Unnamed reporter, 1999, 'Business: the company file arms sales fuel BAe's profits', BBC, 25 February, available here: http://news.bbc.co.uk/1/hi/business/the_company_file/285963.stm

17. Unnamed reporter, 2009, 'Firm admits overseas corruption', BBC, 10 July, available here: http://news.bbc.co.uk/1/hi/business/8144361.stm

18. Hilzenrath, David S., 2011, 'Justice Department, SEC investigations often rely on companies' internal probes', *Washington Post*, 23 May, available here: www.washingtonpost.com/business/economy/justice-department-sec-investigations-often-rely-on-companies-internal-probes/2011/04/26/AFO2HP9G_story.html

19. Pei, Minxin, 2007, 'Corruption threatens China's future', Carnegie Endowment for International Peace, October, available here: www.carnegieendowment.org/files/pb55_pei_china_corruption_final.pdf

20. CRO, 2010, 'German President Horst Köhler resigns', *Der Spiegel*, 31 May, available here: www.spiegel.de/international/germany/0,1518,697785,00.html

EPILOGUE

1. Mackie, J. L., 1980, *Hume's Moral Theory,* Routledge, p.61.

2. Blitz, James and Dombey, Daniel, 2009, 'US claims Gulf donors fund Taliban fighters', *Financial Times,* 25 March, available here: www.ft.com/cms/s/0/b1787f4c-197a-11de-9d34-0000779fd2ac.html#axzz1JgltFTCpz

3. Censky, Annalyn, 2011, 'How the middle class became the underclass', CNN Money, 16 February, available here: http://money.cnn.com/2011/02/16/news/economy/middle_class/index.htm

4. www.census.gov/foreign-trade/Press-Release/current_press_release/exh15.pdf

5. Bull, Alistair, and Zengerle, Patricia, 2011, 'Obama calls for deep cuts in U.S. oil imports', Reuters, 30 March, available here: www.reuters.com/article/2011/03/30/us-obama-energy-idUSTRE72S3C820110330

6. Gates, Robert M., 2010, speech to forum 'Export-control reform: business executives for national security', 20 April, available here: www.bens.org/mis_support/Gates%Export%Speech%4-20-10.pdf

7. www.lockheedmartin.com/news/enr/2010/export-control.html, last accessed 17 April 2011.

8. Wu, Jiao, Li, Xing and Chen, Weihua, 2011, 'New chapter in relations', *China Daily,* 20 January, available here: www0.chinadaily.com.cn/china/2011huvisistsus/2011-01/20/content_11884662.htm

9. Johnston, Nicholas, and Forsythe, Michael, 2011, 'Obama signals closer ties with China's Hu even amid frictions over rights', Bloomberg, 20 January.

10. Lichtenbaum, Peter, 2011, 'A faulty connection: U.S. policy links national security, market access', *Defense News,* 7 February, available here: www.defensenews.com/story.php?i=5636722

11. Cendrowicz, Len, 2010, 'Should Europe lift its arms embargo on China?', *Time,* 10 February, available here: www.time.com/time/world/article/0,8599,1961947,00.html. Read more: www.time.com/time/world/article/0,8599,1961947,00.html#ixzz1Jha3lWH0

12. Spiegel, Peter and Thornhill, John, 2005, 'France urges end to China arms embargo', *Financial Times,* 15 February, available here: www.ft.com/cms/s/0/55da9a64-7f85-11d9-8ceb-00000e2511c8.html#axzz1JgltFTCp

13. Unnamed reporter, 2011, 'European arms embargo out of date', *Global Times,* 13 Janaury, available here: http://opinion.globaltimes.cn/editorial/2011-01/612043.html

14. Minnick, Wendell, 2009, 'Is China stealing Russia's Su-33?', *Defense News,* 4 May, available here: www.defensenews.com/story.php?i=4070484

15. Crutsinger, Martin, 2010, 'China boosts holdings of U.S. Treasuries', Associated Press, 17 May, available here: www.msnbc.msn.com/id/37188970/ns/business-world_business/

16. Miller, Rich, 2009, 'U.S. needs more inflation to speed recovery, say Mankiw, Rogoff', Bloomberg, 19 May, available here: www.bloomberg.com/apps/news?pid=newsarchive&sid=auyuQlA1lRV8

17. Statement from Federal Reserve Bank of New York, 2010, 'Press Release', 3 November, available here: www.federalreserve.gov/newsevents/press/monetary/20101103a.htm

18. 'Pliny', 2010, 'Commentary: Fed's intention in question in monetary easing policy', Xinhua, 17 October, available here: http://news.xinhuanet.com/english2010/indepth/2010-10/17/c_13561190.htm

19. Gertz, Bill, 2010, 'Chinese see U.S. debt as weapon in Taiwan dispute', *Washington Times*, 10 February, available here: www.washingtontimes.com/news/2010/feb/10/chinese-see-us-debt-as-weapon/

20. Knight, Laurence, 2010, 'What's the currency war about?', BBC, 23 October, available here: www.bbc.co.uk/news/business-11608719

21. Leahy, Joe and Pearson, Samantha, 2011, 'Brazil takes fresh "currency war" action', *Financial Times*, 7 April, available here: www.ft.com/cms/s/0/288b4b0a-60a5-11e0-a182-00144feab49a,s01=1.html#axzz1JgltFTCp

22. Nader, Ralph, 2011, 'Waiting for the Spark', Information Clearing House, 19 April, available here: www.informationclearinghouse.info/article27926.htm

23. Bolton, John R., 2010, 'The key to changing the United Nations system' AEI Online, available here: www.aei.org/outlook/101000

Index

Compiled by Sue Carlton